"The greatest trick of the devil is that he has convinced one-third of humanity that he doesn't exist. One-third pretends there is no God so they can indulge themselves, and the other third think they are good enough to do without Him.

"Then there are the few, the quiet, the humble, the unimportant. Those who have sought His truth since eternity and quietly go about moving mountains with faith. Those who invoke the name of God at every turn. Because of those the devil remembers and trembles. Those, my son, are the ones chosen by Him to save the rest."

—*Florencia Martinez Hernandez 1898–1995*
My grandmother

FAITH AMONG SHADOWS

FAITH AMONG SHADOWS

Malcolm Leal

CFI
Springville, Utah

This is not an official publication of The Church of Jesus Christ of Latter-day Saints. The opinions and views expressed herein belong solely to the author and do not necessarily represent the opinions or views of Cedar Fort, Inc. Permission for the use of sources, graphics, and photos is also solely the responsibility of the author.

ISBN 13: 978-1-59955-226-2

Published by CFI, an imprint of Cedar Fort, Inc., 2373 W. 700 S., Springville, UT 84663
Distributed by Cedar Fort, Inc., www.cedarfort.com

Library of Congress Cataloging-in-Publication Data

Leal, Malcolm, 1966-
Faith among shadows / Malcolm Leal.
p. cm.
ISBN 978-1-59955-226-2 (alk. paper)
1. Leal, Malcolm, 1966- 2. Martinez Hernandez, Florencia, 1898-1995. 3.
Mormons--Biography. I. Title.
BX8695.L385A3 2009
289.3092'2--dc22
[B]
2008041847

Cover design by Angela D. Olsen
Cover design © 2009 by Lyle Mortimer

Printed in the United States of America

10 9 8 7 6 5 4 3 2

Printed on acid-free paper

To Florencia Martinez

My Grandmother

ACKNOWLEDGMENTS

It has taken me more than fifteen years to share the story of my grandmother in one complete account. For almost a decade now, those who have had an opportunity to converse with me beyond the pleasantries of protocol have known of "my grandmother." By now she is a household name in many quarters since I have quoted her on almost every subject of the gospel.

I have finally mustered the courage to spill onto paper a few of the vivid memories I treasure about her and my life under her wise, protective shadow. I owe my spiritual restlessness, thirst for knowledge, insight, and inclination for the study of the gospel to my grandmother, Florencia Martinez Hernandez. It was she who pointed me to the truth and foretold the existence of "men that walk with God" when she knew of none. It was she who planted the seed of faith in me and enticed me to approach "her God" for everything I needed. It was she who demanded that I strive for more and seek beyond my borders, for "we are surely more than mere mortals," she said. "Without God we are nothing, and if we are nothing then there is no God." To her memory and now legacy I dedicate with great love and admiration every page of this book.

I'm immensely grateful to Bishop Z. for all his counsel, love, and nurturing. I learned from him some of the things my father should have taught me. I wish he wouldn't have spared the rod. When I grow up, I hope with all my heart to be just like him. To Sister Z., my love and gratitude for her prayers. I heard them.

To my brethren and their families, Andres, Gordon, Felipe, and Paul:

I miss you very much. Please forgive me.

To all who exhorted me to share the memory of my grandmother and her wisdom with my brothers and sisters of the Church, I am grateful.

A thousand times thanks to Jennifer Leigh for your patience with me in editing my account. You skillfully smoothed out the rough and tumble in me that got onto the paper and turned my memories into a truly compelling story. Thank you again.

To the angels that the Father has sent to bring me joy and solace on account of my past suffering: my family.

AUTHOR'S NOTE

I offer beforehand a sincere apology; some of the elements of this account may bruise the sensibilities and tender feelings of some readers. I've avoided descriptions and details that may be offensive and overly crude. I struggled to preserve the truth of my life's story while sharing some of the barbaric scenes and events that I lived through and witnessed.

Some of the events described in this book took place over a seven-year span while I served in the Cuban military. Those dead and wounded were my friends; men who gave their lives not for an obscure cause or distorted political doctrine, but for their friends—for me. I've changed the names of those still living on the Island so that the long memory of the hate-mongers and the merciless may not reach them, even after these many years.

Some of the views and feelings expressed by my grandmother were the result of her direct experience of which I have no specific knowledge. She obviously harbored some resentments toward established religious practices in our country, but she did not share her reasons with me. I preserved those in the narrative for the sake of authenticity, but I harbor no animosity toward any religious tradition. I honor all men who worship God and work in a heartfelt attempt to better mankind.

PROLOGUE

Most people have a romantic and absolutely correct view of the jungle—that it's filled with birds, flowers, butterflies, and plants of incredible colors and exotic beauty. There are also huge bats and small bears; dog-like creatures; creeping, flying, buzzing, and sliding critters; cats of all sizes; and monkeys that believe they're Elvis at sundown. With all the flapping and chirping and squawking, the cacophony can drive anybody insane in minutes.

But in time, one learns to filter most of the clamor out. It becomes background music, and your senses blend with what is normal, depending on the time of day and the season. Amazingly, your brain develops the ability to sense, hear, and feel when something is amiss, and thus worth your attention. This ability to discern the almost undetectable is essential. In the jungle, failure to pay attention is often fatal. I can attest to that.

Such failures are usually precipitated by prior errors in judgment. Survival skills are based on a number of factors, some tangible and demonstrable, others more subtle and elusive. Emotion, on the other hand, is described as the slayer of rational thinking. Anxiety, anger, or anticipation can destroy days or weeks of mathematically designed operational planning. The world-renowned Navy SEALs—the special operations arm of the United States Navy—lost a dozen men during the incursion in Granada under such circumstances. If caution is abandoned, we become reckless, impulsive, and even arrogant.

The rain was unyielding. It had been falling for two days nonstop, making movement in the jungle almost impossible. Trails disappeared. The earth moved constantly, sliding from under my feet at varying rates of speed. Trees, bushes, rocks propelled by gravity, and rivers of murky water flowed in every direction, regardless of the topography. The noise deafened me. Water falling furiously on leaves of different sizes and shapes from hundreds of feet up made a colossal racket. The ear-piercing thunder and the blinding rain pounding on my face exacerbated my frustration. My anger, in turn, dulled my sense of awareness.

I crouched against a clammy tree for a long time and clutched the sopping, smooth green bark. My effort to peer through the rain across the open stretch of the clearing was useless. The time-lapse camera equipment and the ground-level radar sensors were just fifty or sixty yards away beyond the tree line where I hesitated. The gear wasn't needed. It had served its purpose for twelve long weeks. I'd retrieved films and downloaded the readings from the sensors, three times remotely, during the same period. As if in a science fiction movie, moss and vines had grown over the lens of the camera, making it inoperable. By the same token, it was very well concealed. I could come later and retrieve it or just leave it there. It would never be found.

Quietly, I uttered a mild curse. *I should just discard the whole thing and report it "lost to hazardous conditions,"* I thought. It wouldn't be the first time, nor the last. But I'd argued so strongly, and for so long, on the satellite link that I was sure they'd have my skin if I showed up without the gear. *Wicked, cheap, stinking Russians. They are beyond contempt,* I thought.

Something across the small gorge had barely come into view a few minutes earlier. I couldn't make it out clearly because the rain made it impossible to discern anything. But I saw something in the low branches of a tree three hundred or so yards away. Was it an atypical movement, or some color variations that shouldn't be there? I paused, that higher awareness skill signaling, pointing to the threat I couldn't visually perceive. Skittering impatience, the cold, and my poorly subdued animosity finally clipped the wings of my apprehension.

Trying to keep my boots from being sucked into the mud, I moved quickly, stealthily across the clearing and covered the distance to the rock outcropping. The wind was pushing the rain almost horizontally, smacking my eyeballs like fire. I still had to go around the formation of rock, take a step up, and retrieve the gear from a crevice. It would take five or six seconds, but I'd be exposed and facing away from the unnerving tree line. I resolved to execute the maneuver quickly and avoid self-doubt. I stretched my neck and scrutinized the general area where—"The heck with it," I grumbled between my teeth.

I crawled around the rocks and got up in one forceful movement. I stepped up and reached for the camera in the hole of the rock.

It felt like a sledgehammer hit me sideways on the head. A flash of lights, bright and blinding, filled my eyes, accompanied by a high-pitched hissing sound. Then nothing. Utter darkness. No sound, nothing at all, as if I'd been suddenly pushed into space—total sensory shutdown. A few seconds later, maybe minutes, the pounding of my pulse on my temples and the coppery taste of blood in my mouth attested to the absolute fact that my life had come to an end.

PART ONE
GROWING UP WITH
GRANDMA

THE FAITH AMONG SHADOWS

"And Moses told the Egyptian king, 'let my people go . . .' but God had made the heart of the king hard and he was stubborn and didn't want to let go the children of Israel," Grandma said. Her explanations were always pristine and to the point. But one of my favorite pastimes was imagining the whole thing in my mind's eye. I could see Moses, old and wrinkled, clad in a ratty robe that looked something like our oldest bath towels. Grandma had also said that Moses spent much time in the desert where it's really, really hot all the time and never rained. *How do you take showers where there isn't any water?* I wondered.

"Anyway, and the king sitting in this big chair, with a big hat," I said eagerly, having rehearsed the scene in my mind.

I'd seen a picture at Grandma's where this Pharaoh had a big long hat with either a lizard or a snake on the forehead, I couldn't tell. He looked weird, all stiff and important. He also had a mean look on his face. Grandma said anyone who had slaves was a mean, bad person.

"Then Moses said to Pharaoh, 'The Lord God will bring to your people all kinds of diseases and kill your cows and all your animals and bring crickets to eat your food so you'll starve if you don't let my people go.' "

"Whoa!" I exclaimed with excitement, my small hands gripping dangerously tight the glass of fruit juice Grandma had offered me a few minutes earlier.

Although I'd heard the story many times before, it always amazed me that somebody could call God to do stuff like that for him. After all, the concept of "G-O-D" is well beyond the grasp of the mind of a seven-year-old.

"Abuela, can God do things like that for me if I ask Him?" I asked, my voice suddenly quiet and reserved—quite unlike me. She took her time as she looked past me through the window into the night as if searching for the right words. The answer to my question about God came as chapters of my life unfolded year after year while I grew up by her side.

I often wondered if there was something Grandma didn't know. It was an established fact that she was old. How old? Who knew. But she was certainly older than anybody I'd ever known. At least, she seemed to have been around the neighborhood before anybody else. She also knew when everybody had been born, got married, had children, moved, or whatever else was important to know.

Grandma also knew everyone around, and I mean *everyone*. And of course, the whole world also knew Grandma, and what was even worse, they knew I was her grandson. That had several implications—some good, some bad. On the one hand, it certainly had plenty of advantages. If I was thirsty or hungry, I could just walk slowly on the sidewalk around the neighborhood and wait until somebody smiled at me. I could just act cute and polite and say, "Hello, Ma'am, how are you today?"

Invariably she replied, "Hello there. How are you doing, young man? You're Florence's grandson, aren't you? You have grown so much—and so polite as always. It's hot. Do you want some cold water?"

Before you knew it, I was sitting at her table drinking water or soda and helping myself to some cookies, cake, or whatever else was in her refrigerator. It never failed.

On the other hand, when the pranksters in the neighborhood wanted to do something, I had to be the first to hit the road—that is, if I didn't want to be seen with the rowdy bunch. Because rest assured, Grandma heard about it and the outcome was never pleasant. So, jumping fences to grab some mangoes from the neighbor's tree or trying a dip in the water reservoir (it was always cool in the summer) was never a good idea for me. It seemed that after five minutes of happiness, I always had an encounter of the third kind with Grandma's old military leather belt. In any event, whenever the boys came up with something clever and fun to do, I always remembered I had to go do something for my grandma.

The fact remained that Grandma was the local encyclopedia, local property registry, and the living memory of the small, sleepy fishing

Cuban village of Santa Fe, where I was born. Nothing escaped her recollection. You could safely bet that if somebody dared to share a noteworthy event in town and my grandmother didn't remember, it didn't happen—end of story.

My earliest memory of my grandmother relates to her waking me up in the morning. I remember opening my sleepy eyes to find her dark, wrinkled, weathered face staring at me with the most peaceful, soothing blue eyes I'd ever seen. To say the least, the contrast was nothing but astonishing. Grandma had ebony black skin, frosty white hair, and soft baby blue eyes. She had a gentle but incisive stare, which was impossible to hide from, impossible to lie to, and wise beyond understanding. To this day, I haven't encountered a face that bore any resemblance to my grandmother's. She was the mother of my mother's mother, descending from people who claimed to be heirs to kingdoms of royalty in the Horn of Africa and the offspring of those who God scattered away among the isles of the sea, she said. To me, she was just my grandmother.

Life was good, at least from where I stood at four feet, three inches. My world was about two square miles with our home at the top of the hill. It was reassuring to be able to see our house from everywhere. I always thought one of the coolest things about where I lived was that I could come from school into the house, drop my pack, shoes, and shirt, kiss my grandma, and go out the back door in about ten seconds. I ran through the backyard, jumped the back fence, and sprinted down the hill to my dingy in the tide pool to check out my crab trap in the lagoon.

Of course, I had competition with my crab hunting operation. The other kids had no problem ransacking my traps if I didn't get there fast enough. After an hour or so of fisherman bragging, we would decide who was Captain Nemo for the day and then run in opposite directions to lunch and homework. The small country school served less than a hundred children, with kindergarten through third grade in the morning session and the "older kids" up to sixth grade in the afternoons. We all had the same four teachers for ten grueling months. The school ran on a skeleton crew—literally.

Life was truly good for most people, especially the kids, in Cuba. We had no worries or concerns, nothing to keep us awake at night. The hurricane season—May through September—was actually the only thing that brought some upheaval to our lives. But it wasn't all bad. It worked out to be vacation time midway through the school year. I loved the anticipation and the guessing game about when and where the storm would touch down. And not going to school was just awesome. They would blow a loud whistle and all the radio stations would talk about the cyclone coming.

And they always, I thought, gave them girls' names. I reasoned that maybe all of the scientists were girls themselves. I thought something had to be done about that.

Of course, Grandma always had the inside scoop about hurricanes. She made me carry load after load of stuff from the store to the house during the last week of spring. Sometimes I tried to hide, but invariably she waited for me and then informed me casually, "Son, you have about twenty minutes before the store closes, and there are about four bags I need you to bring."

"But, Abuela," I softly protested, "it's going to take me two trips, at least, and the store is fifteen minutes away." (I'd done the math many times.)

"Well, son," she said, "you'd better get going then."

That was Grandma. She'd heard every excuse and claim in the book and then some. You couldn't impress, convince, or argue with her.

"Unless you're dead," she'd say, "then I may cut you some slack and give you more time."

Her theory was, "Excuses are like a butt—everybody has one and usually you don't go around sharing it." So even trying the subtlest form of argument was futile.

As could be expected, life on the bay of Guamá revolved around the sea. Most people fished, or were married to somebody, or had parents, grandparents, brothers, or cousins who fished. It seemed to me, at least early in my life, that if you didn't mingle with fish there was something fundamentally wrong with you. And of course we ate fish—different kinds, mind you—most days.

It wasn't until I was a bit older that I was allowed to wander inland and away from the sea. The bush was dangerous and unpredictable. You couldn't see more than a few yards ahead of you, and there were things that could bite, scratch, and who knows what else. But there was land indeed and plenty of it. I just never noticed.

Surrounding the peninsula for miles stretched very fertile terraces, lush with citrus groves and coffee plants that seemed like an extension of the emerald green of the shallow waters of the bay. And of course, people worked there. I just didn't know any of them until much later. It also never occurred to me that Grandma had anything to do with the big brown bags that were hoisted in the storage shed out back. Or the noisy stone mill across the courtyard, and the donkeys that pulled it day and night for almost two months during the cold season. Or the toasty smell that floated in the air from far away during that time of the year.

THE DEVIL'S BREW

According to Grandma's historical record, coffee plantations had surrounded the peninsula since the late 1700s. The coffee fields were planted by a half-crazed Frenchman who barely escaped the slave revolt in Haiti (he had a head injury and a face deformed by scars). The land was cultivated by his descendants and later by others who came to the region and lay claim to part of the land. It has been in continuous use for at least two hundred years.

The valley beyond the hill was also planted with coffee, and a rudimentary roasting plant had been built in the 1800s. When the wind blew seaward, we could smell the roasting aroma almost ten miles away on the peninsula.

During the harvest season, dozens of small growers came to grind their loads at Grandma's stone mill. The grinding stone spun around and around day and night, without interruption for eight to ten weeks. Four or six pairs of old, battered, sad-looking donkeys took turns pulling the rough, heavy stone.

For some obscure reason, Grandma always kept me away from the whole grinding, donkey feeding, and packing operation. Scruffy-looking men with turbid and restless eyes came and went. A lot of writing numbers, bagging, and arguing took place during those cold months. The long shed across the courtyard was always full of people. Some even slept there for a few days on the floor on dirty mats that smelled like wet rags and "medicine."

When the first donkeys arrived, laden with heavy packs, Grandma got a serious, quiet look on her face and told me as a matter of fact, "No playing across the yard, ever." The whole thing scared the life out of me. Granted, I didn't have a grip on the full story. But even at an early age, I could sense that whatever took place during those weeks a few dozen yards across from my front door was fraught with bitterness and rode on a dangerous edge.

A few years later, I received my first management and business school lesson; I often claimed that I learned about supply and demand and price elasticity from Grandma, not graduate school, as most assume. Economics 101—Cuban coffee style. The price of commodities is always lower during the harvest season if there's no forward-looking information on the markets, weather, or derivatives. The local market is flooded with the product and with not much variance in quality, since it all comes from the same region and is roasted in the same place within a ten- to twelve-week period. Price, for the most part, becomes a function of quantity and depends on whether you're buying wholesale or retail amounts. Profit margins during the harvest season are, therefore, razor thin.

As a practice, Grandma never charged the growers money for the mill service. "Always in spice," she said. It was usually 5 to 10 percent of the total poundage plus the keep of the animals (the donkeys or horses or mules or whatever they brought to carry the loads). At the end of the grinding season, several dozen sealed brown bags of finely ground coffee swung from the beams of the storage shed in the back of the house. The high-ceilinged, split-level roof was littered with ropes and knots holding the toasty-smelling brown bags. The walls of the barn were covered in shining thin sheets of metal in order to deter rats, raccoons, and other crawling animals from getting into the bags and make their own dining room up there.

The bags disappeared little by little. Now and again, people came to talk to Grandma. They were big men with crispy shirts and big cigars that they never lit in front of Grandma if they wanted to live. They would talk and drink cold lemonade or mango juice, and then talk some more. Afterward they would slowly walk to the back shed. Grandma always hesitated, as if she wasn't sure, stopping and scratching her right arm, smoothing the front of her dress, and walking again. Then the bags were gone.

One night a man came. No crispy shirt, no cigar. He had a rushed and restless look on his face, and he breathed short, shallow breaths, as if he'd come chasing his rusty green truck instead of driving it. He spoke fast and labored, but in a low tone, almost like whispering. I sat outside the living room on a crate, not even a dozen feet from the room, and I could barely hear him.

Grandma sat quietly, listening without blinking, and occasionally smoothing the front of her dress softly as usual. She didn't say much: "I understand. . . . Yes, I know, Russ. . . . I know it must be difficult. . . . Sorry, I can't help you right now." The man started rubbing his head and his arms, and covered his sweaty face with his hands. I stood up in an attempt to gain a better view through the open window. He stood and paced between the chair and the wall.

"You can't do this to me," he spoke, with a strident, broken voice. "You can't do this to me," he repeated louder, and Grandma stood up and pointed to the door.

"There's nothing I can do for you today," Grandma said in her customary soft, persuasive tone. "Son, I suggest you go home and rest."

The man stormed out of the house, jumped in his rusty green truck, and cranked it hard, leaving a cloud of dust behind him. Grandma looked at me and smiled. Not an ounce of care in her eyes. She came closer, gave me a warm glance from her blue eyes, and kissed me on the forehead.

"It's past your bedtime, son," she pointed out.

What transpired later that night forever lived in my mind as the most bizarre and possibly the most frightening moment of my short existence. After I went to bed, I could still hear voices outside in the hallway. I could recognize the voice of Calixto, Grandma's gentle-giant friend. They'd known each other since they were young. Grandma had stories to tell about Jose Calixto Valdez, as she often called him to remind him that she knew him well and was privy to stuff about him that should not fall into the public domain. He was a colorful character, even at seventy some years. At six feet plus and a blip below three hundred pounds, anyone could feel their lives were in serious peril if they had to cross fists with him.

The rusty green truck was back. Doors slamming and the hush outside my door gave way to a real riot: shouting, screaming, things breaking, and the heavy breathing of men engaged in a physical struggle.

There I stood, petrified and unsure about whether I should open the door of my room to the hallway. Curiosity was always a better motivator than fear. I cracked the door open one inch and peered outside. What I saw next cemented my notion that Calixto wasn't really human. Maybe a mutant, maybe ET, who knows—just not human. With one hand, Calixto held a man by the neck against the wall for a few seconds. He lifted him effortlessly and left him there until the man hung like a puppet, not moving. A second man rushed from behind and hit Calixto with a baseball bat. Calixto swept backwards with his left arm, grabbed the man's wrist, and pulled him toward the wall. In one seamless motion, he grabbed the man's neck with his left hand and hoisted him up the wall right next to the other one he was holding with his right hand. The short, stocky man struggled for a few seconds and then became quiet, almost lifeless.

Slowly, even gently, Calixto set them down. He held onto their arms and dragged the men out the door. The noise stopped. The commotion was over as soon as it started. Although quite a large crowd had gathered outside our home, everyone was silent. I couldn't see everything from my window, but I could see that some had begun to stroll away down the street. Some men were helping others, one leaning on another, others limping and weaving down the dark street.

The full extent of what transpired remained a real mystery for years. All my begging and pleading with Grandma to tell me what happened didn't prosper. She smiled and declared, "Son, it was nothing—nothing to worry about." Not one word more for years to come. I got the details of the altercation from my mother, who I don't believe was there, although she asserts she was.

After the coffee season was over, prices began to inch up with every passing week. Supply dried up slowly, and the market operators became more and more frantic in trying to fill the demand gap. Just like in the Chicago Board of Trade, speculators hedged against future fluctuation of price. Sometimes they had an order they needed to cover and a delivery to meet on a certain date and supply wouldn't cooperate. The traders became frantic, desperate, even aggressive. Russ, the man in the rusty green truck, had to cover an order and the supply wasn't there. He heard through the grapevine that my grandma had a stock of coffee in store and he came to buy, but Grandma wasn't selling. He became desperate and tried to force the sale. This unfortunate coffee trader stumbled against Calixto, and that wasn't part of the plan.

Days later, Grandma sold some coffee to a third party, which allowed for Russ to cover the hedge. The price was four times higher than they were ready to pay but they had no choice. It was a textbook case of price elasticity in an open, unregulated market. By the way, Grandma never went to school. She learned to read and write on her own, but numbers came to her as second nature.

As far as Calixto was concerned, he was just visiting and the men showed no manners when talking to my grandmother. He didn't hurt them, he claimed. Just showed them a little manners and a lesson for the future.

Calixto was, from what I could discern, one of those people whose name was invariably tied to the history of the community. Depending on who was reporting the story, Calixto had, directly or indirectly, influenced social, political, and (unbelievably) sport events in the region for half a century. Of course, he systematically denied any involvement in those events.

The man practiced plausible deniability to the fullest extent of the word. As far as he was concerned, "It's all the work of delusional and ill-intentioned minds." Now, whatever story Grandma shared about Calixto was different. He shrugged his shoulders, simply adding, "I must be getting old because I don't remember it that way, but I trust your memory better than mine." He shrugged and strolled away

The most memorable story about Calixto related to the Great Depression years. Calixto had found temporary employment as a boxer and due to his natural physical abilities had been successful in six fights all over the provinces. He'd built so much expectation that the Army had offered their best fighter on a twelve-round fight for a grand prize of five hundred dollars. Calixto figured he could support his family for a couple of years on that prize money. One small detail: he had to throw the fight by allowing the favorite to knock him out in the eighth round.

Details about what transpired next get fuzzy. The fact remains that in the seventh round some words were exchanged. According to Grandma, the Army sergeant, reassured of his victory, uttered less than gentle words to Calixto: "Here comes your medicine." The Army sergeant was taunting Calixto who, until that point, was willing to keep his end of the bargain for his family's sake.

The fight ended in a gun battle (everyone packed "heat" back in those days) of epic proportions. Since the boxing match was supposed to have a predetermined outcome, the heavyweight bidders felt cheated by the house bank that held the bets. Unfortunately, there's no footage of the fight, but the accounts match up. After the sergeant's bravado and teasing remarks, three seconds after the eighth round bell rung, Calixto punched him so hard that he fractured his jaw and the braggart never spoke clearly again. It took almost one hour for the man to regain consciousness, and in the ensuing public disturbance, nine people received gunshot wounds and other injuries in various degrees of severity.

Very calmly, Calixto jumped out of the ring, pushed his way to the cashier window, and told the betting boss, "If you don't pay me, you'll have to live in fear for the rest of your days, or otherwise kill me so you can sleep."

Some claim the man at the cashier window had an episode of severe diarrhea. Calixto said he already had bad bowels from so much rum and late-night seafood dinners. Whatever the medical condition responsible for the messy episode, Calixto got paid, his family survived the worst economic depression in history, and he ended a short but memorable boxing career. Not by choice, however. He just couldn't get a match with any sane person. Many years later, as a science experiment during my early high school years, I measured his left straight punch. At age 72, Calixto clocked almost 380 pounds of force in his punch, enough to render anybody of any age out of commission for a long while, and placed a large number of neurons out of service permanently. I surmised that the sergeant-boxer stumbled away from that fight with more than a speech impediment.

That was Calixto. The man seemed larger than life and had a frown that could make you shake in your shoes, but a laugh that shook the leaves out of the fruit trees in the backyard. Where and how Calixto and my grandmother met was lost to memory, but their friendship was born in lean and perilous times. Grandma became a widow at age twenty-three, at a time when "women weren't considered a whole person," she said. She almost lost her property and family possessions to an unscrupulous town lawyer. Calixto, in the process of having an "interview" with the attorney, demolished the man's door and hoisted him by his legs with a rope over a tree branch outside his house. He let him hang for an hour while he detailed what he'd do to him if he ever saw him again.

For a while, Grandma explained, they were all afraid that Calixto had actually killed the man. Nobody heard from him again. To this day, Calixto claims the whole thing is a fabrication.

It's Just a Building

The Church of Jesus del Monte was a tiny, musky, cold church within walking distance from home. If it weren't for the sound of the ancient bells four times a day, no one would have noticed that it was there until Christmas time. It was built in the 1600s by the mother of a wealthy tobacco grower who was murdered during the "uprising of the meadows," as the incident was coined by the colonial authorities. Poor day-laborers who worked the tobacco fields rebelled against the hanging of six of their comrades who had been accused of price fixing during the English occupation of Habana. For years, the story goes, nobody went to church but the old grief-stricken lady since the parish had no priest. That was still true a hundred years later.

The lady died and the building decayed in time without use. Even the ivy that dotted the gray granite walls of the façade seemed lifeless, tired, and lost in time. Nobody I knew went there except on Christmas Eve for mass, or whatever that was that people called "mass."

I stood at the door many times, but my grandma didn't know it, of course. She'd have had my skin if she found out. As far as she was concerned, whatever went on in that building "was not of God." She said that time and again. Light seemed to skirt away from the doorway, as if it lost its shining power just a few yards inward. I just stood there, gazing into the building. I could feel a faint draft coming from within, bringing a humid, dusty smell, like squashed snails or wet dirty socks. There was no sound coming from the darkness either. Nothing moved in there. I knew the long benches, built in rows, sat like sleeping soldiers on the dusty stone floor. I'd seen them at Christmas, but I couldn't see them now.

On Christmas Eve, some people went to the little church. It was always late and I was tired but we went, too. Every year about midnight we arrived with the show already started. Most of the people there were elderly, including many of my neighbors. The children looked anxious, curious, confused, and unsure what to do. Most of them were too short to see over the heads of the crowd. I was usually too far away to hear what was going on. I had to be content with an incomprehensible scene of men, women, and children, dressed in weird, pajama-like dresses, and plastic toy camels, among other props.

Over the years, with the help of Grandma's Bible story reading and repetition, the Christmas show at the old dark church began to make sense. The poorly narrated and adulterated nativity story was rehearsed every year, but the details became coherent in my mind every time Grandma read the Bible to me at home. It was Joseph and Mary looking for a place to rest. There was the innkeeper and the makeshift manger, which in our church was inhabited by plastic sheep and lambs. Mary went into labor and finally birthed the baby Jesus.

And then Grandma and I were gone. As quietly as we came, we left. No matter how much I complained, raved, and argued, we walked out of the church and into the middle of the night, to our home.

The mystery of our sudden departure before the climax of the story was revealed a decade later. By then it had been a few years since I'd attended the Christmas show at the old church.

In Cuba, teenagers had no interest in Christmas stories, much less in a relic of a building that had no social or spiritual significance in the community.

Some years later, a friend invited me to her home to see her brother who had returned from studying abroad. After a couple hours of reminiscing and self-aggrandizing stories about high school girl conquests, I headed out into the cold December night air. The church stood on a soft hill halfway between my friend's doorway and my home.

A "north front" is a twenty-four-hour cold wave that rolls down from New England and across the eastern seaboard, freezes the orange groves in Florida, and sends the surf up ten feet in the Caribbean basin. That's as long as the winter lasts in Cuba. Temperatures drop to about sixty degrees for one or two days every other week. When this happens, invariably, the government declares a state of emergency, parents keep kids home from school, and unless you're designated critical personnel, you don't dare go outside. That's when Grandma took out clothing I hadn't seen for years, it seemed. Most of it no longer fit me, and I thought I looked like a sausage with those tight, checkered sweaters on.

The streets were deserted. Small whirlwinds toyed with leaves and papers, rattling and echoing between the buildings. The few brave souls who had to venture into the streets were huddled in groups, trying to keep warm with the heat radiating from the engine at the back of the bus.

I looked up to the dark reddish sky. I could feel the clouds getting closer to the earth. I could smell the rain in the air, but it was still hanging high up in the sky. I stepped into the street at a brisk pace, sporting a brand new shirt and pair of shoes. In those parts, shoes are sort of allergic to water. They really get disfigured after a splash. Halfway home, the rain came, cold but timid at first, almost hesitating. I held onto the idea that it might stop or that a wind shift would give me a window to make it through the five blocks that separated me from the welcome warmth of my home. Wishful thinking. The rain didn't hold back. It pounded the pavement and the treetops while I ran. But I was only concerned about my shoes. Communism came and shoes disappeared from the store shelves. The average Cuban had access to one pair of "dress" shoes per year. And, they better have lasted you a year. That in itself became the source of significant anxiety, among other mental disorders for most people in Cuba. On the one hand, I had shoes that were completely allergic to water. Mind you, I lived on an island with three cubic feet of rain per year. And I had no way to seal, protect, or repair the shoes once they smelled like water. If you stepped in a pothole, you'd better start making funeral arrangements for your shoes.

As I cleared the hill, there it was: the small church on the mount. It was still dark, but there were people outside and, sliding through the massive doors, a trickle of light coming from inside. I searched the deserted sidewalks, but there was no other place to get away from the cold air and furious rain. My shoes were always on my mind, of course.

Although it had been five or six years since I last stood there, I walked into an all-familiar scene. There were again people playing Joseph and Mary and the innkeeper surrounding the makeshift manger accompanied by the plastic sheep and lambs. Then the baby Jesus, in the form of a doll, arrived. What happened next left me perplexed. Initially I thought of it as kind of gross rather than sacrilegious.

The actor Joseph lifted the baby Jesus doll above his head, and most of the present spectators fell to the ground and mumbled some unintelligibly memorized prayer. I stood there confused, unsure of what was occurring, but there was more to come. Next, the priest pronounced the doll holy and blessed and kissed it. He then approached the participants and commanded them to pay homage to the Jesus-doll. One by one, those present held and kissed the doll, and some uttered praise.

The thought of kissing the doll after thirty-some people had put their lips on it was repulsive, to say the least. But what troubled me the most was the soft encouragement of the priest to the worshipers: "Humble yourself before the Lord or be damned," he reiterated.

I stepped backward quietly and went into the night, my mind still replaying the grotesque scene. The air smelled fresh and clean. The wind had died down a bit, but it was still swinging the rain sideways now and again. Two girls ran down the street past me, giggling under a crumpled newspaper. And then I was home. I'd forgotten all about my shoes.

"Are you okay, son?" Grandma asked me as she placed a plate of hot lentil soup in front of me on the table. She could always tell when something troubled me. I thought, for a long time, that she could actually read my mind. As a young child I, used to hide my eyes from her so she couldn't look into my thoughts. After taking a spoonful of soup, I phrased the idea several times in my mind before it left my lips.

"I stopped at the church of Jesus of the Mount on my way home. It was raining." I took a piece of bread and dipped it in the soup. Seconds went by and no response. "The twins were there. Marcus and his sister too." These were my inseparable friends since childhood. We sort of drifted apart once the girls started to grow breasts and the boys mustaches. There's something weird about puberty that turns your friends into completely unrecognizable, hormone-driven beasts. We were still pretty civil to each other. I just couldn't stomach their constant preoccupation with the opposite sex.

Still no response. After I finished half of my soup, my bread, and a large cup of milk, she finally spoke: "Did you put your wet clothing in the bathroom?" she asked.

I looked up. She was offering me a napkin, while her placid, implacable blue eyes dissected me.

"So?" she prompted softly while she sat down across the table.

Here it goes, I thought. "I saw the doll thing at the end of the midnight mass," I concluded, and kept working on my soup. The rain tapped on the kitchen's window. The whistling of the wind outside was the only distraction, and it filled the uncomfortable absence of words. The silence was killing me. "Is that why we always left before the end every year when I was little?" I pondered out loud without looking at her. She waited for me to lift my eyes.

"What did you think, son?" Her questions poked me like a needle.

"I thought it was just gross." I tried to smile. It didn't work. "Bizarre," I added on a more serious note.

I felt trapped, a somewhat familiar feeling. Verbal fencing with Grandma was stimulating but at times emotionally taxing. Once you started exploring a subject with her, you had to finish. I avoided the whole thing whenever possible. Today wasn't one of those days. She pushed me to think, ponder, and reason until she was satisfied that I'd done my best, until I was clear and secure in my ideas.

"What did you see?" she probed again.

"The baby Jesus' birth—and the doll-kissing business," I replied, again trying to wrap the conversation up, but more like hoping it would go away somehow, or maybe I could go away.

"And what did you think, son?" She was needling me here. I felt like a trout being tempted with the irresistible worm on a hook at the end of the fishing line. As time went by and our conversations got more "adult-like," I noticed she was expecting me to make up my mind, to reason and give her my gut feeling. I hesitated but searched for it.

"Well—I think if God saw the show it would make Him puke. The whole thing was just unreal and the priest was forcing people to do it." She nodded. "I know we aren't supposed to make images or dolls or anything like that. So why do they do it?" I was just thinking aloud. "The whole wall is full of statues and altars and flowers and candles and clothing with blood and all kinds of stuff." I was on a roll by then. "Abuela, we've read the Bible since forever, and it says that we shouldn't do that sort of thing. Why do they have those pictures and statues hanging on the walls?" I wondered. I drew an imaginary frame in the air. Then I shook my head, more or less trying to shake the musky smell and the darkness of the place out of my short-term memory.

Actually, this was a lifelong question for me. Most neighbors and friends had statues of "virgins" and "saints" in their home. The painted clay figures were venerated and worshipped, visual cues that we should pay some attention to them. Countries in the New World became surrogates of the European colonies. In the case of Central and South America, the cultural and religious traditions and social baggage came from Spain. Together with the conquistadors came the priests. It's said that the New World was born under the weight of the crucifix and the sword, the latter to conquer and the former to give legitimacy to the conquest.

Religion in Cuba was and still is, in many respects for many people, a time-honored homegrown recipe that incorporates native indigenous legends, African-rooted cults, and Catholic traditions. Other than Grandma, I wasn't aware of anyone who knew anything about the Bible, or had read one or even owned one.

"That isn't a church. It's just a dark, old building," she concluded. I let go of my spoon softly and made eye contact with her.

"But there's a priest there," I offered.

Her eyes narrowed and took a scary glassy look that I'd seen before, though rarely. "If that man is a priest of God, I'd rather go willingly to hell with the devil." The words spilled out of her mouth like hot lava.

I quizzed Grandma about this issue a thousand times. But she died without ever elaborating on the history of the situation, even though it was evident that her dislike of the man was intense. Years earlier, I'd accompanied Grandma on an errand, as usual, holding onto the hem of her dress so that I could look around and through the fences of the neighbors while we walked, and not be left behind. We turned the corner and there he was, Father Fumes.

Father Fumes, Father Gasoline, and a couple of other less gentle nicknames were the pseudonyms applied to the local priest. Popular wisdom had it that he liked the "consecrated" wine a bit too much, and that instead of a cup, as prescribed, he finished the bottle after mass.

There was also the small detail of the lady who assisted in the rectory. She'd been there for almost twenty years serving "faithfully." She never married but managed to have two sons while in the employ of the parish. And she was still there. Another detail that didn't escape the scrutiny of the neighborhood related to the uncanny resemblance of the children to the priest.

Father Fumes was sporting his usual dusty, long robe made of thick, nubby wool covering his hundred or so extra pounds, the tinkling wood crucifix hanging from his sweating neck. He had small restless eyes that were often hidden behind thick glasses fogged by the vapors of his heavy breathing. His hair, tangled and dirty, always looked like birds were trying to build a nest while he took a nap.

The man saw Grandma and jolted out of the sidewalk across the street with enviable speed for an old man. Grandma uttered a muffled curse.

"What is it, Abuela?" I held tighter to her hem.

Although no more than seven or eight years old at the time, I recognized the intensity of the reactions but couldn't decipher the meaning. The exchange had remained in my mind since then, but my grandma refused to elaborate on it, even though through the years I tried unsuccessfully to pry additional details out of her memory.

That night, while eating my soup, though I wanted more information, all my grandmother said was, "The building is a church in name only."

She got up from the table and disappeared into her room. She soon returned with her old weathered Bible in hand. After flipping through a few pages, she pointed to a section. She read:

> The earth also is defiled under the inhabitants thereof; because they have transgressed the laws, changed the ordinance, broken the everlasting covenant. (Isaiah 24:5)

She closed the book and looked at me steadily. I'd heard the scripture passage before, but for the very first time it dawned on me: Grandma believed there was no "true" church and, in her eyes, the priest was worse than the devil himself. It was no doubt a radical concept. Scary, actually. *If there is no church and no priest, then where is God?* I wondered.

She smiled, came around the table, and kissed my forehead. "Good night, son." I heard the soft soles of her shoes fading into the hallway. My soup was cold, and I was no longer hungry. I felt scared and confused.

"It can't be." I found myself talking to no one.

Could it be that Grandma no longer believed in God? I got up and quietly walked to my grandma's room. I stood in the doorway and listened for her breathing. I couldn't hear a thing, just my own heart pounding in my ears. It was dark, but I could see her bed at the other end of the room.

"I need my beauty rest, son," she giggled from her bed.

I approached her bed and whispered, "Did I wake you?"

She turned and faced me without lifting her head. "I heard you coming," she said. "I always hear you," she added, anticipating my question.

"Abuela, do you still believe in God?" I asked, fearing the reply.

Slowly, she sat up in her bed. I often forgot that Grandma was already eighty-four years old. In the dim moonlight from the window, I held her gaze for what seemed a long time.

"Of course, son. That's the *only* thing I believe in," she stated softly but with the kind of certainty that can knock down buildings.

"God is the same yesterday, today, and tomorrow. He has been my God since I was twenty-three years old and will be my God forever," she concluded.

I tried to organize my thoughts. "But how come you said there's no church and that Father Fumes wasn't a priest?" I asked, clutching the folded bedspread at the end of her bed.

She paused for a few seconds. "God gave men clear instructions of how He wanted His church and His affairs handled. Men, in their arrogance, changed everything. They broke the commandments, they changed how things ought to be done, and therefore walked away from the true way of God. Thus, they're cut off from Him. They have no claim to His mercy or laws, and much less to do things in His name like the priests today claim," she said, accentuating the last few words.

The explanation was transparent but had serious and profound implications.

"So, God isn't with us any longer, then. Are we on our own?" I asked, folding and unfolding the fabric in my fists.

"No, son, He is here," she said with certainty. "He is always here, but we must seek Him with all our heart." She smiled, as if she understood my confusion. "You tell God that you know He is there, that you know you're cut off from Him because we've lost the way, but that you love Him." She smiled, and her white teeth gleamed in the soft evening light. "He will hear you," she said.

She continued: "I know Him, I believe in Him, and I've seen again and again all the wonderful things He has done for me in my life." Her tone was convincing. I felt hope inside where before I had felt bereft, and in despair. The notion that God could actually do stuff for me was radical.

I asked, "Can I actually see or feel something that God is doing for me?"

Once more Grandma measured her words. Meaning was critical to her. "Son, if you didn't see or feel what God was doing for you, how would you know it was Him? When He is working for you and with you, rest assured, you'll know it. Don't forget that you asked Him in the first place." She tilted her head a fraction and raised her eyebrows. That was her "bingo" sign—an indication that the rest was left as my mental homework, something to chew on for later. She was done, at least for the night. She motioned for me to move closer for a moment and touched my face with her warm, wrinkled hand. "Just one thing," she said as I was making my way to the door. "In order for you to deserve His blessings, help, and protection, you have to obey His commandments." I stopped without turning.

"Good night, son," she said, and I heard the ruffle of the sheets.

Sleep eluded me for a long time that night, almost until daybreak. My thoughts turned into worries. *Follow His commandments.* Grandma's words bounced in my head. Nobody I knew followed the commandments any better than Grandma, I concluded. It's true that there is no place in the Bible that says, "That's it, we're done with the commandments." But, by the same token, I believed that Grandma knew what she was talking about. Maybe she had some kind of secret deal with God that only worked for her. But she said it was for everybody. My head hurt. I needed to sleep. I tried for a very long time without success.

At breakfast the next day, I was tired and confused but ready for more. I asked two or three questions in rapid succession. It was a "thought rehearsal" like Grandma used to call it. "You're thinking faster than you can come up with words to express your thoughts, son," she said, while grinding a small ball of cocoa into powder. I thought in silence, while the rhythmic sound of the marble stone kept getting softer as the chocolate grit became powder.

"The day that you believe that He is real, that He can hear you and that only He can help you, then He will reveal His awesome power and you'll know in your heart, without a doubt, that He is God," she concluded.

Again, I experienced the tremendous certainty that day that God had done some great and wonderful things for my grandma. Hungry for more information, I prodded. "What miracles have you seen, Abuela? Please, tell me."

She only smiled and cleared the table of dirty dishes.

A Hand and a Name

My great-grandmother, Florencia Martinez Hernandez, was born about 1895. She was the youngest of sixteen siblings, and because there were no records available at the time, she wasn't sure of the year. She celebrated her birthday on August 31, "but only God knows my real birthday," she laughed. Her father was away during the War of Independence of 1895 and didn't return until she was two years old. Her mother passed away during childbirth, and her older sisters cared for her.

Her father was a revered war veteran nicknamed Lieutenant Maguey (Agave). He was smooth and handsome, Grandma said, but he had nasty hard thorns and a sharp edge when provoked, just like the agave plant.

Grandma married at age eighteen, against the advice of her family and contrary to the desire of her in-laws. Her husband's family descended from the very first emancipated slaves in the country. They had large land holdings and hundreds of workers and had managed to amass a significant fortune in two generations. Her husband had studied law and operated the first printing press in the province. Mercury photographs show him as a distinguished-looking man with thin, rimless glasses. I still preserve fragments of his journal, draft notes, and other personal writings.

After four years of marriage and two children, he fell ill to what was described as possibly tuberculosis or lung cancer. After a brief fight with the disease, he died—leaving Grandma with two very small children and a precarious legal situation. Unscrupulous manipulations of a ruthless town lawyer almost plunged her into total destitution. Only the timely intervention by a lifelong friend prevented disaster.

She managed to sell her holdings and moved away to another province. There she was able to acquire an old colonial house with some land for cultivation, a well, and what later proved to be her most profitable enterprise—a stone mill. There she settled and raised her family. That was the place I called home for more than two decades.

She settled in the small fishing village west of Habana, which became my universe until fate, or the hand of God, took me halfway around the world. In that small village she worked and prayed with equal intensity for almost thirty years, waiting for what she termed "the whistling of the Lord." In her simple but undeniable logic, God had to manifest Himself somehow, somewhere, and dispense instructions to His children about how to "reconnect and rebuild" the relationship.

In her mind, since God had promised to build a temple for all people of the world, new instructions had to be dispensed and received. And for that day, Grandma was ready. In 1948, Grandma purchased an open ticket for sea travel to Israel. According to her reasoning, it was just a matter of time before a temple would be built in the Holy Land. She reasoned that according to Isaiah, one would be built and He would signal for the people of all nations to come and worship.

> For thus saith the Lord unto the eunuchs that keep my sabbaths, and choose the things that please me, and take hold of my covenant;
>
> Even unto them will I give in mine house and within my walls a place and a name better than of sons and of daughters: I will give them an everlasting name, that shall not be cut off.
>
> Also the sons of the stranger, that join themselves to the Lord, to serve him, and to love the name of the Lord, to be his servants, every one that keepeth the sabbath from polluting it, and taketh hold of my covenant;
>
> Even them will I bring to my holy mountain, and make them joyful in my house of prayer: their burnt offerings and their sacrifices shall be accepted upon mine altar; for mine house shall be called an house of prayer for all people. (Isaiah 56:4–7)

We read this scripture again and again over the years. I suppose that it was lost in the symbolism, the poetry, and the archaic language, but the message was there. As Grandma saw it, the God of Israel intended to have a temple built and bring all people into the covenant. It was there, in black and white, and waiting to happen.

Grandma felt mystified, sad, and fearful, since, as far as she knew, this prophecy had not come to pass. By 1988, Israel had been established for forty years, and there was still no temple that she knew of. Even worse, she'd read in *National Geographic* that the Muslims had built one of their churches in the place where the temple mount was. For years Grandma thought it was a tragedy, but later she shrugged her shoulders and forgot about it.

"Forget about it?" I exclaimed, shaking my head in confusion. "Abuela," I tried reasoning out loud, "you said that the temple will be rebuilt and all people will be able to go there and be taken to be part of the house of Israel."

"I didn't say that," she declared, interrupting my tirade. "God said it." She smiled.

"Okay, point taken. God said it. But the Muslims built their own church in the same spot that the temple is supposed to be built again. It would take a war for Israel to retake the place, tear down the Muslim church, and rebuild the temple."

As usual, in a masterstroke that shattered the argument in a second, she stated offhandedly, "Well, son, that's God's problem, not mine. I just have to be ready and get there when He blows the horn." She paused. "Believe me, He will have His temple built in His own due time," she said, tapping on the table with a bony finger.

This temple, and whatever took place in it, was critical to Grandma's view of God. In her mind, God never slept, took a break, went on vacation, or much less forgot anything. He had promised a temple and a covenant, and it would happen. Her fervor and convictions were certainly baffling. She spoke as if this "covenant" was hers to claim. I felt, at times, the very distinct impression that she felt a kinship and affinity for the things of God that were puzzling, to say the least. There were also these weird, time-honored traditions in her ancestral family that had a very Jewish undertone and weren't at all connected to the traditional African roots—not eating shellfish, not working on Sunday, and, the most absurd of all, not eating pork, which is a total anachronism for a Cuban. The pig roast for Christmas is almost a constitutional mandate.

About this last issue I'd questioned her countless times before. Why did we have to suffer the results of many hundreds of years of, now inconsequential, traditions in Grandma's family? Pork is considered more or less a delicacy as well as an endangered species in Cuba. Most families looked forward to the Christmas dinner including a slice of pork roast, black beans, and white rice, and the next day to well-seasoned, crunchy pork skins.

Not us. Not in our family. It drove me to the edge of insanity that Grandma wouldn't cook pork roast for Christmas like all the other normal, pork-loving Cuban families. By the beginning of December, Grandma started her litany: "Well children, let's have a good Christmas this year, okay? Let's not start with the 'but Abuela why can't we have a pork roast like everybody else' song again, okay? There will be no pig roast in my kitchen until after my funeral. And even then if you dare bring one into this house, I promise I'll come back from the dead myself and throw it away, pot and all. And you can try me if you don't believe me."

For years, I thought she could make good on that promise. To this day, we have given up on the whole pork roasting deal. Just in case.

She wouldn't eat shellfish either. Now, that was enough to put us in restraints in a hospital for the less-than-lucid folks. In an environment where most people fished for a living and ate fish at least once a day, we looked like certified kooks. In the Middle Ages, people got burned at the stake for less than that, I heard. In some parts, going against accepted traditions could get you hanged. She didn't care. She cooked shellfish, all right, in a different set of pots specially designated for that kind of food. Exquisite shrimp and lobster dishes, fit for a state dinner. But she wouldn't eat them, not even at gunpoint. She later soaked the dishes and pots in baking soda and lemon water for a couple of days on the patio. This "decontaminated them," she claimed, and only then did she bring them back into the house.

Sunday was special for us. There were no trips to the convenience store, no yard work, no chicken cage cleaning, not much of anything but relaxation. Grandma rose really early and peeled and sliced a bucket of potatoes into wedges, then set the beans on the stove and cooked either ground beef or shredded beef. We were free to eat as much as we wanted, whenever we wanted. But that was the only meal available the whole day. She wouldn't cook, and my mother wasn't even allowed in the kitchen.

We also had to stay close to home. "Parents need their rest," she admonished us. We weren't allowed to loiter at our friends' homes since we'd be disturbing their day of rest.

You couldn't make Grandma work on Sunday. If you had an emergency, you'd better call the Red Cross, because if you were hoping that my grandma would go visit you, there had better be an act of God compelling her to go. Otherwise you had a better chance of being struck by lightning than her going to your house.

"The devil doesn't have enough money to pay me to go to work on Sunday," she'd say. If you were sick and dying, Grandma would visit you—on Monday.

"If you're in such a hurry to stand at St. Peter's gates, then go ahead. I'll catch up with you in awhile. Shoot, I'm eighty-some years old. My number is just about called." That was Grandma.

Her ancestral memory and family history described how the folks who were brought as slaves to the Islands were from Ethiopia. They were a bit different from the other folks from Congo, Guinea, the Ivory Coast, and Nigeria. They were slender, tall, had clear eyes, and dressed in colorful attire. Her folks were fishermen and tradesmen that traveled up and down the river in slim, fast, canoe-like boats all the way to the ocean.

She spoke of how they had just one God, a God who couldn't be bribed, bought, or scared into doing stuff for you, for He ruled the universe. And her forefathers had priests, real priests, that were set aside by God Himself long ago to teach the people, to defend them, and to keep His sacred things. What those sacred things were, she didn't know.

"Nobody remembered," she said sadly. "It has been so long."

Her belief in this God was unshaken, her faith the size of Mt. Everest. She used to say, "There's nothing that God won't do for you if you believe He will, and if it's the best for you."

The scriptures were her anchor and line of connection to this God that she loved and in whom she trusted entirely.

"We're all His children, born in different houses, at different times," she reflected. "But we come from the same root, like the twin wild orchid trees out in the front of the house. Almost a century old and planted on a strange soil, far away from where the seedpods fell to the ground for the first time."

She'd told me that the trees were planted from seeds that came in a pod from Spain inside a book in the early 1800s. The young lady of the house had been brought to the Island to live with her paternal uncle in order to keep her away from an unwelcome suitor back in the old country. Her family reasoned that after a few months, perhaps a year, the young man would desist on his advances, given the distance and lack of contact. Unbeknown to the family, the young lady had enlisted the help of her younger sister in order to stay in contact with her sweetheart. She was able to send and receive letters from him as if they were from and to her sister.

The young man knew that it would take him some time to secure the funds and necessary documents to travel west to the colonies. Contrary to what happened in North America, Spanish Crown servants weren't free to travel to the colonies to settle, except with an endorsement from the court jesters.

Wild orchids take approximately twenty-four months to bloom. If the seedpod survived the month-long trip and made it to the ground, the young man wrote and told her he'd be with her before they bloomed. What happened next isn't entirely clear, and the whole story could have been part of the Victorian era romance climate so prevalent at the time. But what was clear is the moral of the story, that those trees aren't indigenous to the Islands, they traveled long and far, they were planted almost a hundred years ago, and they were there as a witness of the Diaspora. Grandma's point: we are seeds of the same tree, strewn to and fro across the whole earth, planted and multiplied far from the roots. But we aren't lost to the Father.

"The hand of God has scattered His children to the four corners of the earth for a wise purpose in Him," Grandma always said. "And wherever we are, He hears us and succors us and strengthens those that rely on Him and call on His name." Tears welled behind her soft, cloudy blue eyes. "And He knows you too, Son."

Years went by before I got a chance to know the God of my grandmother. I had many nights of reading and doubting the scriptures, but not her faith, not her words.

ISAIAH—GRANDMA'S
PROPHET—AGAIN?

"Abuela, why do we have to read that prophet again?" I asked, a bit exasperated. "The man makes no sense. Besides, it's kind of not really all that important to us right now," I stated, my sense of historicity excellent. At least I thought so. The stuff was clearly not intended for me.

"Well, that's most certainly not true that he isn't talking to you right now." She pointed and read:

> The wilderness and the solitary place shall be glad for them; and the desert shall rejoice, and blossom as the rose.
> It shall blossom abundantly, and rejoice even with joy and singing: the glory of Lebanon shall be given unto it . . .
> Strengthen ye the weak hands, and confirm the feeble knees.
> Say to them that are of a fearful heart, Be strong, fear not: behold, your God will come with vengeance, even God with a recompence; he will come and save you. . . .
> Then shall the lame man leap as an hart, and the tongue of the dumb sing: for in the wilderness shall waters break out, and streams in the desert.
> And the parched ground shall become a pool, and the thirsty land springs of water: in the habitation of dragons, where each lay, shall be grass with reeds and rushes. . . .
> And the ransomed of the Lord shall return, and come to Zion with songs and everlasting joy upon their heads: they shall obtain joy and gladness, and sorrow and sighing shall flee away. (Isaiah 35:1–4, 6–7, 10)

My head was buzzing like a beehive inside an old hollow tree, of course, but her explanation was transparent, almost too simple to be true. After all the suffering, the difficulty, and the strife, the Lord will reward the righteous of every land. They'll find rest and protection in the fold of the Lord.

"There are many things I don't understand," she admitted. "But it's my hope that the good Lord will allow me to understand some of them before I die. If not, then at least I will have read them in case they quiz me in heaven," she chuckled. But maybe she was serious.

"Son, for some reason, the Lord allowed this prophet to live a very long time and to write more than anybody else. He wrote about things that no one else wrote about in the whole Bible."

Again she slid her fingers over the old, faded Bible. By then her eyes were clouding with cataracts, and finding the passages she wanted to read took slightly longer than before.

> Thus saith God the Lord, he that created the heavens, and stretched them out; he that spread forth the earth, and that which cometh out of it; he that giveth breath unto the people upon it, and spirit to them that walk therein:
>
> I the Lord have called thee in righteousness, and will hold thine hand, and will keep thee, and give thee for a covenant of the people, for a light of the Gentiles;
>
> To open the blind eyes, to bring out the prisoners from the prison, and them that sit in darkness out of the prison house.
>
> I am the Lord: that is my name: and my glory will I not give to another, neither my praise to graven images.
>
> Behold, the former things are come to pass, and new things do I declare: before they spring forth I tell you of them. (Isaiah 42:5–9)

"Son, remember that there have always been millions of people on the earth. But only the folks in Israel knew the real God," she said, accentuating her words. "The rest of the folks were worshiping stones, wood carvings, bull-men, scorpion-men, elephant-head women, killing people for sacrifices, and only the Lord knows what other kinds of abominations." I loved the faces she made for effect, stabbing the air, flapping her hands around her ears and protruding her lips pachyderm style in her best characterization of Dumbo.

"And they thought they were in the clear," she continued, making the "OK" sign with both hands and rolling her eyes. "They didn't know that they didn't know." She let it sink all the way into my fertile but still shallow brain.

"So God, the *real* God," I said, using the same emphatic manner-isms, "won't approve of what I'm doing even if I do it with faith?" I asked.

"Nope," came her response like a bucket of cold water in the middle of summer. "Not if it's wrong and He hasn't prescribed it that way," she added conclusively.

"That's messed up," I concluded, confused and disappointed. She had killed my whole argument, which I thought was a good one: faith.

"Son, if you cook for all us with love and care and the best desire to help, but we end up dead of food poisoning, you're gonna have an appointment with the judge and a change of address to a place a lot less pleasant than the current one." She knew how to make a point that helped clear my mind and leave me hungry for more.

"Look here," she said:

> And Nadab and Abihu, the sons of Aaron, took either of them his censer, and put fire therein, and put incense thereon, and offered strange fire before the Lord, which he commanded them not.
> And there went out fire from the Lord, and devoured them, and they died before the Lord.
> Then Moses said unto Aaron, This is it that the Lord spake, saying, I will be sanctified in them that come nigh me, and before all the people I will be glorified. And Aaron held his peace. (Leviticus 10:1–3)

I was shocked. God just literally smoked these guys in public for a first offense, and their dad couldn't even be mad about it. But the point was made evident and without room for misunderstanding: God is in charge. He decides how things are done, and there's a penalty for trespassing. In their case, failure to obey was fatal.

"So . . ." I hedged, "how come God doesn't flame Father Fumes?" I asked, trying to keep the smirk off my face. After all, it was a legitimate question.

The mere mentioning of his name brought my grandma to the verge of physical illness. Although I probed, scrutinized, and begged for some historical background on this issue, I was never successful. I imagined that some juicy story must be behind such strong reactions, but she took the secret to her grave.

"Men like him can't escape divine justice. In His due time, God will deal with them. Christ saw right through them and put them to shame in public," she explained while flipping through to the end of her Bible. She paused for a few seconds and then read:

> But he that is greatest among you shall be your servant.
> And whosoever shall exalt himself shall be abased; and he that shall humble himself shall be exalted.
> But woe unto you, scribes and Pharisees, hypocrites! for ye shut up the kingdom of heaven against men: for ye neither go in yourselves, neither suffer ye them that are entering to go in.
> Woe unto you, scribes and Pharisees, hypocrites! for ye devour widows' houses, and for a pretence make long prayer: therefore ye shall receive the greater damnation.
> Woe unto you, scribes and Pharisees, hypocrites! for ye compass sea and land to make one proselyte, and when he is made, ye make him twofold more the child of hell than yourselves.
> Woe unto you, ye blind guides, which say, Whosoever shall swear by the temple, it is nothing; but whosoever shall swear by the gold of the temple, he is a debtor!
> Ye fools and blind: for whether is greater, the gold, or the temple that sanctifieth the gold? (Matthew 23:11–17)

"So, what's going to happen to him? Father Fumes, I mean," I asked.

I could feel a timid smile trying to push aside my poker face for a second. Grandma's face, on the other hand, was expressionless, her eyes taking the now familiar, almost scary glassy look.

She was silent for what seemed like hours. With her eyes fixed on the wall, she answered. Of course, it wasn't what I was looking for. "That's God's business." And with that she was done with the topic.

Grandma's love for the writings of Isaiah was centered on his recurring themes. On one hand, again and again, this prophet pointed to the Gentiles (all of us not born in Israel and who lived away from the teachings of God and His laws). The other involved Grandma's belief that in order for God's teachings to be complete, a tabernacle or a temple needed to exist. Her argument was pretty convincing, at least for me.

"As soon as God was able to get the children of Israel away from Egypt, He gave them instructions to build the tabernacle," she explained. "The place was beautiful, with colored linen and embroidery, curtains and carpets, as well as sections for different things and ceremonies. It was a place where they could find Him and He'd speak with them. It was a place of worship as much as a place for them to learn to communicate with their God. A sacred place."

She read quietly for a few minutes. She'd read the account in Exodus countless times in her lifetime. But every time she read it, she found renewed faith and hope. She relished the images of the description: so many cubits of purple fabric and green fabric and silver thread, and golden rings. But the description of the temple of Solomon almost brought tears to her eyes.

"Oh, son, how I would have loved to walk into the temple of God," she exclaimed, overflowing with excitement. "A place like no other on earth made for God, according to His commandments and for His own purpose. A place, son, where His presence could be felt and the knowledge that His Spirit dwelled there. . . ." Her lips trembled a little with emotion.

"There are no places like that on the earth anymore," she said softly. Her gaze moved away from me, hiding the tears that finally rolled down her face. She got up slowly from the table and walked quietly into the kitchen. After some slight chinking of dishes and silverware, she was back with some cheese and fruit preserves on a small plate. I felt my own tears burning my eyes. I don't know why, but Grandma talking about the temple always made me feel sad, happy, and uncertain all at the same time. It was like I was missing a vital part of something that I needed to understand but that was still beyond my awareness. Why was this temple so critical? And if so, why had God not caused Israel to build another? After all, Grandma said that in 1948, Israel became a country again and the Israelites returned to their homeland.

I'd read with her that even the apostles went to the temple after Christ was crucified. But then the temple was destroyed and never rebuilt.

Another theory of Grandma's was that Israel hadn't come to understand that Christ was their God, that He came because the old laws didn't work anymore, since they failed to realize what it was all about.

"Killing goats, rams, or doves couldn't save anyone," she reasoned. "The whole idea was to show them that the penalty for sin was death. That only through the shedding of blood and sacrifice we could be restored," she explained.

I'd seen animals being slaughtered, and it wasn't pretty. As a younger child I stopped eating chicken when I found out that we were eating the ones that had been pecking only hours before on the patio.

"Sin brings death," Grandma explained. "After awhile, the Jews became almost mechanical about sacrifices. They didn't regard them as

critical to salvation, but they became a tradition. Thus, a great and ultimate sacrifice was needed to save the nation and bring the world to God
so that all His children could be saved. That was Jesus Christ, but it went
right over them. They were so obsessed with the law that when the Law-
giver came, they killed Him. They thought He had broken the law!" she
exclaimed, raising her hands. She pointed to another scripture in Isaiah:

> But now thus saith the Jehovah that created thee, O Jacob, and he
> that formed thee, O Israel, Fear not: for I have redeemed thee, I have
> called thee by thy name; thou art mine. . . .
> I, even I, am the Lord; and beside me there is no saviour. . . .
> Thus saith the Lord, your redeemer, the Holy One of Israel; For
> your sake I have sent to Babylon, and have brought down all their
> nobles, and the Chaldeans, whose cry is in the ships.
> I am the Lord, your Holy One, the creator of Israel, your King.
> Thus saith the Lord, which maketh a way in the sea, and a path in
> the mighty waters . . .
> I, even I, am he that blotteth out thy transgressions for mine own
> sake, and will not remember thy sins. (Isaiah 43:1, 11, 14–16, 25)

She read slowly, sliding her wrinkled fingers over the crumpled pages
of the book, accentuating the word *Lord* every time. In Spanish it was not
translated as such; the word *Jehovah* appears instead.

"There it is in black and white, son. He was and is the God of Israel.
But they didn't believe because they no longer had faith. They had traded
it for a bunch of useless rules and regulations they couldn't even keep."
She shrugged her shoulders and shook her head in disbelief.

"But, Abuela—" I asked, taking my time since I was still phrasing the
question. "How come you can read the Bible and understand it so well
and they couldn't?" I was really looking for an explanation rather than
questioning Grandma's ability to understand Isaiah.

Actually, nobody else I knew read the Bible, much less understood it.

She tapped slowly on the table for a few seconds. Again, she was
sifting through her endless repertoire of responses. Through the years, I
realized that her responses were always designed to leave no doubt in my
mind of her certainty. It was as if she were expecting my complete surety
regarding these issues.

"God will reveal Himself to all people of all nations that truly seek
Him, obey Him, and worship Him in their hearts. He is available to all,
everywhere, anytime, and you never need to wait in line." I couldn't wait

to see that. Most Cubans believed the line at the pearly gates would take weeks. She smiled tenderly and caressed the side of my face.

Well, that was encouraging. At least I had a hope to be able to connect with this God at some point in time. However, I felt that I was staring at the horizon through a piece of PVC pipe. It seemed small, far, and as fuzzy as an old black and white family picture.

The problem with Grandma's God was that He spoke a long time ago, through prophets who lived eons ago, and the language especially was a killer. But beyond the obvious, I struggled with the notion of "descending from Israel." I failed to see the connection or why the fate of Israel was tied to ours.

God also seemed like a cognitive impossibility—an all-knowing, all-powerful God that you can only feel when you're at your wit's end; a God that you must obey at all times, think of and pray to at all times, and follow His every commandment. And boy, He had many of them.

All the reading and all the teaching sunk deep into my brain and stayed there, like sediment at the bottom of the river. It wasn't until many years later, when my very existence was threatened by one of life's storms that the silt was stirred up. But amazingly, it made it all clear. No doubt fear played a significant factor in my resistance to approaching this God. What if He really zapped me or something? According to Grandma, He was a jealous God, quick to forgive and slow to wrath. But if you found yourself "on His left hand" for whatever reason, you were as good as space dust. Such thoughts sent chills down my spine.

I turned away, trying to shake the thoughts out of my head. It was just too much. *How does she know so much? How come God never spoke to me?*

But again, if He did, I was sure I would die on the spot of sudden teenage death syndrome.

Look Me in the Eyes...

My understanding of the importance of money in everyday life as I was growing up was rather fractured. I'm mystified by my prior ignorance when I compare and hear children discussing their allowance and purchase choices today.

A peso, or "chavo" as Cubans often refer to money, was usually a dirty, torn, scribbled piece of paper, usually of little use to children, except in the grocery store or the bakery. The candy lady, of course, was different. She just took coins, and coins weren't real money as far as I could tell.

Adults seemed to need money quite frequently. Since these kinds of discussions weren't the purview of children in my household, I mostly overhead conversations between my grandmother and others from our village about "needing a little bit of money until payday." It was confusing to me, to say the least, and the whole subject was still light years away from me being able to make sense of it. My grandma's face always remained impassive as she spoke to Lena, a hyper, razor thin, fast talking neighbor. On one particular day, she nodded and said things like, "Yes," "I understand," and "I can see how . . ."

Then, after several minutes, Grandma leaned forward on the edge of her seat and said softly, without blinking, "Look me in the eyes and tell me that whatever happens, you'll pay me back."

One day, I saw Lena cry. It scared me to see this vibrant, energetic woman break down and drop to the floor while sobbing uncontrollably, so much it almost made me cry. Beats me if I knew why. The intensity of the situation, I imagined. I felt the desperation in our front room.

I once saw a man kneel down, hug my grandma's leg, and cry. She held his head for a while until he managed to get up and clean his face. Most of the time she got hugs and kisses. What it all meant was well beyond my comprehension. These actions were emotionally charged, and at times, people did things that were total anachronisms for grown-ups.

As time went on, these episodes began to take shape in my mind more coherently. Life was hard for most families. Unbeknownst to me, Grandma's small but diverse enterprises provided employment and sustenance for many families in our tiny community. But at times it wasn't enough. And they all knew that help was always available.

"God blesses you, son, so that you may remember that it is Him who blesses you, and later, that you may share the blessing with others," she almost always said when the topic of conversation was money.

"The notion that you got things just because you earned them is a fallacy," she pointed out. "All we are and have belongs to Him. And whatever is given us, we must administer wisely to be worthy to continue to receive in the future. And because it belongs to Him anyway, who are we to deny others when they are in need of a portion of it?" Once more, it took some time, but she hammered it through.

"Don't get attached to stuff. It's not ours to begin with, and although you may have provided effort and sacrifice, it's by His will and kindness that you got the stuff. And, if by any chance there's a neighbor in need, you should share. Thus, we become worthy to continue to receive from Him in the future."

That was deep. I scratched my head and tried to reposition my line of reasoning. It made perfect sense to believe that a man had the right to enjoy the fruit of his labor, unencumbered, unconcerned, and free of guilt. After all, people often ripped their hands working so they could make a name for themselves and stake a claim to something. Acknowledging God, however, for success or accomplishment, seems to steal the thunder out of "personal achievement." But it made sense. It's His entire domain. We don't discover anything but simply become aware of that which has been there from the beginning of time. Observation, research, or inspiration leads us to it. But it's not new. These concepts were just mind-boggling to a twelve-year-old.

Grandma described the Great Depression as the bleakest period of economic activity ever in the country. There was no food, no money, no employment nor prospect of it. Millions of people struggled for survival on a small ration of corn and wild vegetables. Even fish was hard to come by because fishing staples were nonexistent. Life was hard and painful.

Frugality and austerity were innate traits in my grandmother. She managed to keep a fairly large plot of land in production through this ordeal. Also, salted fish (which can last for years in storage) complemented our family's food staple. Trading was very limited; simple and otherwise readily available commodities like cooking oil became scarce.

Lack of food forced many parents to leave their children with relatives who could care for them until the situation changed. In her case, and for many years, dozens of children stayed in my grandmother's home at different times during the Depression years. Parents left them in the care of Grandma for months, and even years, until they could find employment and a more stable source of income.

More than half a century later, and since I can remember, Mother's Day was a reminder that many of those Grandma cared for during those horrible years hadn't forgotten her. No one in the neighborhood received more letters and postcards than Grandma. The postman, Gustavo, came very early in the morning with large bundles of cards crudely wrapped in construction paper.

"This is a special delivery run just for you, Florencia," Gustavo said, smiling and carrying a brown paper bag tied with a thin rope. Grandma said they had known each other since Gustavo was little. Of course, she was the senior and founding citizen of the community. She'd seen everybody in diapers, more or less.

Gustavo wasn't very old, but he always looked tired. His parched, shining face was friendly and inviting. He carried a brown oversized leather bag that stained his white shirt on the shoulder. The postman's bag held a certain mystique. It was the container for news from far away, or a reminder of a painful obligation: like the gas or electric bill. Gustavo always stopped to talk to Grandma. During the summer he stayed longer, savoring cold mango juice with ice squares in the tall glasses we almost never used.

They talked for a long while. She always asked him questions about other people who lived up or down the hill beyond my visual range. Grandma never got to see these people because she couldn't take on the hills anymore. Neither could they.

But on Mother's Day, Gustavo would come at daybreak. Sunday mail delivery on Mother's Day must have been instituted in Colonial times because it has existed since anyone could remember. With bundles of letters and festive-looking greeting cards, the postman whistled right before he strained his vocal cords and called your name at full volume. It was usually to arouse the attention of those living in the back or second stories of the neighborhood buildings. On Mother's Day, that unmistakable whistle sent us at neck-breaking speed down from our bed to the doorway just to watch him stride down the garden stairs with the roped brown packs of cards and letters. Some of the letters were from people and places we had never heard of. Others were from familiar people whose stories had been told many times.

Grandma always prepared homemade cocoa with toast for Gustavo. He ate quickly, gulped the last drop of the warm drink, and sat and talked, never looking at the letters—never once. He was content with bringing them and being the bearer of good news, distant news. And of course, there was hot cocoa. My grandmother's cocoa, with a hint of cinnamon dusted on the top, was the best I'd ever tasted.

Gustavo went on and on about "so and so" and "her and him" and on for what seemed an endless tirade of meaningless names of people who lived nearby. How could they know so many people? Then I remembered. Gustavo was the postman. He got to read the names of everybody who lived everywhere since the last Ice Age. But Grandma? I know she'd never delivered letters. So how did she know so many people?

After Gustavo was gone, we opened the door to the morning air to allow the light to flood the living room. Grandma's eyes were getting weak. She strained, trying to read the sender's name. And we waited in suspense, watching her lips as she murmured the name softly and then break into a colorful laughter.

She handed the card or the letter to me, for careful reading.

"Dear Florencia," it always started. It went on to describe how grateful the sender was for Grandma's help.

Grandma always listened quietly and stared into the wall, as if searching deep into ancient history and memory for the details. They always came back vividly, clearly as noonday light. Dates, places, people, the weather, and a myriad of small snippets that made the story feel real. At times, it felt like the day's light faded away and a film rolled into view, in full color.

My favorite letter was about the sick twins. The boys were left in Grandma's care right after the rainy season started in 1944. Their mother had been "sick of black lung's disease," as folks described tuberculosis in those days. She was weak and yellow, unable to speak, and too feeble to stand, much less care for a couple of toddlers. She could only swallow a cup of soup and some chamomile tea a couple of times a day. Coughing fits lasting five to six minutes left her drained and faint. The sight of the blood and fluid that followed these fits was hair-raising. Her husband couldn't stand to look at her anymore and avoided her eyes whenever possible. He'd cried in the beginning, but he was fresh out of tears.

He felt hopeless, lost, resigned to see her die sooner or later. Sooner would be better since he couldn't cope with it any longer.

The decision was made to take his wife to the sanatorium. It was an interesting word, I thought. Since nobody ever healed there, it was most likely a parking lot for the sick and dying—the last stop before the grave. It was the land of the hopeless and the destitute.

Her husband came looking for some work in order to feed his children, but there was none. Not for him, not for anyone. The whole business and industry had come to a standstill. There was no fuel, no spare parts, no seed, and no fertilizers. A few lucky farmers had managed to have seed and dehydrated vegetables in store. Fish was always an option if you happened to live on the coast. Hunger was rampant and unabated on most of Cuba during those years. People resorted to eating things they never later admitted to consuming.

The father and his children brought nothing to Grandma's. He shuffled into my grandmother's yard, pulling a tired, old horse behind him. His twins were asleep, tied onto the saddle. He didn't know where he was, nor did he care. They'd been on the road since daybreak, but he wasn't sure how many days they'd traveled before. Nor did he remember when he last fed the children. They had cried until he couldn't hear them anymore. They had stopped for a few days in a fruit orchard and ate until the fruit made them sick. Then they moved on.

Grandma invited him in. He seemed tired and broken, with a look on his face that she knew and feared—the look that signals when someone has stopped trying and no longer has any desire to continue. Grandma fixed one of the rooms in the house for him and the boys. They were four years old at the time, she said. "And a noisy pair," she added. She fed them that evening. It was the first of many suppers. And after they had put the twins to bed, she and this weary man spoke for a long time of his life, of his home, how he met his wife, and how he had nothing except the twins—a painful reminder and ever-present memory of what was now gone.

"He cried," she said, "for a long time." And he talked, biting his fingernails till they bled, about his country school, the town's children who got sick, and how his wife had cared for them until she got sick. He cried about how the folks turned their back on them once they found out about her illness and how the townspeople ultimately burned their home one day while the little family went to the doctor.

They had gone to her sister's house for help. Her sister had fixed the barn for them but wouldn't allow them into her home. They placed some food in a basket by the front door and left. First the heat and later the rain and the humidity had taken its toll on his wife.

She seemed to get worse every day. The food eventually ran out. Their relatives wouldn't even open the door. All his pleading and begging was in vain. His wife was dying a little each hour.

Pity helped for a while. Now and again neighbors dropped some food at the door of the shed, but it wasn't enough. Then, it was the business of keeping the twins away from their mother. But how? She'd cry and call to them constantly in her tormented sleep. The rags filled with blood and the bedpan with urine and vomit were dangerous for the children to be around. He had resorted to building a small compartment to keep the children away from her. Or was it that he didn't want to see her?

They got on the road, but it was unbearable for the dying woman. They had consulted a vet, since they had no more money for a regular doctor. He suggested the sanatorium in the nearby town. The old colonial building was a former convent later converted into a hospital early in the century. There they went and there she stayed. He wasn't sure if she understood where she was. He wasn't sure if she could even see him anymore. It had been weeks since she'd spoken his name.

Grandma hired the man. He recovered some of his strength with the passage of time. He was diligent and able, but didn't say much. There wasn't much to do in the orchard around the house, "but it gave him the sense of earning his keep. Every man needs his dignity," Grandma asserted with sadness.

The twins tore around the house and chased the chickens until the children were exhausted and happy—for the most part. Children are resilient, void of pessimism, and without a past to torture them. They called for their mother occasionally, but it seemed like a distant memory to them, more like a flash of images not quite real in their mind. Their father didn't answer them when they asked questions about her.

After the rainy season, word came that the sugar mill a few days' journey away was hiring a few hands. The man spoke with Grandma about going over and "earning some real money" for a few weeks. He wanted to buy shoes for him and the boys, another horse, and a few other things. Grandma told him to go without fear. She'd care for the boys until his return.

Five long years passed before Grandma or the twins saw the father again. By the time he arrived at the sugarcane mill and the much-coveted job, more than a thousand men were already crowding the place, hoping for a few week's employ. Heartbroken and ashamed, he dared not come back empty-handed. He kept going a few more days to another mill, again only to stumble on a similar scene. There he found a horde of destitute, hungry men, desperately hoping for a hair-thin opportunity to earn a day's meal. And once more he went on to several more mills until he found himself almost at the other end of the country—four weeks away on horseback.

Men, in general, have a low tolerance for failure. Despair is like a long tunnel without an exit but with a possible end. Usually death seems like a noble, even appealing end to failure. He found himself staring down a cliff. His soul was heavy with sorrow, and his blood was filled with cheap sugarcane rum. He knew the twins were safe with Grandma. No matter what, she'd care for them until they were able to fend for themselves. She was gentle and even tender with them. That was his only concern. His wife had certainly died by then. If he had nothing to provide, he shouldn't be a disgrace either. He had nothing to offer to anyone, not even to himself.

He jumped, in silence, with tears trailing down his face. It seemed like a long time, but he felt peace, not fear. He was unconscious for days. He awoke choking on bat dung and with cockroaches crawling over him. A web of vines and dead branches entangled his body. He thrashed and pulled and yelled until he fell to the ground, exhausted and crying. He cursed everybody and everything, including his birth. He faced the ultimate insult: that he was so useless, he was incapable of ending his own life.

He walked for days after that. He washed at a nearby river and walked without aim until his strength failed. He finally collapsed in a shed, among the sticky, acrid smell of some tobacco leaves stacked high on drying bars hanging from the ceiling. There, he cried himself to sleep amidst thunder and furious rain.

The farm workers found him. He woke up to find the edge of a sharp machete pressed against his neck. He looked like a lunatic, disheveled, ragged, dirty, and reeking of bat dung. He cried again. He tried to explain, but his hungered mind was incoherent. They fed him stew and some fried bird. He swallowed it all in two minutes.

He showered in the pool of the floodgate down the slope from the well. They gave him some faded clothing that was too big for his starved frame, but it was clean. He'd forgotten how long it had been since he'd used soap to wash. And then he slept for almost two days. The farmers came now and again, fearful that he'd died in his sleep. He had many dreams, disturbing and confusing dreams, like his own life had been.

He worked in the tobacco meadows for a few months. His mind had locked away his past existence. He didn't remember anybody or anything for many weeks. He seemed content with the safety of his sleeping corner in the barn that doubled as a smoke house. He was also pleased with the food twice a day and the peacefulness of the place that seemed to have escaped the famine that scourged the land in those days.

The trail that came into town from the main road was hidden by a sharp bend in the road. You couldn't see anything beyond that point. In more than one way, the geography of the place seemed to protect him from whatever was taking place "out there." Routine was a welcome relief to the emotional brutality he'd endured for so many months.

Before he knew it, the weeks became months, and soon years. He found solace in a small garden that he planted next to his barn. Most days he worked and toiled in it until sundown. Life had a familiar rhythm that appealed to him and helped him compartmentalize his existence. It helped him carve the rest of his life out of his conscious mind and push him into the present, unencumbered and free of the torturing memories of the past. And for a long time it worked.

Then, unannounced, the past came crashing down violently, accompanied by the bitter taste of regret. The expectation of the new year brought exuberance and renewed, unfounded hope to impoverished, naïve people. The air was filled with futile expectations and magical thinking. It was almost infantile and good-natured, if it weren't so tragic and heartbreaking. People in Cuba literally have almost nothing in terms of possessions and a future that doesn't exist for all practical purposes. The alcoholic excess of the year-end celebration had nothing to do with hope. It was but the adult Cuban version of Cinderella. It helped them find solace for a few hours, a few days every year, which incidentally could be their last.

People arranged for the trip of a lifetime back to the place of their birth, usually never to return. They offered sacrifices of stone or shells to ancient African gods, virgins, or saints—hoping for help with a non-reciprocal love interest, a coveted dead-end job with paid lunch, or just trying to mess with someone's fate for sport. All in the hope to pacify, entice, cajole, or manipulate life, people, or whatever into their favor and pleasure. These hybrid traditions provided ample opportunity for intoxication and all the irrational and grotesque behavior that came with cheap sugarcane rum and emotional depravation. Hunger and poverty had symptoms other than malnutrition.

The twins' father stared at the old woman, a former neighbor. She stood before him stoic, her wrinkled face swathed in a solemn stare, not just trying to recall his name but also his life. She knew him well. She knew everything about him. His name fell from her lips slowly and softly, fearfully perhaps. She seemed tentative and unsure of what else to say. She waited.

He heard his name echoing inside his ears. She knew his real name, not just "Teacher" as the people in the township came to know him. For a second, he wondered why nobody ever bothered to ask him his name. It dawned on him suddenly—nobody cared. They were all refugees, transients, and runaways from somewhere. They were all trying to escape their past, their pains, and the tragedy of their own lives. All of them had come to this place at some point in time. They had different reasons at different seasons, but all were eager to slide out of the hurt that precipitated their exodus.

He felt contractions rising like a wave and his mouth filling with bitter saliva. He turned away and stumbled into the bushes to hide. He stared at his half-digested dinner scattered on the grass and leaned on a tree as the memories came, inundating every recess of his mind, assaulting his brain relentlessly, with an intensity that was foreign to him. And then the tears came. He ran down the side of the storage sheds and into the tree grove away from the houses. There he screamed out his pain, which he kept at bay through the daily work, the vegetable garden, and his own denial. He cried out his loneliness, his regret, his shame.

Five years later he retuned to children who didn't really know him but missed him. He spoke to Grandma for a long time that night. The next day they left. The twins returned every summer with friends or relatives to see Grandma. The father never came back.

"God forgives, but some folks manage to deny themselves of it for some reason," Grandma observed.

Even when they no longer looked like twins, they came. They always brought food, lots of it, in bags, sacks, and boxes. They brought their own children, who grew up calling my grandma "Abuela," something that not only baffled but also infuriated me, since I believed that was a privilege saved for a select few . . . mainly just me.

There were always stories when they came, shared memories of long ago accompanied by tears, hugs, and laughter. The twins seemed big, rugged, and loud. They also appeared curious, looking everywhere as if they were trying to take the place in and match it to a picture frozen in their minds. They asked for people I never heard of and things that no longer existed; every year they asked the same questions.

They were an attachment to the family that preceded me, part of the thousand histories that make the tapestry of which Grandma was the common thread.

THE SHRIMP WAR AND NATIONAL GEOGRAPHIC

Summer in the Caribbean is pretty benign. For one, it's the heart of the rainy season, and no matter how relentless the noon heat may be, a tropical storm usually swings by and dampens the bravery of the sun with a fresh downpour.

Still, eighty-five degrees makes for an unhealthy bacterial soup on any food item left out of the refrigerator, especially meats and fish. Without ice, fish has four hours of shelf life during the day. Beyond that marker, only the ignorant or the suicidal attempt to eat it. Nobody in their right mind eats leftover fish purchased from the local market after 11 AM.

In the absence of Benadryl, the most common antihistamine in history, food poisoning can be a terrifying ordeal—if not a fatal one. For years, some of my friends bore the signs of their gluttonous foolishness on their faces. Literally. They walked around town with no hair on their heads, sporting a weird, purple-pink glossy look. It wasn't an easy thing to endure—that is, after you overcame the violent vomiting spasms and projectile diarrhea that you had to endure for two or three days. Then, you faced years of storytelling and public humiliation about how many times, where, and in front of whom you stained your pants. Lifelong nicknames resulted for the ones who ate the rotting fish.

The fish market was by the waterfront, within walking distance but far enough from our home that we didn't have to wake up every day with the roaring of the boat engines clanging in our heads. The smell was a different story. Every day at noon, they hosed the fish market down in order to sweep away the guts and waste from the day's activities. The biological sludge was driven by gravity toward the sea through a canal of sorts that made its way in between the old, dilapidated boathouses that dotted that side of town. The stench of dried blood and guts, fish parts, and the like was overwhelming. If the breeze was right, we got "wind of it" for a few minutes. It was enough to make you contort your face and stop chewing if you happened to be having lunch.

The market had been housed in an old colonial building for almost two centuries: thirty wood stands set on both ends of a long, cold, dim corridor with fish of all kinds arranged in wood boxes full of ice that dripped water into a narrow drain underneath. A strong fish smell permeated the building and one full street block in every direction. The place was a hazard in its own right. The hallway was full of local and foreign buyers, the fishermen pushing their catch down your nose and into your shopping bag, screaming, "Fresh! Fresh, people. Just out of the ocean!" They also gave out pricing information, weather forecasts, seasonal fluctuation of the species, and other tidbits of information.

The wholesale buyers from the towns round about—restaurants, fish stores, together with brokers and speculators—made our small fish market a scary-looking swarm of activity. Everybody seemed to be pushing or holding a homemade cargo device of some kind. Once weight and price were settled, the fish was dumped quickly into a man-powered rolling apparatus, propelled at terrorizing speed through the narrow corridor, and onto old smelly trucks on the back street of the market. The constant sound of nylon crackling and sliding from the vendors wrapping the fish snapped above the tumult, and the hand gesturing of the people made for a constantly shifting landscape in sound and motion.

"Fishermen are some of the hardest-working people on the planet," Grandma pointed out. But they were also some of the most impoverished and stagnant families in the world. Weather pattern changes, toxic spills, oil shortages, and economic upheaval dominated the lives of fishermen in the Islands. They scraped by with a living as fishermen because that's what they had done for four hundred years. They felt they had no viable choice.

Truth be told, most fishermen in town had a meager existence. The sea claimed a life now and again, and living became a Dante-esque nightmare for those left behind. They worked harder and longer than anybody else, only to remain in miserable poverty. The situation went from bad to worse, depending on the season. There were hurricanes in the summer and north fronts early in the year. According to Grandma, nature took its time and pleasure disenfranchising these people.

Most fishermen inhabited simple, sparsely furnished homes. One out of four lacked a refrigerator, and television sets were considered luxury items. Just a few years later we were fortunate enough to purchase a color TV. We set the appliance atop the black and white set we used for every-day watching. My mother decreed that "the color TV was for the weekend and special programs." She defined a "special program" on a case-by-case basis. The host of people who paraded through our home to see the color TV was unmatched by any previous event. We turned on the TV, and since Cuba had only five hours of programming per day, there was nothing to see except the color calibration bars and the annoying audio signal test tone. Mrs. Matisse, an old neighbor and Grandma's friend since for-ever, came to see this new contraption. She approached the set hesitantly, her hands clasped in front of her as if in prayer.

"How do they get the colors in there?" she asked innocently.

She stood at arm's length and stretched her hand coyly to touch the screen. The tips of her fingers grazed the brightly colored screen for a second; then she withdrew her hand with a snap. She inspected her fingers for any trace of color. "It doesn't paint," she marveled. That was 1980, mind you.

Life was simple in every respect for these folks. "Other than the bounty of nature through the hands of God, we were hard pressed to keep any skin on our bones." That was one of Grandma's favorite mantras. Irri-gation was almost limited to the greenhouses, if I dare to use such a term to describe where they grew and cared for the seedlings. The greenhouses were creepy-looking, wide, barn-like buildings with rusty pipes dripping water into long clay pots.

Rain was the only way to water the crops, and waiting for it to fall from the sky was an ulcer-provoking pastime from October to May—if all went well. Sometimes too much came too early and flooded the fields.

Other times it was too little too late in the season and the harvest was anemic. A few times in the century, Grandma said, it didn't come at all. "And people walked around just skins and bone" because of a protein-rich diet that lacked vegetables and fruits. Some people lost their teeth, she told me, reflecting sadly on dry spells of years past. That only left fish, in all shapes, colors, species, and varieties.

It seemed like we had a never-ending supply of fish, and since the fishermen saw no reason to get more than they needed, there was still plenty in those years. The only problem was that the brokers and wholesalers were the only ones getting rich in the gig. Grandma had that figured out years before, but the locals seemed unable to grasp the higher laws of supply and demand. They also seemed to lack the know-how to break away from the poorly designed supply chain in which they were such a critical and medullary part.

Because of the lack of industrial refrigeration in the area, most of the catch of the day had to be sold within hours. Such constraints put the buyer in a clear advantage, to the detriment of the fishermen. All they did was wait for the sun to advance in the zenith, and as it rose so did the anxiety of the fishermen who invariably relented to the low price offer of the brokers and wholesalers.

For years, Grandma despaired at how high-quality seafood, including lobster, crayfish, shrimp, scallops, and abalone were sold in our local market at 80 percent the price it fetched in the city.

The problem at hand was systemic, she had reasoned years before. There was little ice around in commercial quantities. The only ice plant within a reasonable driving distance was four hours away. The price of ice had increased slowly, but consistently, for twenty years—a fact that escaped her understanding. There was also the issue of local demand for additional ice. It had remained the same for the last five or six years. The ice used to cool fish couldn't be recycled or reused for other purposes, and additional ice couldn't be stored safely for later use.

On a fateful day in the mid-fifties, Grandma was thumbing through an old issue of *National Geographic* and read that in Scandinavia they built underground cold storages to store fish and food stock. The article described in detail the origin and common use of said facilities.

The physics and overall mechanics of the storage facility were a bit fuzzy in her mind, but the concept and application were clear. Building a cold, underground storage facility would solve the storage issue of excess fish and give the fishermen a fighting chance to increase the price for the catch of the day.

On a bright spring day, Grandma awakened earlier than usual. She pulled out one of her fluffy dresses adorned with lace and embroidery that she saved for important occasions, her black mahogany walking stick, and a wide hat. As usual, she seemed subdued, but I could sense her urgency and anticipation underneath. Her eyes flickering with excitement, she left before sunrise. I wandered about the kitchen for almost an hour, hoping to hear or see *something* that would give me a hint about her mysterious outing. The information came to me a bit here and there, but within days, life took a very unsuspecting turn for most people in town.

Her mission was fairly simple, she thought: find an engineer. A "real" one" would probably be too expensive to hire to replicate the cold storage facility described in the magazine with sketches and all. Her plan was to find a half-starving engineering student who could take on the job quickly and at a fraction of the cost of a "real" one.

As usual, she found a willing, hungry student who was able to start on the project the following weekend. She never mentioned to me how much it cost. Grandma believed that "the less children worry about money the better." I should be content knowing that "it sometimes costs blood to earn it and you should conserve it at all cost."

George, the quasi-engineer came on Saturday, equipped with long rulers, pieces of drawing paper, metric tapes, and other strange but supposedly useful tools. He was tall and skinny, with sparse reddish-brown hair, and pale, dry-speckled skin that seemed to me like a poorly fitted ghost mask. He seemed shy and spoke slowly in response to Grandma's questions, always pausing to search for the right words.

Immediately, I became his assistant on the job. At age twelve, I took my first managerial experience to heart and informed my curious friends that this was a serious enterprise and loiterers weren't welcomed. They could watch from a distance, of course, and I was available to answer questions later in the afternoon. There were no details given regarding what the work was about until it was ready. These were Grandma's orders, which were inviolate, with penalty of banishment from our home forever. My friends recognized the gravity of this endeavor and kept their distance. Break the rules, and no more fruit preserves, no more cold drinks, and—the cruelest punishment of all—no more fries on Sunday at my house.

Building the storage required a small bulldozer that had seen better years. Both the diabolical-looking mechanical contraption and its ragged, intoxicated operator appeared on the verge of total breakdown. The fearful operation of digging a hole with the bulldozer's monstrous metal shovel lasted forty-five torturous minutes. Afterward, a huge gaping hole faced the afternoon sky like a large grave. A small crowd had gathered around to gossip and speculate about Grandma's latest endeavor.

Grandma discussed something quietly with the scrawny soon-to-be engineer, and they both nodded with subdued satisfaction. After the earth mover was gone, I assisted again, placing small wood stakes on the edge of the pit according to the instruction of my temporary employer. Careful notes were taken and measurements rechecked.

George stayed with us overnight. Grandma brought an old military cot and some blankets and set them up in a corner of our spacious living room. He seemed jittery, anxious, and unsure, and walked slowly but constantly. He had big, puffy eyes that looked as if he hadn't slept for a month. He struck me as being lost and out of place. He had a voracious appetite, however. Judging by his scrawniness, no one could have guessed that he could put away so much food as quickly as he did.

The kids had a blast sliding into the pit on a rusty piece of tin from a nearby roof. It was a fairly competitive process, requiring hustling the tin from the other kids who were obviously reluctant to part company with it. I also got pretty dirty, which earned me the get-in-the-shower-now-if-you-want-live-to-be-eighteen look from Grandma.

At daybreak, the carpenters swung into action. Long boards and beams formed a double box of sorts at the bottom of the pit. Among the kids, speculation ran like a mud slide downhill in the rainy season. "Abuela Florencia is building a neighborhood pool," they whispered. I wished it were true. I pictured myself rolling in the money earned from charging the kids admittance to my pool. Not a chance. Grown-ups also whispered about the ongoing work. They came and went at different times of the day, making small talk with Grandma, and trying to pry some small detail about the "thing" being built. All to no avail. Grandma just kissed her old friends and patted the young men on the back but didn't speak a word.

By the time the work was done, most people had pushed the affair out of their minds. Since it was all built with prefab concrete slabs, the outer shell of the storage facility went up quickly, and the rest of it went on underground and away from public scrutiny. The dozen or so men who formed the construction crew worked from sunup to sundown every day but Sunday. They installed a drainage pump and concrete shelves with gutters that moved the excess water to the end of the storage into a lower deposit where it could be collected and siphoned out with the pump. This pump had underground and aboveground hand levers. The crew also installed a chain-pulley cargo lift to carry the stock. It had a narrow stairwell that opened to a metal door on the surface.

The day the ice truck arrived, the expectations of the people bulged with tsunami-like force. Most people had no idea what the ice was for, or that we had built an underground cold storage in our backyard. They had no concept of such structures or their use since they had never even heard of such things.

In the tropics, ice has a very short life span. Actually, short is an understatement. Children savor it like a delicatessen sandwich from heaven. Nine months out of the year, the temperature remains over eighty degrees and a glass of cold anything is always a welcomed indulgence after a few hours under the tropical sun. I always thought ice had a mysterious aura. Water that can become strong as concrete, sharp as steel, and burn like fire? Just awesome.

Using folded hemp sacks, a group of local men carried the ice blocks on their shoulders from the truck to the underground storage. After they were done, Grandma had prepared a number of large pitchers with iced fruit juice to give to the men. After their work, they sat around enjoying the cold water from the melting ice blocks that streamed down their backs. It's not every day that one gets a really cold shower!

The conversation was lively and inclusive. The initial excitement had given way to a more familiar friendly exchange between neighbors. Without warning, the question interrupted the conversation: "So, Florencia, what is the ice for?" someone asked. It caught me by surprise. I thought that the issue was already settled. Not so, apparently.

Everyone became silent almost in an instant. I looked for my grandma's eyes, but she was facing away from me. Holding her hands behind her back, she paused for a few seconds and replied slowly, "Well, I think the devil may set up camp nearby, so I have to find a way to cool down my house." She smiled, her white teeth flashing.

The whole group broke out in hearty laughter. Some didn't quite hear what Grandma said. But it didn't matter; it was sure great to have a good laugh anyhow. A few minutes later the crowd slowly dispersed, some walking with the typical careless swagger of the Island folks, some avoiding looking suspicious but glancing nervously toward the earth mound next to where this strange building was buried. Whatever the case, no one uttered another word about this peculiar afternoon.

Nighttime brought hard and warm rain. It was not a particularly strong storm, but it was enough to clean the dirt and people from the streets. As Grandma and I dodged puddles and mud cakes on the edge of the sidewalk, I could hear my splashing echoing through the empty porches and alleys. We arrived at the social room at the far end of the street before anyone else. The social room was a dilapidated building that used to be a corner store. No one was actually sure about what happened to the actual store. One day it was there and the next it wasn't. Grandma's theory was that the storekeeper was put in jail for embezzlement. She had her sources, but as usual, she declined to elaborate. The store was taken over by the neighborhood and often utilized for sweet sixteen celebrations, weddings, funerals, graduations, or whatever social event took place in the community. "The darn thing is a watering whole," Grandma would remark with a frowning face. "Beer is still running down the street a week after the party is over."

That was an undeniable and historically documented truth. Most social events in town, and in Cuba for that matter, were just excuses for public intoxication. Often less than neighborly situations, fostered by alcohol, resulted in people going to the local medical clinic.

Early in the day, Grandma and a few others had gathered in our dining room for dessert: fruit preserves and cheese. That, without a doubt, was food that Adam and Eve ate before they stopped being vegetarians. There was nothing in the world I would have rather had than fruit preserves and cheese in front of Grandma's conspiracy partners at our dinner table. But that day I suffered unjustified torture since I was not allowed to get near the table. I sat sulking, within earshot of the conversation, but I was entertaining revenge plots of my own. Of course, they involved benign acts of truancy like trampling flower beds and flooding yards with garden hoses. That was the extent of my criminal master plans. I managed to catch loose phrases here and there. "Okay, at six then? . . . Yes, the food will be ready by then . . . yes, everybody knows . . " I was mad and despondent. Denying me dessert amounted to child abuse in my book.

People began arriving in small groups, clusters of lethargic people in static-charged shirts and pants. Some of my friends were there, looking sleepy and dying of boredom. They all spoke quietly, sitting huddled together, lighting cigarettes in unison while passing somebody's trophy Zippo lighter around. The room filled with people enveloped by blue smoke. Grandma grunted softly and opened the window. She looked across the room and gestured to Julio to do the same. He smiled and pushed the swivel window up and propped it with a stick.

A few minutes later, the room was packed. People started to shift anxiously in their seats. Grandma moved to the front of the room and tapped on a nearby chair with her cane. All the faces turned at once. The murmur died down slowly. The silence was thick with smoke and anticipation.

Grandma paused a few more seconds, scrutinizing the crowd. She smiled and then frowned slightly. She looked straight at Julio, who at over six feet five inches, was by far the tallest man in the room. He had driven an old taxi in and out of town for years. He enjoyed sugarcane rum a bit too much, and one rainy night he wrapped the cab around a cedar tree at a fork in the road into town. He almost lost an eye in the ordeal. Since then, he'd returned to fishing. I didn't think they made cars his size. He walked with a hunch after so many years of driving a poorly fitted vehicle.

"Julio," Grandma started, and he blinked quickly several times. "How long have you been fishing? Since . . ." She hesitated for a second, searching for the right words. "Since you left the taxi?"

He scratched his head nervously. "About three years?" he answered tentatively.

"More like four," she pointed. "Do you have a TV yet?" He shook his head side to side slowly, fixing his gaze on the floor.

"It's okay, Julio," she comforted him gently.

"Mario, how is your son?" she asked another man in the room. He was a short, stocky man who had a reputation for having a deadly punch and a bone-crushing grip.

"He is getting better, Florencia. Thank you for asking," he replied softly, also looking downward.

"Can you tell Theresa that I have something for the boy at home?" she asked, crossing her hands in front of her dress. He nodded.

Mario Jr. had dislocated his hip a few weeks before. Regardless of the touted medical care in the country, pain medication was rarely heard of and aftercare was almost nonexistent. The boy was in excruciating pain for twenty hours a day. The prescription for pain, whatever little the doctor gave them, didn't help much. Grandma had arranged for a consultation with a pain specialist in a clinic in a town two days away. That helped, and Grandma had gotten her hands on some pain pills for him a day or so before.

The gentle inquisition continued for a few more minutes. Her questions were genuine and expressed real concern, but unquestionably stressed the point that followed.

"Boys, I've known most of you since you were born. In fact, I was already an old woman when some of your parents were born," she said, holding her walking stick out as a silent witness. Her words traveled the distance across the room at a measured rate but heavy in content. The mood was reflective, somber.

So, Abuela Florencia (everybody called her that, much to my disagreement since she was *my* grandma), decided to take matters into her own hands.

She combed the room and smiled. Slowly at first, she went on to describe how she'd seen many of them and their families suffer with illness, lack of money or food, punishment from the weather, and other perils. She spoke in general about how many of them had come to her to borrow money in tough times. And they knew they could always come to her—always. The exchange was filled with love and compassion.

"I know there's a reason, although I'm not quite sure, why God has been good to me. So I'm just returning the favor to you. He doesn't really need my help." She paused, took a deep breath, and glared. Her demeanor shifted to that sharp edge visible only now and again when she needed to make a point without room for misunderstanding.

"Aren't you sick of these bands of thieves robbing you blind of your day's work?" she blasted. Grown men jumped in their seats at the sharp, strong voice of this frail old lady. Some raised eyebrows, others had diverted looks. The statement made everybody uncomfortable.

"Aren't you ill to your souls that these drunk degenerates come here in their white starched Sunday best and yank from your broken and tired hands this gift from God that supports your families?" She drove the question into the crowd.

"Some of you have left your blood, pieces of your bodies, and even the lives of loved ones at sea. Some of you can no longer fish." Now she was getting personal. "Gerardo, you can't even walk three days out of five. What will you do when you can no longer stand on a boat for six or eight hours?"

Gerardo had nothing to say. He shifted in his seat, uncomfortable from her reference to his physical condition. The rain had subsided a few minutes before, and only the rhythmical *tap, tap, tap* of the water dripping from the roof onto the metal flaps that doubled as windows broke the silence in the room. After a few seconds he sunk on his chair, his eyes nailed to the floor. Although directed at him, the question was a rhetorical reminder of the collective fragility in Santa Fe. The fishermen were all mangled and exhausted, withered and torn by the years of backbreaking work at sea.

Grandma was just getting started. "I've seen some of the most despicable, repugnant men in the world come in broad daylight and break your will and take your dignity without remorse." Anger seemed to have found a ledge now. There I stood, gaping mouth and all, unable to digest the scene. I'd never seen Grandma on a rage like this—ever.

"When you give away for pennies your day's sweat because you're afraid, you make a mockery of the God who keeps you alive. When you can no longer see the lights of town and there's nothing but water and wind between you and your family, who brings your skin unharmed back to land? Why do you then allow this band of robbers to steal your life away, day after day?" Her voice quivered, but her demeanor spewed lava front and back.

She paused for almost a minute. A fine mist had started to fall again. The tinkling of the water on the tin-covered windows was the only sound in the room. Grandma swallowed hard, took a couple of steps to the right, and sat on an empty chair.

"Boys, I love you like my own children. I've loved and cared for your families like my own, so please hear me," she said, slowing her pace now.

The mood took on a more conciliatory feel. People breathed, I thought, for the first time since she started her diatribe. The group moved a bit, seeking to resettle in the room. Some match strikes snapped in the room and columns of smoke climbed to the high ceiling.

There was a large piece of construction paper taped to the wall in the front. On it, Grandma had scribbled some numbers. I could also see the name of some fish, the word *gasoline*, and more numbers. She talked about how much money fish, the same fish they drew from the sea, cost in the towns.

"Oh, now you're going to turn our minds to mush, Florencia," somebody said, and a few timid giggles spattered through the crowd. Grandma turned in that general direction, and they ceased almost immediately.

"That degenerate Carlos Rutgers has the largest fish store in Santa Fe. Out the back door he sells to most restaurants and small fish stores up town. Now, Gerard, where do you think he gets his fish?" she asked poignantly. Again, the question wasn't meant to be answered out loud. Everyone knew, and they nodded in unstated agreement.

"And, that God may strike me dead right now if he doesn't sell his fish for five times more than he pays you," she said, holding her gnarled hand up, her five fingers splayed out. Somebody dropped a glass in the back, while a not-so-mild curse was muttered loud enough for all to hear.

Grandma went to visit her doctor monthly in Santa Fe and used these visits to be like James Bond, scouting and spying in the bigger town that had the fish buyers. This is how she knew about the notorious Carlos Rutgers and his store—aside from the fact that she knew he had a pregnant mistress in a nearby town, plus several illegitimate children all over the place. "Wealthy men can afford to be wicked," she used to say. She despised the man.

In a quiet voice, she explained slowly what so many of the fishermen already knew. "After years of pondering and praying," (since she said she did fear doing something her God wouldn't approve of) "I stumbled onto the solution in an old *National Geographic* magazine. There it was, the subterranean cold storage housing." Her next announcement fell on the audience with the force of a wrecking ball. "Tomorrow we'll double our prices for fish," she stated, a subtle, almost playful smile dancing on her lips.

The crowd broke into a turbulent mix of optimism, suspicion, fear, and plain shock. How was that possible?

"That will never happen," blared somebody from the back of the room. They started moving closer to Grandma. "There's got to be more to this story," somebody else argued.

"Listen, boys, this is what we're going to do," she whispered in a totally conspiratorial tone this time.

What followed was a bit complicated for me. I heard some children's voices around the building and I went to the door. There I saw a couple of my friends dodging puddles. I stepped outside and called them.

"Andy, where are you guys going?" I asked while walking fast to close the distance.

"It's movie time," they said almost in unison. They didn't stop and I broke into a short run to follow them into the dark, humid night, going back to the world of children and the cool things in life for a few hours.

Morning proved to be unusual, to say the least. I heard a crash—a big one. Then something that sounded like firecrackers—*pop, pop, pop*—and ear-piercing, horrifying screams. I jumped off my bed and ran through the long hallway that separated me from the front door. Grandma was standing at the window but the front door was locked, which was very unusual.

"What happened? What happened out there, Abuela?" I tugged at my grandma's dress. The window was too high from the ground for me to see.

"Stay down, son, it'll be over soon. The police are here," she replied calmly, not an ounce of care in her tone.

I made a run for the other window but she insisted: "Son, stay down and away from the windows, please." This time she had that look that meant business. I'd considered whining but decided against it. It never worked anyway.

I stood next to her, listening to the screaming and shouting, which seemed to decrease gradually with every passing minute. Grandma pulled a chair and let me climb onto it. "What happened?" I asked with excitement.

"Ah, nothing. Just some folks that can't deal with a little change," she replied with a faint touch of sarcasm.

"But what happened?" I kept asking, my feet bouncing on the chair seat.

"Well—" she started slowly, choosing her words. "These folks are mad and somebody crashed a truck into a storage shed at the market." The whole thing was vague. I wanted the juice: who hit whom and where? Was there any blood?

She didn't respond, but gazed at me tenderly, as usual. When she was done speaking, you couldn't pull anything else out of her with a crowbar. It took me half a day to figure out what happened, but I had my sources. Richie, one of my boyhood friends, spilled the beans over saltine crackers and orange juice and gave me the details of what transpired beyond my window.

Grandma had devised a plan to post prices for fish in the market. Every fisherman was free to sell his own at whatever price he wanted, and that included lowering their own prices, but then he couldn't use the cold storage facility. The rest agreed on the bottom prices to avoid undercutting each other. They made out large red signs with prices and refused to bargain with the brokers and wholesalers, who couldn't believe these ragtag fishermen had gotten the upperhand. Prices were no longer negotiable, and it "had been set by the co-op," some said matter-of-factly.

"What co-op?" the buyers screamed.

In order to teach the fishermen a lesson, the wholesalers and brokers left the market. The fishermen sat idly, overcome by anxiety. "What if the plan backfires? What if we lose the catch of the day? What if they seek other sources?" These and many other questions floated in their minds. But two hours later, a delivery truck belonging to one of the wholesalers came flying down the street and crashed against the pillars of the fish market. The driver pulled out an old gun and shot a few rounds through the air. The shouting and screaming that followed was what I heard from my bed.

The parish police arrived, and the angry brokers left in a rush, baffled and enraged by the fishermen's strategy. Evaristo, nicknamed "El Colorado" Redman, a small fish market owner in Santa Fe, walked slowly away to his truck, shaking his head in disbelief. He dealt with the same fishermen for years and always came early, got his merchandise, and left. He often came before daybreak and before the mob of brokers and wholesalers. He sat in his blue and green truck for a long time and tapped on the steering wheel unfocused, absent. After a few minutes, he turned the key in the ignition and cut through the alley, away from view.

A couple of my older friends came to my house, peddling furiously on their old bicycles.

"They're all gone," they shouted. "They're all gone! The fish buyers, the cops—gone."

I dashed to the middle of the street, anxious to see what had happened. To see what? Who was gone? Oh, it burned me up! What did my friends know that I didn't? They were on a secret mission that I knew nothing about. This was unreal. Grandma grabbed her umbrella and snapped it open to keep the sun at bay. I tugged at her dress.

"Abuela, where are we going? What's going on?" I asked, fidgeting like a hungry cat.

"Oh, we're just going to chat with the folks at the fish market," she answered casually, twirling the umbrella.

Whatever was brewing had to be good if Grandma was involved. We entered the damp, shadowy building that occupied the fish market. Even before we arrived, we could hear voices: excited and colorful, with intense, anger-filled, aggressive language.

"Geeeez!" I commented timidly about it.

Grandma looked at me with a frown: "Never mind their language. They don't mean it; they're just mad. It'll be okay in a little while."

Gabriel, a razor thin, usually mild-mannered fellow, was unrecognizable as he paced like a caged tiger. He kicked the wall rather hard a few times, and I wondered if he'd break his toe.

My grandmother clapped her hands together, getting the man's attention. "Gabe, cool down and quit hitting yourself. It's Friday and the doctor won't be back until Monday." Some people laughed.

"It's not funny, Florencia. This is serious. We're talking about our families here," he stressed loudly, pointing a menacing finger at Grandma.

His shirt and pants were of an indistinguishable color: dirty with fish blood and faded by too many washes and the blazing sun. They hung on him as if he were a scarecrow. Grandma didn't reply immediately. She fixed her gaze on him like a hawk about to fall upon a dove. It worked. Gabe lowered his finger and put his hands in his pockets.

He relaxed a bit. "Sorry, Florencia, I just don't know how this is going to work and I have to feed my family," he said.

Having served her purpose, she walked up to him and put her hand on his bony shoulder, squeezing just a little.

"Gabe, come to my home and take whatever you need for your family. That stands for all of you." She raised her voice. "And know this: If I have to sell everything I have to feed your families while we see this through, I'll do it in an instant." She approached Mario and whispered something in his ear. He motioned to a few others and they left the room.

"Okay, boys, let's get to work," she exclaimed, making a spinning gesture as she spoke. "Let's take all the fish to the back. Don't forget to mark your crates. Let's not get into a fight about my fish was bigger than yours and stuff." They laughed more amiably now.

I looked at Grandma and motioned to her that I was going to the back of the market. She nodded. "Don't get in the way—let the men work," she added as I turned and ran to the end of the dimly lit hallway.

In front of the fish market were four small trucks and Grandma's old Johnson tractor with a pulling cart. The men loaded crate after dripping crate of fish onto the trucks and the tractor cart. It was only a few blocks to our home and the underground cold storage. Grandma was just a tactical genius. That Friday morning not one pound of fish was sold to the usual buyers. They left on accord thinking that they could come around a bit later and scoop the catch at rock bottom price at lunchtime. They were in for a surprise.

After they had placed all the fish down in the storage, the men congregated in the social room. Grandma had arranged for a few women to fix a meal for all the fishermen. The sweet aroma of home-cooked food filled the room. Pots and pans full with all kinds of tasty dishes were arranged on a long table at the front of the room. The men lined up eagerly and served themselves, later to sit in groups on the chairs arranged in clusters.

Of course, not only the fishermen showed up to get their fill. Everybody else and their cat stood in line to join the banquet. As usual, no one was turned away. Halfway through the meal, Grandma walked to the middle of the room. "Enjoying the food boys?" she asked playfully. Lots of satisfied, unintelligible growls signaled agreement.

"Good, good," she said. "Today is the first day of a better life for all. Enjoy; you deserve it," she added emphatically. "Listen now. Go home, you hear? Go home to your wives and your children. Don't loiter around town today. Stay home and don't talk to the fish buyers. No matter what they say, no matter what evil threats they breathe against you, don't respond."

She mimicked fat Carlos Rutgers's pouncing walk, and the crowd laughed, some nervously.

"Don't answer them. If they bother you too much, just tell them to come back during business hours, like it says on the door of the market," she instructed.

They were all quiet, attentive, hoping to see through her visionary eyes, hoping this would work. "I tell you this—God has never let me down in my ninety-some years."

"More like hundred-some," came the hidden comment of someone in the back. A thunderous laughter rolled through the crowd. Grandma laughed too.

"If it's not Cristobal the comedian. Stick to fishing, Chris," she said, giggling.

"Oops!" More laughter.

"Boys, seriously now." Her wrinkled face became grave. "God will bring to your door what you ask Him for. You just have to stay the course," she promised.

There she was speaking to this group of pagan men about a God that none of them knew. They worshiped a mixture of African deities made of stone, shells, and wood, with white plaster saints that had many names. Some African, some Spanish, some both. They usually required some form of blood sacrifice to be enticed into doing men's work. "Kill me a goat and I'll scare your neighbor? Frogs will rain again before I catch myself doing any of that," Grandma would say. In her mind, there was only God, and He wasn't the father of chaos or confusion.

You couldn't bribe her God with the blood of chickens or doves or anything. He had already required the blood of Him whom He had chosen so that no more blood needed to be shed. Whenever Grandma spoke of this subject, her eyes welled with tears. Her words came from somewhere deep. You couldn't help but feel that this was, for her, as real as daylight. But how did she know, I wondered. "It's all in the Bible," she'd say. But how have I never heard anyone but her talk about this? Did anyone else know about this?

"Sure, son," she countered with optimism. "I know in my heart that there are men on the earth today that can hear the voice of God," she declared matter-of-factly.

This assertion was nothing but disturbing to my young mind. The notion that there was a man like Moses, a prophet, walking around today, had mythical proportions.

"So how come we haven't heard about him, this Moses-type guy?" I'd ask carefully. She thought for a while. It killed me to wait for her responses, but I had no choice. I folded a piece of old newspaper in squares again and again, trying to make noise. Grandma glanced over my head out the window for a few seconds. "Well, remember when Moses took the children of Israel from slavery in Egypt?" I nodded yes. "They were about half a million people. And they were probably the only people in the whole earth then that knew anything about the true God."

It clicked. "So maybe we're in the wrong country!" I exclaimed.

"Yes, we most certainly are, son. And we don't know where to find Him," she added.

"Should we go to Israel, maybe?" I wondered how we'd get from Cuba to Israel.

"He isn't there. I already checked." Her voice sounded flat but resolute.

Then I remembered the brown faded paper she had shown me—the ticket she'd purchased in 1948 to go to Israel. She'd secured it soon after the United Nations acted to ensure the establishment of Palestine as the homeland and place for the return of the Jews. It cost her a year's worth of wages, but she thought nothing of the expense. However, she found nothing—no temple, no prophet. Instead, she came home with great disappointment.

Still, her faith in her God was unshakable. "It's His world, His domain, and we breathe at His mercy. So, I'll just wait and see without fussing," she said now and again.

Some of the fishermen present had heard Grandma speak of God before. It was clear to them that she was a woman of faith, although most likely they didn't understand the depth of it. Most people in our town had a primitive awareness of God—either an acquired notion that there was one, or they had been told of God.

Lazaro, possibly the oldest fisherman in town, stepped forward. "I'm with you, Florencia. Let's do this thing and teach these sons of the morning a lesson they'll never forget," he offered. Similar statements followed. In the end, the position to stay consolidated and fight was almost unanimous, at least in public.

Grandma combed the room with her eyes. She was looking for the quiet, unspoken disagreement, the hold ups of doubt, the pessimists, and the weak. "A chain is only as strong as its weakest link," she said. The people in the room were silent, as if unwilling to let my grandma down.

"Okay, okay, boys, then we're ready." She seemed pleased. "Now, we have to play this by the numbers. Please don't improvise, because it can get complicated." They took the admonition at face value.

"We've prepared signs with prices depending on the kind of fish, size, weight," she continued. She paused at small intervals. She wanted to gauge their reaction, assess their fear. "Fear is the wiggling room that the devil needs to do his deed." Another testament of her own personal doctrine.

"Saturday is the busiest day at the markets in the towns, but not for us," she explained. "There's no way on earth they won't be back today. So you must be prepared."

Schooling in the Islands, or for that matter, education, was almost nonexistent when my grandmother was a young girl in the 1800s. In most towns, there was some kind of communal instruction that might extend to the equivalent of a third- or fourth-grade education. Grandma never went to school. She described how one of her older sisters had taught her how to write a little and do math. She could read fairly well, although slowly. But numbers were her domain. She could add, multiply, subtract, and divide in seconds, while staring at your forehead.

Many years later, while in graduate school, I marveled that many of the business principles addressed at this level I'd already heard from her.

She continued, "They're hurting now. They lost already maybe two hours' worth of business. Their only choice now is to come back and deal with us," Grandma said, her tone providing reassurance. Her plan began to sink in for the rest of them.

She cautioned, "They're now mad as rabid dogs. Don't get into a fight. It's their anger, so let them keep it." She wanted to avoid violence. Some of the folks were known to have a short fuse.

"We've set the price and they'll take it. They can't afford to lose today's and tomorrow's sales on account of our price." She was instructing them: Business 101. "They need fish for the weekend, so they'll swallow it." She smiled.

"But what happens on Monday?" shot one of the fishermen from the back of the room.

"Yeah, what about Monday? They can go to Isla Verde for fish, right?" came the questions from the back of the room. The noise level increased, doubts and trepidation finding space in the group.

"Boys, I don't have gray hair as a fashion statement. Like I said before, I've been around half a century before any of them." Her words were strong, but she looked like a peaceful, little old lady. "I already talked to some people in Isla Verde." The room roared. People got up and smiled; others seemed confused. "Listen, boys," she tried to keep them focused. "Isla Verde is four hours away. They'd have to buy iceboxes and more fuel to go there on Monday. It will be a costly ride, and somebody is going to have a heart attack when they get there," she said, holding her chest. They all laughed boisterously.

Julio stood. He'd grown up fishing with his father and his grand-father, who was a friend of Grandma's since his youth. "Hey, boys, we went to Isla Verde two weeks ago," he said, his voiced thundering above the chorus of animated voices in the room. "The prices over there will be exactly the same as here on Monday," he smiled with gusto.

"Okay, boys. Go home now and let's be back at the market by 1 PM," Julio continued, on a more serious note.

The crowd moved out in small groups and walked briskly down the street. The whole town simmered with excitement and anticipation. This gambit had the potential to radically change their lives, or starve them to death in the process. For some, it was long-awaited revenge for years of ill-treatment and abuse at the hands of the buyers. For others, it provided justice and the opportunity for a new beginning. Grandma said, "In due time all things come to fruition." And it was about time.

Morning in the Caribbean is a magnificent display. A fine mist blankets the land, depositing dew on every leaf, every window, and everything else that stood vigil outside during the night. At daybreak, the sun sends light beams through the millions of drops of dew that rest on the land, creating a million rainbows everywhere you look.

Early morning brings low tide. The ocean seems also to be in a peaceful state of rest, almost immovable, like a giant glass gently resting on the warm white sand. Picking up clams on the shoreline was one of my favorite pastimes. It was simple but exciting. I also discovered that I thought a lot during this mostly solitary activity. Walking along the edge of the water, eyes scanning for shells barely visible on an inch of water, I thought about a thousand things. It helped clear my mind and flex my "reasoning muscle," as Grandma described the brain.

By 11 AM, the sun had climbed almost to the center of the zenith. The heat was usually intense, but the cool ocean breeze dampened the radiation. It was rather strange to see the fish market in town open beyond this hour. Most activity was usually wound down by then.

That day, high noon was different. The townsfolk looked different. They moved with a strange energy—animated and awake. Gone was the midday stupor that often dominated the hour. Most people didn't have a clear idea of what was unfolding. Conversations between husbands and wives that day were full of "I don't know, but Grandma Florencia says—"

As predicted, the buyers started returning trucks driving along in small caravans. No doubt they also held meetings and strategized about how to deal with a bunch of ragtag, illiterate fishermen from a tiny coastal town. Santa Fe had a couple of *pilotos*, sidewalk beer bars that gather the less than outstanding citizens of the town. You could smell the rancid stench of beer blocks away. "The trough of the hosts of hell," Grandma had coined those dark and raucous places. Small businessmen and more than a few of the locals gathered there to strike deals or just to socialize.

Grandma sat quietly reading her Bible in her favorite rocking chair.

The house was cool, a soft breeze running unimpeded throughout. It was peaceful and inviting, but I was dying to get out there. I could feel the effervescence, the exigency of the moment. But Grandma insisted I stay in. As usual, no further explanations were offered. I complained and argued for quite some time—unsuccessfully. "Are you finished, son? Get a book then."

The kitchen window became my theater balcony. The buyers kept coming, and some of them went into the fish market, yelling and cursing. Others seemed shocked and distraught for the second time in just a few hours.

The approaching sound of an engine broke the quiet of the late morning. I jumped out of my seat and into the chair by the window. "It's Redman," I announced, boiling with excitement. Grandma didn't move a muscle; she didn't acknowledge my report. She read quietly, whispering the words to herself.

The engine stopped. I looked intently to the door, eagerly waiting for the visitor to appear. Redman took a long time to cover the distance to our doorway. Every step seemed uncertain, tentative. Was he afraid? Unsure of what he'd say, or what to expect?

He stood right outside our door, his head hanging on his chest, his hands toying with a few coins in his pockets. After a few seconds, he lifted his head and looked in. His eyes locked with Grandma's. I was expecting sparks to fly, fire to rise through the walls, something spectacular, I supposed; but instead, nothing. There was no animosity, no ill will. There was no discernible emotional energy.

Grandma motioned him to sit across the room. He stepped in and sat quietly. He rested his back on the oversized chair, legs crossed. He changed his mind and leaned forward and locked his fingers between his knees, his eyes fixed on the ground. Grandma rested inert, waiting. Her gaze was soft, almost casual. Redman stood softly, hands in both pockets and walked to the open window.

"Big mess out there, Florence," he stated, pointing outside.

He didn't turn, and Grandma didn't answer. The scene was confusing to me. I couldn't gauge the situation, nor could I read the emotional temperature of it.

Redman turned. He walked to the chair next to Grandma but remained standing. "What do you need so that we can carry on with the business?" The question seemed simple but underlined with urgency.

"The prices are set by the fishermen, Redman. A slight change of plans, I know." She sighed. "Have you ever gone fishing, Red?"

"Yes," came the hesitant reply, "a few times."

"Well," she rolled on, "sometimes there's only a light south breeze. It isn't dangerous, but it gets in the way. It will push you off course until you find a cove and can make land. The only problem is that by then you'll be in Yucatan, Mexico. Just a minor inconvenience," she smiled.

"So, this is the new price for fish here in the Cove?" His words were barely audible. The question was uttered almost in fear.

"That's the new price, Red. Would you like some fresh fruit juice?" Grandma asked as she got up and moved to the kitchen. He didn't answer. In turn, he moved toward the window.

The faint clicking sound of glasses in the back reminded me of a big clock ticking. A few seconds later, Grandma appeared with three glasses of freshly squeezed fruit juice. I waited until they both had served themselves. Grandma nodded and I helped myself. I sat quietly back in the corner.

The juice's sugar seemed to give Red courage. "So what happened? What changed here?" He was still trying to make sense of the most unusual business situation he'd witnessed in his twenty-plus years as a storekeeper. He spoke softly. His pronunciation was precise, crisp. He sounded like no one I knew. He always wore fluffy beige pants that flapped in the breeze as he walked and white or tan *guayaberas*, the traditional tropical shirts with embroidery and big pockets in the front. Very clean and stylish, I thought. I wondered how he managed to stay clean while dealing with fish.

"Red, no science here. The folks took a look around and woke up. It's that simple." Grandma sipped her juice as if he were only on a social call. She figured if you were too dumb to grasp the core of the issue, you were even less apt to discuss it.

"So it's a settled issue then," he offered, half question, half tentative assertion. Grandma smiled her usual "I've finished talking, so should you, and move on," kind of a smile. He got the point and offered his hand for a handshake. Grandma reciprocated and the fish buyer was gone.

The cranking and rattling of the engine faded as Red's old Chevy truck clunked down the street. Grandma didn't move from her seat. Her part was done, and after all the uncertainty, the plan worked. The strategy rested on forcing the buyers into a unique position. The cold storage served its purpose and continued to do so for twenty more years. The

National Geographic article and what it led to became a legend told for a generation for miles around.

Every day at the close of business, remnant fish was stored. The market hours were extended and the number of customers doubled.

For the first time ever, families were able to plan. Per capita income rose every year for a generation. The quality of life of all people improved in real and tangible ways. The fishermen's understanding of self-reliance, communal effort, and their relationship with nature transformed their existence forever.

"Envy is the burden of the lazy," Grandma said frequently. Those who envied whatever their neighbor had and gazed with wanton eyes were wasting their time. And according to Grandma's dictum, committing sin.

"Get to work and get it, if you want it so bad," she explained.

If the wholesalers wanted cheaper fish, they could find it. It was going to cost time, effort, energy, and initially money, but they could find other sources. But often, people weren't inclined to do the difficult thing, which was frequently the right thing. Robbing, scamming, or plundering was always easier. Many feathers were ruffled by these assertions over the years.

LET THE DEAD BURY THEIR DEAD

Esperanza died. She was a chunky, white-haired old lady who lived a couple of blocks from home. She always dressed in white and always covered her head with a scarf. She knew who I was—everybody did—but she wouldn't talk or even look at me, ever. I'd asked my grandma about this strange behavior, but her response wasn't very enlightening.

"Some people just chase their own tail," she offered. In Grandma's lingo, that meant that some folks did irrational things again and again for no apparent reason and without any visible gain.

Esperanza also avoided Grandma. She would cross the street before she reached our corner, and left the store if we happened to arrive when she was there. These oddities lingered in the back of my mind for years, even after her death. In time, I found some answers and some history, but not from Grandma.

Esperanza's husband was originally the owner of the local meat market. The couple enjoyed prosperity for many years and were respected and well-liked by all in the town of Santa Fe. There was only one issue that seemed to tarnish the picture perfect family: Esperanza couldn't bear children.

Although I'm the product of a different generation, the stigma and pain caused by infertility, especially for a woman, was still significant at that time. Esperanza waited for years, more or less patiently, to conceive but didn't see any results. As medicine and science advanced, she sought medical advice and treatment. Some of these treatment options were novel and promising, but untested. Esperanza pursued these options for years, at tremendous costs.

Esperanza's husband, Bernardo, or Benny as Grandma referred to him, had been her friend for years; as far as I can tell, they were friends before he and Esperanza got married. Grandma was a good fifteen years his senior, but a good friendship ensued. It was said that Grandma loaned him funds to start his butcher shop some twenty years earlier. For years, Benny came to visit Grandma at least once a month. He delighted in Grandma's world-renowned hot cocoa with caramel syrup. Initially, Esperanza accompanied Benny to visit Grandma.

When Esperanza died, at least fifteen years had passed since Benny and Grandma had spoken.

Apparently, between Esperanza's fertility treatments, doctors, and trips to the city, the butcher shop went bankrupt. They also lost their home, along with Benny's pride. In an act of desperation, Benny hung himself in the backyard. But he left a note in his pocket, which the police found. The contents opened a chasm between Esperanza and Grandma that lasted a long time.

It was clear that Esperanza's obsessive pursuit of maternity was the catalyst. Grandma had spoken with them months before and tried to comfort them in their anguish. She offered them words of encouragement, words of faith. For her, the story of Abraham and Sarah spoke volumes about faith and trust in God.

During one of those long conversations well into the night, Grandma posed the question to them: "I know you have tried the doctors. Esperanza, have you tried God?"

Perhaps in frustration and resenting what she perceived as Grandma's condescension, Esperanza yelled back, "I don't need God, what I need is a child!"

Silence followed—that profound and uncomfortable silence that invited reflection on what had been said.

"Esperanza, not your will but His. You'll spend all the money in the world, destroy your marriage and your life, and still won't have a child if it's not His will. Now, your task is to find out what His plan is for you and your husband, and how you can be happy within the boundaries of that plan, and pray that it pleases Him."

Esperanza got up and left the room. She returned a few minutes later and told her husband it was time to go.

"Esperanza, you can't demand anything from God," Grandma tried to explain. "The very air you breath belongs to Him, your life belongs to Him, and if He sees fit to keep you from having a child, you should humble yourself and pray day and night until you come to understand what you are to do. Then, maybe then, He will be merciful and give you a child. I promise you, even if you're one hundred, He will give you one if your test is done and your faith is sufficient."

Esperanza didn't answer. She pulled her husband violently by the hand and left. A few months later, Benny was dead.

The suicide letter spoke of how her obsession had bankrupted them, how his pleas to stop going to doctors and witches had been ignored. He also spoke of how her constant anger and animosity had killed the marriage. He saw himself just as a money machine, totally irrelevant, except to pay for her insane drive to have a child.

> We tried everything; we had nothing else except God. But you couldn't try God. You were above it all. I was not enough. Not even your desire to have a child was enough to force you to your knees. I tell you something, there is no doubt in my mind that God would have given us a child, just like Florence said. I have tried going to God many times.
>
> You have killed my love for you and my desire to live. I can't do this anymore. I will pray that God will forgive me, but I can't live like this anymore knowing that you are the reason that everything I worked for is lost.

Malicious people speculated about Benny and Grandma on account of the note. Most folks knew that it was just a rumor, but the truth was lost to many. Grandma tried to show Esperanza the way to cope with her situation, the way to develop the attitude and the faith to face life on God's terms. Esperanza failed to realize it.

Esperanza sold her older guesthouse and moved to a smaller home she and Benny had bought early in their marriage. She purchased a handful of boats and entered in a partnership with young fishermen to share the proceeds of the catch. It provided a living for her without her having to go to work every day. She spent her days in the dark Church of Jesus of the Mount. She never visited anybody and very few people visited her. And then she died, alone and sad.

When she died, the church was full of people. It wasn't every day that somebody died in town. I guess there was this morbid curiosity about how people look when they're dead. That was at least what my friends said about going to the funeral.

"Grandma, aren't you going to the funeral?" I asked, wanting to join my friends there.

"Let the dead bury their dead," she said without looking at me.

The expression didn't make much sense to me. "How is that going to work?" I asked, thinking about literally, how a dead undertaker was going to bury a dead Esperanza. I tried picturing the scene. It was just too bizarre. I shook my head trying to discard the image.

"Here, sit." She gestured to a chair while holding a plate of french fries. Part of my brain just switched off from the salty, greasy, delicious smell. I obeyed and sat, but my eyes were glued to the fries.

"Think about what the whole funeral is all about," she began. "They all go, walk around to see the made up face of Esperanza in a pretty dress, and then what?" Grandma dramatized her words by "walking" her index and middle fingers over the table.

"Then Father Fumes is going to say how nice Esperanza was and how much people liked her and blah, blah, blah . . . ," she trailed off.

She fixed her eyes on me, gave me a quarter-smile, and continued. "The fact is, the woman was neither good nor did she live a good life. Most people didn't like her because she was a bitter, bad-mannered little old lady. She didn't offer a glass of water to a thirsty soul if she found one. On top of that, she was arrogant and proud, a woman of little faith."

There it went. The "F-word" again, an intangible essence that permeated everything and everywhere I looked, as far as Grandma was concerned. But really, what was it? For Grandma, everything started and ended with *faith*.

I thought for a couple of minutes while she started to brush her long white hair. "But, Grandma, what is faith?" I asked, accentuating the syllable. "How do you get or grow faith?"

She stopped her grooming ritual. She tied her hair behind her back and placed both hands on the table. She looked over my head through the window without blinking. She was scaling down her thoughts. She was a master at bringing everything to my level.

"Can you see the air, son?" she asked.

"Of course not," I responded, thinking she might be patronizing me.

"But you know it's there, don't you?" she asked again.

"Sure," I said. I was lost.

"Interesting." She was smiling now. I braced for the killer blow.

"You say you know that the air exists; you haven't given it too much thought ever in your life. You can't taste it unless it's carrying some other smell. You can't grab it, but you say it exists."

I didn't dare say anything. I actually didn't know what to say. I was holding my breath.

"Well, son, that's what faith is all about. You haven't seen God. You never said that He has spoken to you or we'd have heard about it. And last I checked, He doesn't give out interviews. So how do we know He is real?" It wasn't a rhetorical question; she was, in fact asking and waiting for a reply.

"We . . . believe?" I asked, not entirely sure of my own answer.

"Yes! We believe," she exclaimed lifting both her arms high above her head. I took in some air for what seemed like the first time in an hour.

"Son, you must believe. Faith is about stepping into the dark without fear. Why? Because you trust in Him who made the light and the darkness. And if your heart is good, what you desire is good, and He approves. He will guide you safely through the dark to the end of the tunnel." She shifted on her chair. She was just getting started.

"Son, we can't find God without faith. Heck, we can't pray without faith. Otherwise it's just a boring litany and good for nothing. We kneel down and we pray to the God Most High and ask Him to help us, protect us, feed us, and everything else we ask. And for what? Well, because we have faith in Him that He will answer our prayers and grant our petition." She stopped for a few seconds and pointed her index finger at me. I could see her eyes welling with tears.

"Son, I tell you today and promise you that as the sun will rise again in the horizon tomorrow, if you have faith in God, then you know that He won't hold back anything from you that is good. He will guide you, show you things, protect you, and open your eyes to things hidden to others around you. If you have faith in Him, there's nothing you can't do, as simple as that."

The concept wasn't so simple. It wasn't just a matter of believing in God and asking Him for stuff you need. As far as I could grasp the idea, you had to close your eyes and believe that He was going to do for you what you couldn't do for yourself. You had to sort of delegate to Him the things you couldn't take on and believe that He would bridge the gap for you.

I thought it might be fun to see how far Grandma's faith went, so I planned my next question.

"So, Grandma, if I had this huge, humongous, impossible problem to resolve and I went and asked God for help, He would take care of it for me?" I asked, trying to hide my smile.

She saw right through it but decided to ignore it. She smiled. "Well, it depends," she answered.

"Oh, Grandma, you see?" I started to complain. It didn't last.

"Son, in life things happen contrary to how they happen in school, for example," she posed. I was lost again but she continued.

"Problems, just like in math, are designed to teach us things. The difference is that in school they teach you the lesson and then you face the test. In life, you face the problem, and as you struggle with it and you see that you can't solve it, you go to God and say, 'Good Lord, this is too much for me. I can't do this on my own. Please help me.' If you're sincere and really sad and desperate, and if you believe the Lord will help you, then He will work his magic and help you solve your problem." She watched as I nodded in agreement. She wanted to make sure I got this point.

"The beauty of the whole ordeal is that in the process you have to learn a few things," she continued. "One: that you don't know everything; I don't care how old you are and how much you think you know. Second: that regardless of how much effort you put into something, you may not be able to handle it. You'll tread water for a very long time.

"Ultimately, the sooner you realize that it is in fact a test, the sooner you'll kneel down and plead with God for help. You're then on the path to solving your problem, having learned some very valuable lessons in the process."

Slowly, very slowly, the pieces began to assemble in my mind. Faith was large, larger than I initially thought. It had roots that had to go deep in order to sustain me through the violent assaults of life's hurricanes.

My next question was simple but dealt with more practical applications. "So, Grandma, how do you use faith?"

There was no need for her to think. She shot from the hip on that one. "Everywhere, all the time, for everything," she replied.

"Son, the day will come when faith will be the only thing that can save your life or the life of others. When all is lost, when your spirit is low or your strength spent, faith will be the pillar you need to lean on. God will be the only hand available for support. But remember, you must absolutely believe that He will see you through."

Her words sank deep into my mind. These same words proved to be prophetic years later.

We sat quietly for a few minutes. The notion of an almighty, all-seeing, all-knowing God was a tad scary. A God we could only approach if we had faith in Him, a faith that required our whole heart. The notion that faith in Him could heal everything, solve everything, and overcome everything was very attractive.

Adults were supposed to know these things. They were supposed to have experience and knowledge. Why didn't our neighbor Esperanza have any faith? How did she manage to live so long without really knowing God?

"So, Grandma, Esperanza died an old woman and had no faith. What is going to happen to her?" My grandmother kept silent, her stare fixed somewhere else, memories dancing before her eyes.

I shook my head and pressed the issue. "The woman was always in church, all day long," I stressed. "It must count for something, doesn't it?"

"She went to church every day to ask God why He hadn't given her a child and why He allowed her husband to kill himself," Grandma said, a sliver of anger cracking her voice.

"Now, you tell me," she continued, "in the eyes of God, she's dead. Those who have lived and haven't come to understand that they'll have to stand before Him to render an account for their lives are in serious trouble. If you don't believe in Jesus Christ, you're dead and you'll be dead, for all practical purposes, at resurrection time," she concluded. "She may have one last chance, I think, but I wouldn't bet on that one," Grandma said as an afterthought.

"But she's dead!" I exclaimed. I got no answer. Grandma got up from the table.

She went into her room. I knew she was looking for her Bible; she always did when she was trying to illustrate a point. She returned to the table and had the cracked volume in hand. She rifled through the pages until she found the passage.

> No man can come to me, except the Father which hath sent me draw him: and I will raise him up at the last day.
> It is written in the prophets, And they shall be all taught of God. Every man therefore that hath heard, and hath learned of the Father, cometh unto me. (John 6:44–45)

Once again, I found myself trying to grasp concepts and doctrines that weren't the subject of everyday conversation. In fact, I'd never heard Grandma discussing these things with anyone. I guess most folks weren't interested.

For them, God in general was an ethereal figure, more like a force or influence than a real character. He was "there somewhere" in space or another dimension. He wasn't connected to us or in contact with us. But it wasn't so for Grandma. Her view was much more expansive.

"But, Grandma, should we seek Jesus, or God?" I asked, grappling with the subject.

"Son, Jesus is God," she said, smiling. I could feel smoke coming out of my ears and the sizzling of what was left of my brain. She laughed at my grimace and stroked the top of my head.

"Let me show you," she said, rummaging again through the pages of the Bible. She stopped, read silently for a bit, and then continued.

> But now thus saith the Lord that created thee, O Jacob, and he that formed thee, O Israel, Fear not: for I have redeemed thee, I have called thee by thy name; thou art mine.
>
> When thou passest through the waters, I will be with thee; and through the rivers, they shall not overflow thee: when thou walkest through the fire, thou shalt not be burned; neither shall the flame kindle upon thee.
>
> For I am the Lord thy God, the Holy One of Israel, thy Saviour . . .
>
> I, even I, am the Lord; and beside me there is no saviour. . . .
>
> Yea, before the day was I am he; and there is none that can deliver out of my hand: I will work, and who shall let it?
>
> Thus saith the Lord, your redeemer, the Holy One of Israel . . .
>
> I am the Lord, your Holy One, the creator of Israel, your King. (Isaiah 43:1–3, 11, 13–15)

She looked at me with a soft smile dancing on her lips. Of course she knew I couldn't understand, but it pleased her that I wanted to know. I sat there and actually asked her questions, trying hard to slip some of the teachings into my undersized brain.

"Son, Jesus Christ is known as the Savior, the Redeemer, the King of Israel, right?" she probed. I nodded.

"Okay, so here Isaiah is speaking for the Lord and the Lord Jehovah calls himself the Creator and the Father." She paused for two seconds to check my pulse, I supposed, since she then touched my wrist.

"So, if Jehovah is the Savior and the Creator and also the Redeemer, when Jesus later used the same 'titles,' then there's no other explanation. Jehovah and Jesus are the same person," she announced triumphantly.

"The rest is simple then," she continued. "There is a Father in Heaven that sent Jehovah (Jesus) to the earth to do His will, and Jesus did just that. And the Father spoke from heaven when John baptized Jesus in the Jordan River and again in the mountains."

She was done, for now, and was still smiling and sensing I was on the verge of losing consciousness. At times, I thought that Grandma totally forgot that I was still in junior high.

She continued. "Father and Son, the first Almighty and the second, the one that worked on behalf of the Father, the Only Begotten Son, needed to complete and finish the work of salvation for all."

Now it made some sense. I said, "I still have to resolve a few—" I paused. "That can't—!" I exclaimed. "Two Gods?" I asked, sure that my heart was pushing up my throat.

"Yep," she said, smiling.

"Are there more than two?" was my next question.

"Well, it doesn't look that way from the Bible, but—" She was thinking out loud rather than responding to my question. "Jesus said we must be perfect and then we'll inherit everything the Father has. That part I don't understand completely, but I'm working on it." She smiled again, her blue eyes gleaming.

And with that, the lesson was over. Grandma disappeared into the kitchen, leaving a very confused boy behind and a mountain of complex theological wrangling for a landscape. Many of these conversations remained with me, oftentimes for years. A situation, a phrase, or a reflective thought brought those conversations to my awareness, and they lay in the deepest recesses of my mind until triggered by an event.

These conversations prepared my mind; they gave me reasoning space and the ability to question things I heard in different churches I visited later in my life. For years, the assumptions Grandma had made and the insights she'd gained from reading the Bible were unassailable. I became convinced that Grandma had access to truths that came from God. Someone would have to bring significantly compelling evidence to the contrary in order to persuade me to explore a different viewpoint.

LIBERTY: GOD'S GIFT TO MEN

My great-grandfather's name was Gilberto Lamoreaux; he was the son of second-generation emancipated slaves. His grandfather had received a land grant in 1868 and settled the region. They had developed a large sugarcane mill operation, employing many former slaves and even latecomers to the colonies from Spain and France.

The Lamoreaux family owned and operated the first printing press in the region and edited the first regional periodical. The youngest of the three boys was sent to law school in Santiago de Cuba, the largest city in the eastern part of the country. There was also a brief stay in Key West that gave this young lawyer a view and concept of the world that impacted generations to come.

Grandma's marriage didn't last but two and a half years. Her husband died of what seemed at that time an obscure and poorly understood lung disease, leaving her with two small children. Because his family didn't sanction their marriage, she found little support after his death. The situation was compounded by the fact that in the early 1900s, women couldn't legally own property. Grandma found herself a widow and on the verge of losing everything she had. An unscrupulous town lawyer attempted to seize her land and property. If it weren't for the intervention of her lifelong friend Calixto, she'd have ended up destitute.

Within two years, Grandma managed to sell her landholding and other properties and moved away, never to return to her native town.

Lamoreaux had lived a short life but had a glimpse of what men could accomplish when they were guided by principles instead of greed. As a young lawyer in his family's business, Lamoreaux traveled to Key West in the United States. It was a sparsely populated outpost at the time with only a few traders, fishermen, and the legendary cigar makers who had traveled across the straits for a hundred years. There he had a chance to read the Constitution of the United States.

The document changed his views on the definition of country and what constituted true liberty. He came to realize that for a good portion of the century the islanders had been waging a war, though they had no guiding philosophy. The notion of expelling the colonial troops was noble, but it had no clear foundation or overarching principles.

The island-born landowners wanted to be free from taxation, but they in turn weren't willing to offer the same benefit to the newcomers. Emancipation had been declared some forty years before, but most free slaves and their descendants lived worse than dogs. At last, what was freedom? Who decided who was bond or free? How could we guarantee that all were free forever?

The Americans were still struggling with the practical application of their Constitution. The notion that God made all men in His image and equal before Him was clear to the Founding Fathers. This issue became thorny when they had to reconcile the fact that thus all men are born with the right to be free, and that freedom is commanded by Him. That was simply groundbreaking and without parallel in recorded history.

From that point on, Lamoreaux's writings were peppered with quotes and paraphrasing of the US Constitution. Its ideas and principles permeated every paper, every thesis, and document he committed to print in his journals, letters, and articles he published in his small provincial newspaper.

With passion, he explored the possibilities of sound principles to govern people. He envisioned ideals that were above convenience and greed. He advocated that the mind and the mandate of the people were an expression of the designs of God.

It seems fair to conclude that before his death, he spoke of these things with Grandma. He convinced her that, although foreign to them, God, the true and everlasting God of the Bible, was the answer to the illness of men. He had the answer to the riddles of time and the solution to the troubles of the past and the conflicts of the future. Grandma was inspired to save many of his writings and one of his journals. It provided not only a window into his thoughts and life perspective, but an inspirational pillar for future generations.

HONOR THY FATHER AND THY MOTHER

Divorce showed its ugly face by the time I was eleven. I never saw my parents argue; I never heard loud or unkind words. My father was a bureaucrat in the government news agency. He traveled frequently and seemed more interested in the corporate climb than in his family.

The government demanded total loyalty. There was nothing more important or significant than the individual contribution to the collective good. It sounded enticing. The problem was that the government typically defined what constituted "collective good" and what should be done in that regard.

One day my father didn't come home. After countless inquiries and questions, reality set in that he wasn't returning. From that point on, Grandma became my only emotional refuge. I came to depend on her for just about everything.

My mother, on the other hand, wasn't able to navigate the transition very well. She became increasingly angry, bitter, despondent, and distant. She returned to work. Finding work wasn't difficult—she was a college graduate and spoke several languages—but finding balance between work and family became impossible for her. She worked from sunrise to sunset, which made interaction with me infrequent and almost limited to the weekends.

In retrospect, martial arts training and most likely the hand of God, as well as the comfort of my grandmother, kept me from making a wrong turn during those years. Opportunities for straying abounded, but I stayed my course. Barely. Drinking, together with baseball, is Cuba's national pastime. From the thick, rancid tap beer sold in the corner bars, to the sugarcane-based rum, which seems more suitable for airplane fuel than human consumption, to a surprising number of garden varieties of alcoholic beverages, Cubans seem capable of extracting alcohol from just about any plant. I kept my involvement with such flammables at a minimum.

Another rather trivial occupation was trafficking in black market goods: pants, shirts, shoes, perfume, food, whatever. Everybody seemed to be either buying or selling something. And it was all contraband, rest assured. Grandma shook her head, murmuring some "mild burning" curse every time I'd show her something somebody had offered me. Again, that kept me from making a serious incursion in the illegal trade.

In time, Grandma completely replaced my mother as my primary caretaker for years to come. Since the divorce when I was eleven, until I became an adolescent, I lost emotional contact with my mother. I avoided her because I saw her as demanding, removed, and domineering. Her verbal aggression and frequent hostile demeanor created a schism that wouldn't be closed for years.

On a bright Saturday afternoon, I was on my way to the movies with some friends. High school had broadened my social circle. I still enjoyed the company of my lifelong friends, but I'd come to know many more people. On my way out, my mother intercepted me and questioned my outing. She pointed to the fact that she didn't know about my plans and demanded that I stay home. I didn't argue with her; I just walked out the door and left her shouting from the front doorway.

Grandma was troubled, and she waited for me to return that night. She asked cursory questions about the movie, my friends, and the weather while she warmed my dinner plate. She was serious and constrained. I could always tell when she was worried.

"What happened with your mom earlier today?" she asked hesitantly. Grandma was never casual when she asked a question.

I stopped eating my chicken and rice for a few moments. I tried to gather my thoughts but had no explanation. The incident with my mother was simply a bidirectional exchange of strong, unresolved feelings. I had a difficult time explaining to Grandma how I felt.

"I—am not sure," I stuttered. You couldn't say, "I don't know" to Grandma and live. So I switched gears mid-sentence.

"Try harder—you have to do better than that," she responded.

I kept eating to make time. I pushed a couple of spoonfuls into my mouth until she held my hand. I took my time chewing, while I listened to the drip of the kitchen faucet. I looked at her wrinkled hand holding mine but avoided her stare.

"Grandma, I don't know what's happened to Mom. She hasn't been the same for years. She's always angry, upset. Nothing good comes out of her mouth anymore. It seems like she only wants to make sure I know she pays the bills and she's in charge."

I tried to keep eating, but she gripped my hand again harder.

"And?" she asked. She wouldn't let go.

"Well, I already told you about going to the movies. You knew about it; you even gave me money. Why did she have to get in the middle? She doesn't have the right to tell me, 'You can't go.' "

"She's your mother, son," Grandma pointed out. "I'm not sure what she was trying to do, but she is your mother."

I felt anger rising in my throat. "Grandma, what is the purpose of telling me I couldn't go? I'd already cleared the thing with you. I always do. I think she does it for kicks, just to show me she's in control. Well, she's wrong," I spouted, my trembling voice showing my lack of bravado.

"I want you to be polite to her. Don't respond to her in anger," she demanded. Her request seemed like an emotional impossibility. "Son, remember that God commands that we honor our father and mother. You don't even have to like her, but you have to honor her."

"But how do I do that?" I shot back. "It's almost impossible to have a civilized conversation with her," I added, my voice gaining a decibel or two and not caring much if my mother heard me across the hallway.

"All I ask, son, is that you respond to her with respect and not confront her," she said, her tone soft and inviting as usual.

I felt like crying now. My mother seemed to go out of her way to humiliate me, impose herself, and force her opinion and viewpoint. There was no room for negotiation.

"I'll try, Grandma," I said, barely holding back the tears.

"I know you will, and God will bless you for your desire to please and obey Him," she said, smiling. "Son, God expects us to be kind, gentle, humble, and meek. Jesus said it was easy to like our friends and to be nice to them. It was harder, however, to be kind and gracious to our enemies." I knew she was paraphrasing the scriptures. It was hard to swallow, but I remained silent.

"God expects you to be righteous, to exhibit qualities that demonstrate that you're above the rest, that you're willing to do the difficult thing because it's the right thing to do. To subdue your anger and animosity is evidence of the fact that you're upright and that you're willing to sacrifice."

"Grandma, do I have to obey all the commandments, all the time?" I asked, more or less rhetorically, since I knew what she was going to say. We'd had this conversation before.

She smiled and stroked the top of my head. She got up from her chair and took my plate. "Let me warm up your food," she said.

In spite of my willingness to appease and avoid antagonizing my mother, the situation didn't improve much. During the next few months, we had a handful of less than amicable exchanges. The situation deteriorated, at least from my perspective, to a point where staying at home was almost unbearable. By the summer of my senior year in high school and my seventeenth birthday, I'd resolved to leave home and the constant tug-of-war with my mother.

ALWAYS ON THE RIGHT HAND

There's something to be said for seniority. For many years, I thought anyone with white hair had a certain aura of respectability. But I came to know that women, especially, don't share that notion.

Either way, for years, a long line of people paraded by Grandma's kitchen, looking for counsel, or just her apron to cry on. The whole scene looked bizarre to me, of course. I couldn't imagine what could reduce an adult to tears. In the limited realm of my understanding, tears were only allowed when frustration—or, occasionally, Grandma's old military bel—got the best of you.

Crying and adulthood appeared to be a tremendous incongruence. However, I was never surprised to find someone sitting at the lunch table, with Grandma's napkin in hand. Immediately, Grandma gave me "the look" and away I went, hunger pangs and all, until the counseling session was over. The whole thing was irritating, especially since they had the whole house to cry in. Why did they have to cry in the prime real estate and occupy the food court?

Anna was, more or less, every boy's impossible love interest in Santa Fe. She was at least ten years older than I, and lived a few blocks away from my home. She was *beautiful.* She had long light brown hair, almost blonde, and piercing green eyes. Those eyes, yes. They could melt you like an ice cream cone on a summer afternoon. Our mothers had been schoolmates an eon before and still talked about it. Weird, I thought.

Even as a very young boy, I could engage in the most elaborate fantasies about Anna. She was sick and I was her doctor, or her home was badly battered by a hurricane and I was the architect. Freud was onto something, regardless of all his other bad habits. Fantasies do play a very important role in coping with emotionally intense realities. On account of being ten years my senior, Anna was unreachable. Fantasies were all I had.

The day I found her crying in my grandma's kitchen I was shaken to my core. My girl—in distress? No! Who was the culprit? For all my bravado, curiosity was burning within me like a blowtorch. After "the look" from Grandma, I managed to leave just far enough to be out of her sight but close enough to stay within hearing range.

What I heard scarred me for years to come. She was in love and it wasn't with me. To add insult to injury, the man was already married! She seemed to be baffled about the fact that God hadn't intervened in strengthening the relationship, turning the affair into a more solid and official engagement.

Cubans are extremely superstitious people. They have this primitive sense of deity that has evolved across five hundred years of a very convoluted cultural and social history. The native inhabitants of the Islands worshiped in very obscure and, until now, not very explicit ways. The Spaniards brought the cross in the right hand of the Franciscan monks. The sword and the musket were close behind, in the name of the crown, but with soldiers who had no compulsion to use them. The slave trade fused the earlier traditions and colored it in a vivid European pantheon. All saints and all gods from everywhere for all people. They're still there, behind every door, in secret compartments, in an inconspicuous shed in the backyard.

They're always worshiping to some saint, African or European, which is the same as far as they're concerned. They make sacrifices to some stone, shell, bones, or wood statue—all in the hope that the saint will intercede, change, manipulate, interfere, scare, or whatever is required. And, of course, God is always around, somewhere. He is there but not in charge, not really, but He's there in some distant corner of the cosmos.

The conversation between my infantile love interest and Grandma was long—not in words, but because Anna's crying spells lasted a couple of minutes each. The rest was just a blur. It didn't matter much, and I resolved right then and there I'd never see or talk to or about Anna again. I was a fallen knight, rejected and mortally wounded.

"Anna, if you dance with the devil you'll get burned," I heard Grandma say.

Anna said something, but I could only hear her sobbing. I wanted to either hug and comfort her, or get away.

"What did you expect?" Grandma continued. "You knew from the beginning, but you held on to your fantasy."

There was a pause, followed by more sobbing. Then I heard Grandma's voice again. "Girl, if you have a couple of eggs in your hand, it doesn't matter if you boil them, scramble, or poach them, you'll never get a steak out of them. That's just insane, to keep doing the same thing again and again, hoping that somehow you'll get a different result."

Tears and the napkin she kept pressed against her face broke Anna's speech. I couldn't hear anything she said.

"Child," Grandma persisted. "What were you thinking? Since when does love justify madness? I've been in love, you know. It isn't a disease. Please don't abandon your brain to the wind and claim it was swept away in the bliss of love. The idea probably will sell well as a soap opera, but it doesn't work in the real world." Her tone was sharp and the sobbing increased.

I could hear chairs shuffling and the chinking of glasses. I remembered how hungry I was and imagined Grandma serving Anna a cold glass of fruit juice. My mouth started to water.

"Look here," Grandma said, "feelings aren't real. They're just the result of whatever is in our minds. You fabricated a fantasy with this boy and forgot that, regardless of how you felt, it was still wrong." The pause was longer this time. I bet they were drinking more of that cold fruit juice.

"My girl," Grandma said, "you can't do wrong and later ask God to help you turn things your way. That's simply impossible. To plead with Him for His help, you have to find yourself on His right hand. He can't look with approving eyes upon what you have done; there's no way." The rebuke was still there, but the tone was softer, almost soothing now.

"I'll help you. It's going to take some time, but you'll be okay," Grandma added.

Since I couldn't hear anything else from that point on, I left. I couldn't get any closer without being discovered. I tried later to inquire about the details of the drama unfolding, but she just gave me "the look."

What a disappointment for a twelve-year-old boy to realize that in fact angels could only be found in heaven. The ones walking around on the earth, although beautiful, had lost their wings.

Grown men also cried at my grandma's table. This was an even more bizarre and confusing scene to witness. Men weren't supposed to cry. That was unheard of and probably illegal, I thought. Besides, you ran the risk of people finding out how soft you were, and the teasing you invited became chronic torture for the next century.

Manny was a handsome guy who I actually sort of envied. He was extremely popular with the girls in the neighborhood. And judging by the number of girls he brought by, his fame and good looks were also known in neighborhoods beyond my own.

He had sleepy green eyes and a warm smile. He was a regular chick magnet. Eventually, he said, one of the girls wanted him so bad that she ended up having his baby.

I was fighting to get the last of some preserves out of a jar when he walked in through the patio door and into the kitchen. I jumped out of my chair to greet him and playfully boxed with him, as usual. He was a familiar face. To this day, I have no idea which cat dropped him at our doorstep. Manny just showed up one day and kept coming. At times, he ate with us and showered at our house. He even spent a few days and nights at home with us, for some reason. The bathroom was saturated with his cologne for months after that.

I wanted to be just like him. Well, in the girl department, anyway.

"Hi, Grandma," resounded his radio announcer voice in the kitchen. "What's cooking?" And he meant that literally

He walked over to the stove and kissed Grandma on the cheek. "Go brush your teeth and wash your hands. I don't know where you've been and don't tell me either," she said, breaking into her best laughter.

He walked slowly from the kitchen and into the dining room. He sat quietly at the table and waited. The strong, silent types don't disclose their pain, at least not at the beginning of the movies. You have to get it out of them as if it is abdominal surgery. Men keep their pain under wraps, deep inside, or so I'd been told.

Grandma came out of the kitchen into the dining room, and placed an icy container in front of Manny. Her fruit juice was legendary.

"What's eating you now, Manuel?" Grandma asked bluntly. He took a minute and a couple of sips from the glass.

"Theresa said she's having a baby," he said, his voice cracking a high-pitched note, tears waiting to spill. He shook his head in disbelief.

"Did she tell you that?" Grandma asked softly.

"No, her sister Vivian told me," came the broken response. His tears began to flow now.

"Are you sure it's your baby?" asked Grandma, stressing the last two words.

"Well, I think—I'm almost positive it's mine," Manny responded, acquiescent.

It was Grandma's time to shake her head. "How many times have I told you, Manny, that you were in dangerous water with that girl?" She left the phrase bouncing in the ear canal.

She wasn't ready to let him off the hook. "You had to go pee at the electric fence, did you? Couldn't you see the bones right next to it? Isn't it enough to signal to your brain that there's something terribly wrong with that fence?"

She waited a few seconds. He kept drinking slowly, his eyes fixed on the glass in front of him and tears still spilling down his face.

"The writing was on the wall, but you think you can swim with sharks without losing a body part. Son, the wrong tastes kind of good long enough to make you forget the bitter that follows." She drove her point home. He had nothing to say.

They sat face-to-face for a long time. Only his tears broke the silence.

For years to come, such scenes repeated themselves with only slight variation in theme. Grandma's response was always similar: "God will succor you only after you turn right."

Her philosophy was simple: there was safety and peace if you always found yourself "on the right hand of God." If you turned any other way, you were on your own and walking on dangerous terrain. In time, the teaching found its mark in me.

I Send You out in the Hands of God

High school was a blur of disjointed and incoherent social exchanges. It was just too much agitation and very little movement, an atmosphere charged with emotion but little meaning. I was relieved when it was over.

Telling Grandma that I'd registered to enlist in the Armed Forces was, in all likelihood, my most difficult decision to that date. How would I explain that I was leaving her and the comfort of our home, my lifelong friends, and the safety of the community?

I had no satisfactory rationalization. In truth, I'd agonized over my decision for months. Without success, I'd tried my best to develop a relationship with my mother. I had no energy left to sustain the tension that the relationship with my mother generated. I needed to leave.

"Grandma," I said without looking at her. She was in the kitchen, stirring some delicious smelling stew. "I have to talk to you," I continued.

She turned and blinked quickly several times. She lowered the flame on the stove and sat at the table. I think she could now feel the weight on my chest.

"I signed up for the Navy," I said in one swing. I was afraid I wouldn't be able to say it if I delayed the news any further.

She sat there quietly. It was impossible to say what was going through her mind.

"Have you thought about this carefully?" she asked softly, her gaze fixed on mine as if she were trying not to miss a second of my reaction.

"Yes, I have. I actually signed up more than six months ago," I added.

Her eyebrows lifted an inch on her forehead and descended slowly, but she didn't let go of my eyes.

I felt sad. I'd kept this significant decision from her for many months. I hadn't made her a participant in the process. I felt like I had robbed her in some way.

"What happens next?" she asked, her voice low but still not letting go of my eyes.

"I have to report to my base on July fifteenth. They'll tell me there what happens next." My answer sounded slow, unconvincing, and void of enthusiasm. She picked up on it.

"You don't sound very excited," she pointed.

My answer was, in a way, honest. "It wasn't necessarily my first choice, but—"

I couldn't tell Grandma that the ever-increasing tense atmosphere between my mother and me had precipitated my choice. It didn't seem an honorable excuse.

"I think I need to go and try to make my own way, Grandma," I offered, nervously shifting my weight on the chair and not leaving much room for debate.

She was quiet for several minutes. Taking a deep breath, she caressed the pages of her open Bible and meditated.

"I love you, son. I've taught you everything I could in these few years so that you can become a man I can be proud of. If you believe in your heart that this is something you have to do, then go ahead" Her words were firm, but a faint sense of sadness infused her statement.

She thought for a while longer. Then she smiled at me with tenderness and motioned for me to get closer. I did, tears burning my eyes.

She held me for a few seconds, then looked closely at my face. "I send you out into the world in the hands of God," she said, a certain air of solemnity accentuating her words. "I urge you to seek Him and His direction in everything you do. Have faith and use your faith, because I guarantee you that the time will come when your life and the life of others will depend on how much faith you have been able to gather in your heart."

I was used to Grandma's advice, but this was different. This was an everlasting message, something she wanted me to carry forever. It was intended to weigh against all odds and situations that I might encounter. This was to be part of me, to shape and to craft a new vision of me and of the world that would last a lifetime.

"Son, you're going to war and I want you to understand what that means," she continued.

Those last words surprised me. I thought I knew what war was, but her insight went much deeper.

"War is the devil's weapon of choice. He maims and destroys, robs and plunders, frightens and disrupts the lives of peoples and countries like nothing else in the world. Millions will go to their graves not knowing why they were born in the first place."

Her description was clear and shed light and knowledge that I came to appreciate many years later.

"The devil drives otherwise normal and reasonable human beings to commit the most horrible acts of violence. He robs you of your humanity under the false pretense of a threat, while intoxicated by power. Keep your heart clean and your eyes open. Go serve, do your duty, but never wield a weapon with the desire to spill blood for vengeance or dominion."

Her words stirred feelings in me unknown until then. Tears continued to roll down my face.

"I'll pray for your safe return day and night until you come back. But keep silent prayers in your heart always. Listen to His voice, and you'll be safe. God hasn't revealed His purpose for you yet, but in due time He will and you'll know it. Until then, go and do your duty to the best of your ability and trust in His strength. He will see you through until you return home."

We embraced for a long time. I could hear the quiet rhythm of her heart and her even breathing. She was about to see me go into one of the most brutal civil wars in recent history on the continent, and she was unafraid.

Off I went to boot camp and a nightmare of twenty-six weeks of military training. The next seven years opened my eyes to a reality that seemed atrocious, absurd, and totally irrational. Wounds, hunger, terrible weather, and armed conflict filled those years, but it was the prelude of what my life was destined to become.

PART TWO
THE UNSEEN WARS

AT LARGE

In the eighties and early nineties, Central America was the theater of the bloodiest and longest civil war in recent history. Depending on whose statistics you prefer, between two and five million people lost their lives in the region. An equal number of people were displaced by the conflict, some never to return to their native lands.

The root of the conflict can't be traced to just one seed. As usual, a number of factors conspired to turn the region into an explosive cocktail. Latin American countries, with very few exceptions, had suffered from the same maladies and social infirmities for the last two hundred years.

Without going into a political science dissertation, it would be fair to say that ignorance on both sides about history, psychosocial realities, and poor military intelligence were primarily the reasons for the "dirty war" of Central America.

The Cold War found fertile ground in the region. The US, on one hand, was politically and logistically training and supporting the military in those countries in order to ensure their interest. On the other hand, the Cubans, with full military and financial support from the Soviets, embarked in wholesale export of doctrine and de facto revolutions to the insurgents and irregular militias operating in those countries.

This resulted in millions of civilians being caught up in the middle of a battleground with poorly defined ideological camps. They became the innocent recipients of the mayhem and violence galore dispensed by a handful of warring factions.

After basic training in the naval academy, I was assigned to officer's training at an underwater demolition and special operations unit. These units operated as surgical strike forces in the region, intelligence gatherers, or as means to neutralize high interest targets in the area.

As a military intelligence officer, I was assigned to a reconnaissance unit with my team deep into what was considered hostile terrain. Our job was fairly simple—if such a thing exists in a war scenario. It consisted primarily of following enemy troops and gathering as much information as possible in every aspect of the unit.

Guerrilla warfare represents a war scenario diametrically different from conventional military conflict as seen on CNN. There are no missiles, tanks, airplanes, or armed personnel vehicles. The jungle doesn't allow for the deployment of such modern wonders of the arsenal. Uneven terrain, foliage, and uncooperative weather render large-scale modern military equipment totally unusable in such circumstances.

In the jungle, war is waged between small cohorts of men in surprise attacks and hit-and-run operations. The objective isn't to destroy your enemy in one powerful, crushing blow, which is practically impossible. The strategy rests on your ability to exhaust, demoralize, and scatter the enemy unit. Operational deployments are planned for small units to launch lightning-fast strikes with overwhelming firepower in short intervals—the primary aim being to wound the largest number of enemy combatants and destroy communication infrastructure and supplies. Our intention was to "decapitate" the enemy unit's chain of command, thus reducing their ability to operate, and making their movement slower (carrying the wounded is extremely cumbersome). Without food and communication, their response is limited to defensive maneuvering.

Typical recon and intelligence gathering entailed less than glamorous activities such as collecting human waste samples in abandoned campsites, recording internal and external enemy radio communication traffic, identifying and photographing unit commanders and leaders, and documenting visits and encounters with other subjects of interest.

This information served as the foundation for the intelligence briefings prepared by our analysis unit in order to plan further operations. One of the most critical tasks was securing members of the enemy unit's high command. That was just a euphemism for a highly complex and precisely executed kidnapping operation on foreign soil of enemy military personnel for interrogation. The above designation was loosely used for any person deemed of interest.

Once the extraction was complete, the subject was transported to a secure location, usually a friendly country or isolated enclave. Because most of the material and logistical support to the armed forces of Latin American governments were provided by the CIA, the Soviet NKVD (Narodnyi Komissariat Vnutrennikh Del) handled the interrogation.

The NKVD is best known for the Main Directorate for State Security (GUGB), which succeeded the OGPU and the early Cheka as the secret police agency of the former Soviet Union. These agents had been specially trained in Central and Latin America. They were fully bilingual in Russian and Spanish, and many of them had years of experience in guerrilla warfare. In a horrific sense, these agents were good at what they did. Most of the time they could, without spilling any blood, get a confession from a tree trunk if they happened to be interested in it. Enter the KGB.

Military operations in the Central and South American rain forest were fraught with dangers: from insects that could drill and burrow into your skin in seconds to nest and leave larvae behind, to two-hundred-pound cats that could sever a limb with one bite and keep running without losing their stride. Spiders, scorpions, poisonous beetles and snakes, toxic plants, and obnoxious fumes completed the menu.

Besides that, there were hosts of well-armed, functionally illiterate government soldiers and paramilitary squads, all bent on killing anything they suspected of being or collaborating with the insurgents. Otherwise, the landscape is absolutely beautiful. The tropical rain forest is home to thousands of species of flowers and birds, one-hundred-foot tall trees and waterfalls towering ten stories high.

The jaguar is one of my favorite jungle dwellers. It is a feared member of the feline family, venerated and hated for two thousand years by the people of the region. The landscape is littered with ruins bearing exquisite paintings and carvings of this elegant cat. The jaguar looks majestic (and innocuous) in *National Geographic*, but in real life its presence can trigger sudden episodes of unavoidable bodily functions.

We had been trailing a twenty-four-man unit deep into the Honduran territory. The men were tired and were running low on supplies, but because they were on their home turf, they seemed unconcerned and lethargic.

They began to settle in for the night, noisily setting up campfires and tents. It had been raining almost nonstop for ten hours. Mud slides had forced them to circle around and avoid the narrow path across the

Nacaome Mountains. They had missed their extraction point by more than a day. It would be another twenty-four to thirty-six hours before they could reach open space for an airlift. It was almost impossible to sleep when it rained at night, but the rain began to subside before nightfall. The jungle seemed to hear my prayers.

In the jungle, the transition between light and darkness happens rather suddenly. Sunlight disappears with an amazing speed, swallowed up by the haze and the tree line. On the leaf-covered floor, a million critters begin their nocturnal dance in search of food, home, or a mate. Nothing stands still—ever.

Early in the afternoon, we'd heard the call of the jaguar deep in the jungle. My company and I assumed, given the amount of rain and the conditions of the soil, it was doubtful that he would venture in our direction. According to my grandma, assumption is the mother of all disasters.

We set up the scanners and shot a few pictures before the last vestiges of the day sank deep into the west. The enemy unit fanned out in small six-man groups. They managed to get fires going, and the sweet smell of beans floated in the dusk-soaked breeze. The aroma of cedar and eucalyptus resin can cover just about every smell, but my hunger had sharpened my senses. I could sniff the pots on the fire a quarter of a mile away.

We took the high ground over their camp. We set our perimeter alarms, and I took first watch. Our small three-man unit was, in most respects, almost invisible in the jungle. Through my high-power binoculars I could see the dirty and haggard faces of the soldiers, some of them still in their early teens, gathered around the small fires. Some of them were busy arming their tents for the night, others checking their weapons. But most were holding tin plates and anxiously looking to the impromptu kitchen in the center of the camp.

I glanced at my food allocation for the night. Since there was no chance we could build a fire so close to the enemy, I was scheduled for another ration of cold canned beans, Spam, and wheat wafers. I had nothing else left but sardines, and I'd eaten so many of them in the previous week that I felt scales coming out of my skin already.

I kept observing. The soldiers were moving slowly and haphazardly around. There was no watch, no defense perimeter, no situational awareness. They were a prime target for a night assault. Under such circumstances, perhaps only a handful of them would escape from the attack to tell the story.

Suddenly one of them moved away from his group into the brush.

With laughter and fingers pointing at him, the man ran softly into the bushes. He stopped forty or fifty feet from his closest group, unbuttoned his pants, and began to obey the call of nature.

The jaguar must have been on the prowl near the camp. No noise, no struggle. The cat jumped down from a low branch and in one skillful maneuver seized the man's neck in a paralyzing bite that must have severed his spinal cord. The soldier lay there, his pale, naked lower torso breaking the harmony of the green and brown cover of the jungle.

The jaguar dragged the body slowly away from the camp. In a few seconds the soldier was gone, engulfed in the shadows that began covering the land, leaving on the ground just a trail of blood over the wet, dead leaves.

It took almost an hour for the rest of the soldiers to notice the absence of one of their comrades. Shouts, flashlights, the cocking of weapons, and the unnerving alarm lasted all night. The troop searched in vain for hours deep into the night but dared not venture too far from camp.

The cat was most likely a few hundred yards from the killing zone. It had probably hoisted the prey high onto a thick branch in order to avoid being disturbed by scavengers. Jaguars can lift prey twice their body weight thirty or forty feet into a tree. The animal gorged on the kill for two or three days unencumbered. The remains were never found. It wouldn't be the last time I crossed paths with the king of the South American rain forest.

During the rainy season, finding shelter became a vital task. Rain fell for twenty-four or thirty-six hours nonstop, at which time trails disappeared, roads became impassable, and mud slides were an ever-increasing danger.

Pre-Columbian ruins made excellent shelters. The whole region was littered with them, large and small, sunken in caves or covered with overgrown brush, massive granite buildings, or small grottos carved into the rocks of mountains. Either way, there were thousands of those structures from Mexico to Peru, the vast majority of them unexplored and lost to modern civilization.

During my years of military work in the region, I developed extensive and detailed maps of such structures. We used them repeatedly, depending on the need and the time of year. It was always possible to hide weapons, food, supplies, and other logistical materials in those structures as a dead drop, days or weeks before their intended use.

I saw the most beautiful paintings and carvings on the walls of those ruins. It was evident that the native inhabitants at the time of the conquest had inherited those marvelous constructions and buildings. Historical accounts point to centuries of warfare as the most likely reason for the extermination of the earlier inhabitants of the region and the original builders of the structures. Later civilizations had reverted to the worship of birds and animals, thus demonstrating a more primitive and less technologically advanced social enterprise. In places like Colombia and Peru, there is strong religious opposition to the excavation and archeological study of Pre-Columbian culture and history.

Granite and basalt only partially exposed or covered by vegetation are still easily discernible in aerial or satellite infrared photography because the rock holds heat or cold longer than the surrounding terrain, thus offering in the infrared a temperature variation of ten or fifteen degrees at dusk or dawn. The ruins and other buildings become easily visible due to this temperature variance on the jungle floor.

From one end of the continent to the other, thousands of these ruins wait, just a few feet from the surface, for the day in which they'll see daylight once more after a millennia in darkness.

The highlands of Peru and Bolivia are at the center of what must have been grand civilizations. I stood in awe when faced with the magnificent pyramids and temples of these ancient enclaves. There, at ten thousand feet, in its entire splendor, lay the Luxor of the Western Continent, full of mysteries and magical appeal, above the clouds and the fray of everyday life. It is a hidden, rather than forgotten witness to perhaps hundreds of battles, and a pillar of an ancient world whose remnant is scattered across the continent.

The history of warfare is written everywhere along those ruins. The Amazon has no borders and the empires that saw their dawn and sunset in the region moved across that expanse also without restraint. Walls thirty feet high and fifteen feet wide stand today, even after thousands of years and waves of warriors pushed against it. The land is littered with debris of weapons of every kind, human remains, pottery, and even fossilized grains.

At some sites we stumbled onto in our many comings and goings. The footprint of warfare was clearly evident. The scene reflected a departure in haste, people in flight. No time to plan or gather—all was left behind as if time was also the enemy. The whole region was a silent witness to the millions of lives that faded into the past as a result of war.

I Awoke and It Was Not Morning

I always wonder why violence is glorified. People in western societies are obsessed with guns and the unavoidable death that must follow. Is it because they're so removed from real violence and mayhem that they fantasize about it constantly? Or is it because they live safe and guarded from danger, so a constant reminder that there is such thing as evil is required?

Real violence overwhelms the senses. For the uninformed, real gunfire is extremely loud. It takes hours to recover normal hearing after a gun battle. And then there's the smell—intrusive, strong and overwhelming—from the smoldering gunpowder, the fiery barrel of the gun, and burns on the forearms.

And then there are horrific wounds, torn flesh, and the ivory white of bones that refuse to return to their place. Blood stains the grass, the earth, clothing, hands—everything it touches. Dried blood, dark brown like filth, can remain under your fingernails for weeks, as a silent witness and a mute accuser. On a crime scene, even thirty years after the fact, blood can be detected and found.

After the battle is over, you're left with the contorted faces of the dead and dying, and the broken voices and cries of the desperate, voices calling for God or familiar names in their last breath. All those voices are crying desperately to be heard one last time, hoping someone is there in the moment of departure. All this death is at the end of the barrel of a weapon. Sometimes your weapon.

Training isn't designed to achieve perfection. Training's full intent is to desensitize you from the horror and the rigors of war, and later to learn how to respond to the unimaginable. Training has to do with being able to expect the best but being ready for the worst. But nothing prepared me for the blood, cries, anguish, and pain of death—that I had to learn one day at a time.

Our mission was simple: take out an enemy communications post in the middle of the jungle to create a radar window. That would allow us to sneak in a couple of airplanes with supplies without being shot down by the surface-to-air missiles and the anti-aircraft guns.

We moved on the target under the cover of night and persistent rain. Stealth was our most precious weapon. Surprise was our best friend.

In less than two minutes, our snipers neutralized the lookouts; the four station operators went to their graves before they knew what had happened. Close quarter battle is a precision game. Six to twelve men must enter a room and manage to hit multiple targets in a matter of seconds without poking holes in each other.

The encounter is up close and quite personal. You come face-to-face with your enemy, and within the blink of an eye either you or your enemy will no longer breathe again. Silencers and noise suppressors work well for small weapons, but trying to reduce noise on a forty-five caliber automatic machine gun is practically impossible. At close range, the bullets scorch the flesh of the enemy, the room fills with smoke, and the man falls to the ground at your feet, his eyes fixed on yours.

Although it was absolutely necessary to push those incidents out of my awareness, the struggle remained for weeks to come. For a normal human being, the business of killing had a very high price. Anxiety and insomnia were just the down payment.

Coming home after four or five weeks of deployment was always a welcome relief. War was transforming me and I couldn't help it. Grandma saw these changes. She sensed my uneasiness, my anxiety. She saw my insomnia, my long stares into nothingness, and my almost fanatical devotion to physical exercise.

Martial arts training had been my emotional refuge after my parents' divorce. It gave me discipline, focus, and, especially, an outlet for my frustration and diffused animosity. In training, I found the means to quiet the voices from the deep. After deployments, I always returned to the basics in order to regain balance. Grandma saw my struggle.

March is the month of the trade winds that blow steady and strong from the southeast. Children looked forward to weekends of kite wars. Most living rooms became impromptu workshops with kite-making materials: paint, thread, and fabric. For almost two months, all other games ceased and kites ruled the homes and the skies.

My time for such pastimes had come and gone. My mind was filled with unpleasant thoughts, disquieting memories, and the remembrances of strange faces. I sat at the dinner table and stared at the wind ripping the leaves out of the trees in the backyard. That avocado tree had been in our yard more years than I could count. The year before, it didn't produce much, but Grandma said the tree had sentimental value and she refused to cut it.

Grandma had tried to make small talk all morning. I'd been back, my body at least, for about a week. Emotionally I was still making my way home. I felt distracted, unable to concentrate. I'd barely heard what she said, but I looked at her and smiled. She stopped talking and sat beside me.

Besides the wind outside, whistling through dry leaves as it tried to squeeze through the window, all was quiet. I searched for something to affix my attention to, but there was nothing. Well, almost nothing. The old blue Westinghouse refrigerator was gasping away. The thing was forty years old and still worked. At least it made ice.

"You're home, son," Grandma said, softly touching my arm with her wrinkled hand.

I smiled. How could I tell Grandma about the nightmares, the fretfulness, and the faces? I couldn't. I wouldn't. It was my burden to carry. Besides, she'd never understand.

"Son, you must be able to leave whatever happens in the wilderness, there. No need to bring it home. It is, after all, just your job. It isn't who or what you are," she stated convincingly.

I hesitated, sweeping minute bread crumbs from the table with my hand in slow motion. "It's ugly, Grandma, very—" The phrase hung there.

"I know. My father told me stories about the war." She looked through the window, into the restless wind. She had my full attention.

"What did he tell you, Grandma?" I asked, feeling my pulse quicken a bit.

"He had no wife, remember? Mother had died and he was fresh out of love. He didn't remarry, so it was he and I when it came to talking." She paused and I waited.

"He told me about the blood, the screaming, the smell, the nightmares, and the rest of it. So, son, I know and I understand."

Grandma always soothed me, including this time.

"So you understand how I feel?"

She just nodded, no words. She was waiting for me to unload.

"It's the faces," I said, taking a breath. "I just don't know what to do about it." That was the best I could come up with. I didn't want to get into the details.

She nodded and frowned a little. "Son, you're a soldier. You do what you're told because you trained for it. You don't get to choose the battles, and on the other side there's another soldier ready to do the same. I know it's complicated, but for now this is all we have."

She continued. "Son, war is ugly, with no clear winners or losers and, at the end, mothers lose their children, wives their husbands, and siblings one another. But you must make peace with what you're sent to do."

She got up and brought back two glasses of ice water. I didn't touch mine.

"Son, I know that being involved in this dirty war doesn't bring you pleasure. It isn't by choice that a soldier takes another soldier's life." She was careful to word the phrase. "Since you're a soldier, you go there for your country and only remember that you have a family that loves you. All you have to do is complete your job and come back."

She took a sip. "As long as you don't delight in the shedding of blood, as long as you don't shed innocent blood, you're just doing your work. Remember, just keep a prayer always in your heart."

It was convincing. Or at least it made me feel better. She promised to make me a chamomile infusion with lemon leaves to help me sleep.

Her words did offer me solace. We never spoke about the subject again, but from then on I was able to deal with the contradictions and incongruences of my work as a soldier, or at least it got somewhat better.

Life didn't become a panacea overnight. But my ability to cope and deal with the realities of military operations improved remarkably. I was able to understand that my situation was transitory and what I was doing didn't necessarily reflect my core belief system and personal preferences.

In fact, life would place before me a number of significantly difficult settings. I'm not a believer in conspiracy theories, but I believe in circumstance conspiring to create truly complex situations.

During war, life is worth very little. The struggle for the means to control becomes the ever-elusive target. Quickly, increasing war casualties force the opponents to enlist more and younger combatants, with shorter training cycles and little time for indoctrination. In essence, armies become hordes of hungry men with weapons, fear permeating from every pore. The men hardly have the faintest idea of why they are risking their lives.

The cocktail is dangerous. More than armies, these military groups soon turn on the civilian population and on each other. They're alone in the jungle, cut off from their central command structure, ill-equipped and frustrated because they fight an enemy that won't face them. Wrath becomes their purpose—anything that moves becomes a fair target. I saw hundreds of graves, silent and forgotten, but a witness to such brutality.

We had worked our way to the border with Guatemala from a four-week incursion into El Salvador. Blending with the natives was fairly easy. We spoke the same language and were ethnically very similar to them. This gave us an opportunity to recover our strength and feel normal again after so many days. Border towns are always colorful and animated. Since it's expected to see folks from all over the country, and in most cases from other countries, movement is fluid. On the other hand, the local authorities are always on the prowl. Contrary to what happens in the developed countries, in some places, people fear the local police and the Army more than thieves.

We were traveling light: a canvas bag with some used clothing, a piece of coarse soap, and an assortment of hygiene products, all purchased locally. For all practical purposes, we were peasants going north to attempt passage into Mexico and hopefully the US.

Our trio moved at a normal pace. My eyes constantly scanned the surroundings under the blue baseball cap I'd acquired a day earlier. It advertised a sausage brand, but lucky for me, the Fifth Avenue fashion arbiters didn't frequent the alleys of the neighborhood we were crossing. No one noticed, and that was exactly the way we preferred things.

Humberto was a communication specialist. At twenty-four, he was the oldest of our group and had been around the block a few times. He was the Cuban version of MacGyver. If a trinket had wires, he could make a radio out of it for sure. If he could make it spark, you'd better hold onto your socks. He was always smirking, always enjoying some private humorous situation. He delighted in planning, and his sardonic smile was often connected to something he was plotting.

He was lightly built, but his hand-to-hand combat skills were excellent. I'd chosen him for my team a few months before and could rely on his precision; he wouldn't accidentally shoot someone in a gun battle. Of course, this was unless someone touched his gadgets—then we'd find ourselves among the dead rather fast. He was quite protective of his "toys."

Vladimir was Russian and Cuban. He was the team's chemical freak, and that is no exaggeration. The kid was raised by a food-deprived Russian mother and a maneater-take-no-prisoners Cuban special forces lieutenant. The kid was really a psychiatric case on leave. Imagine a kid that grew up without candy, he explained, pain in his eyes.

Vladimir redefined the meaning of economy. He could find, make, and save food out of a squirrel for the three of us. He could also be counted on to find whatever it was you sent him to find, even if he had to spend a week on it without food. He was a bulldog; once he caught the scent of something, he couldn't let it go.

He was an expert marksman as well. Perfect score on every weapon. It was rumored that his father gave him a gun at age five. He didn't get any other toys after that. He denies the tale.

They were all older than me, but I'd earned their respect. They trusted me and I them. At the end, we were three brainiacs brought together by strange circumstances. We spoke the same language: critical thinking. The plan was to wait until after dark, move to the coast, and radio for instructions. Our link to the extraction team was a small but powerful satellite radio we carried. It was concealed inside an old scratched GE portable radio in the bag of one of my team members. He'd stripped the original unit out and replaced it with a more modern but much smaller AM/FM receiver. The rest of the case was utilized to conceal the real radio and our lifeline when in the field. It had passed inspection for months and in multiple scrutiny stops. The setup was airtight—literally.

We selected a small family restaurant on the northwest corner of the intersection in order to get a glimpse of the landscape. We sat in the shadow of the small one-room improvised eatery. We ordered light, which implied that we had little money and we were in a rush. All seemed well, in general. We had seen a military patrol four blocks behind, but it didn't appear they noticed our unassuming trio.

We enjoyed the local delicacies and asked simple questions about the local river. We avoided the main roads whenever possible. Military roadblocks, police checkpoints, and bandits that frequently assaulted the public transports to loot the passengers plagued them. Country roads and horseback were much more secure and, consistently, a significant source of local intelligence. People loved to talk, especially about what they hated the most.

The sun was moving fast toward the ocean, and so were we. After praising the restaurant matron for her food, we were on the move. We paused for a few seconds to arrange our belongings and glanced in all directions. And there they were: two soldiers casually leaning on a porch rail a hundred or so yards from our stop. Their green pants and the long tip of the rifle bayonets announced their position.

In the intelligence business there's an old maxim: there are no coincidences. I felt my jaw tense and my pulse shift gears.

"We should move sideways," I said quietly to my team members. That meant we would just travel in a lateral direction rather than with the main flux of the people, and force those who may be shadowing us to show themselves. This we did.

On the second L-turn, we found a public restroom and went in. The stench was almost intolerable. Whoever was in the stall had to be dying. We exited the location three minutes later, and there were the soldiers, a block away.

What did they want? Was it something they heard from somebody, or was it random? I doubted they were that good. We kept our normal pace but were now aware of their interest.

"Let's go west and watch for a taxi; they're on foot," I whispered.

We had to find a way out of the location without abandoning the main thoroughfare. If the soldiers were onto something, they dared not do anything in public. I was convinced they were still on our tail but I couldn't see them. There were no glass windows or mirrors to glance back. We pushed west, hoping to be able to reach the end of the street after dark and slip away in the shadows. It wasn't meant to be. Dusk was coming upon us, and the street was crammed with vendors, animals, trash, and children. It was Saturday.

The last rays of sunlight dropped over the dilapidated tile roofs. We stopped in a corner, pretending to get our bearings. We asked for directions and glimpsed down the narrow road. The soldiers were just a few feet away and walking slowly now. The chase was over.

"Let's get it over with," I said, a bit unnerved.

I couldn't get my finger on it; it just didn't make sense. Sharks don't come unless there's blood or frantic movement. We had sent neither signal.

I hissed, "Let's look for a spot to stop and wait for them." It was the only way to deal with it.

We traversed the street diagonally and stopped near the alley that cut across the way into the block. We mimicked a bit as if lost. They closed in.

"Hello there," the chubby soldier said, his mouth full of cheap chewing gum. He carried his cap slanted back, revealing a sweaty forehead. He was laboring to breathe. They had been behind us for a good half hour.

The other soldier was younger, no more than twenty perhaps. He was thin like a scarecrow inside the ill-fitted secondhand military uniform. He was also breathing heavily, but in his case, it was anxiety. His rifle was almost at waist level. He was scared.

"Where are you folks from?" the chunky soldier asked.

"San Sebastian, Captain. Just passing through," I said with an impeccable regional accent. They loved grades and titles. It implied you recognize their command of the situation. It puts them at ease.

"What are you carrying?" he asked. I was waiting for that one.

"Just a change of clothing and soap, not to offend, Captain. You know we're trying to go north. Lost everything with the storm last season; we have no choice."

It made sense. After the latest devastating hurricane, more than one million Central American refugees made their way across the Isthmus through Mexico, hoping to get to the land of milk and honey.

After years of civil war, UN mediators, and an exhausted Soviet Union, Central America saw the first inklings of peace. The geopolitical map of the world had changed radically, but the regional conflicts persisted. Without a clear agenda, or clearly defined political future, Latin American countries sank into chaos and bloodshed. Military units broke into paramilitary squads. Local governments disappeared or morphed into chieftains and tribal coalitions. As hunger increased, weapons became the commodity of choice. The soldiers behind us could just be looking to score some cash. Immigrants and transient peasants were choice targets for extortions.

"What's in your bag, friend?" asked the soldier, this time to Humberto, while poking his bag with the tip of the bayonet at the end of his rifle.

"More or less the same, Captain, and an old radio. We use it to try to hear news about what's going on back at the ranch. Things are pretty bad back there," Humberto said while unbundling the old discolored radio.

"Turn around and put your hands on the wall, all of you," instructed the soldier.

The young one began to shake visibly. I guessed they skipped the part where they teach them shake down techniques at the Army depot. He wasn't ready for this.

We turned to the wall. I frowned to my companions and we spread out. That would force them to separate from each other to cover the three of us. That also forced them to make slow, wide arch motions with their rifles in order to point at any of us.

We didn't carry much money, at least noticeably. We had some large denomination currency neatly folded into the stitching of the dirty canvas bags we were carrying.

"Captain, we don't have much, but whatever we have, you can take. We just want to keep going north. We'll be out of town tonight," I said, using my much rehearsed peasant speech.

I glanced back and the fat soldier had lowered his rifle across his chest on the arm sling and was holding the radio. This wasn't going to end well. No matter what, we couldn't let go of the radio. We'd be just as dead and stranded if we were cut off from the extraction team. It could be days or weeks before we could send a message to somebody that could relay it back to the island.

"Is this your radio?" he asked.

Humberto answered also his well-rehearsed lines. "Oh my God, Captain, we got it at a bazaar in Jutiapa. It's all we have so we can hear some news and the weather, my captain." He was pleading.

"The radio stays," he said. I started to turn and he shouted, "Keep your damn hands on the wall!"

I felt my body tensing as I flexed my legs a little, looking to get into position. Things went downhill from there.

"Captain, please, there's a little bit of money in my right pocket. Take it," I said.

"I have some, too," Vladimir added, his eyes on me. I blinked slowly. We had no choice now. They waited for me to make a move.

I saw the shadow of the fat soldier lean onto the younger one, and I barely heard a whisper. He shook his head in the negative.

A slight tingling ran over my back. I heard a muted curse, and the shadow of the fat soldier launched in my direction. The rest happened in a blur.

I took a step sideways to the right against the wall and felt the blade of the bayonet pierce my shirt. I also felt a slight burning on my skin over my left hip as I spun around and away from it. My back-kick hit the soldier on the base of the skull and thrust him against the wall. I heard the blade of the bayonet snap.

I hit him again as he bounced back from the wall. This time I buried my fist into his puffy neck. I felt the cartilage in his trachea collapse. His eyes bulged as he fell.

I turned and Humberto had his right knee on the chest of the other young soldier. "Is he dead?" I asked.

"No, but he could be," he answered without looking at me.

"Just take the side arms and the pants. Let's put them out here in the bushes," I instructed while I scrutinized the street.

It was already dark and we were a block away from the main street. It all happened so fast. We needed to get going. We dragged the bodies into some bushes and picked up our pace. We discarded the clothing into a garbage bin in the corner and blended with the passersby.

We moved faster now. People usually did at nightfall. Streets weren't safe after dark. We jumped into a rundown taxi and made our way out of the town's commercial center. We got out and walked another three blocks and boarded another to the edge of town.

From there we walked. There was no moon. Extractions are always planned around the same time in order to avoid undesirable contacts. The moon has a strange effect on people.

As we walked in silence, except for the ocean breeze toying with the trees around me, I couldn't ignore the burning in my back and my blood-soaked pants. I felt the wound with the tip of my fingers a few times but decided against alarming my companions. The wound was not deep, and I anticipated going home in a few hours. I couldn't help but think that it could have gone very wrong that night. A fraction of a second, or an inch, and I could have been dead in the back alleys of Guatemala.

Luck or fate? I slowed my pace and gazed at the bright star rising in the east. "Wherever You are, thank You," I said quietly to the God of my grandmother.

I could smell the ocean. Even when I was lost in unfamiliar territory,

I could always find my way to the sea. We walked double pace for about an hour. After we were sure we'd left the last houses behind, we broke into a soft run. We covered the rest of the way in less than two hours.

We arrived at the coast without incident. We could see scattered light here and there across the landscape. We turned away from the main path and made our way over small sand dunes. It was quiet. Lizards moved away as we advanced through the bushes.

We stopped on the top of a dune covered by sage-like shrubbery and scanned the horizon. No movement at all. Above the bushes I could see the shadows of dark houses but no lights. I signaled to Humberto to go to work on the communication link.

I took out the pistol I confiscated from the soldier. An old Berretta, scratched and weathered. I inspected the magazine and put the safety back in place. I hoped we would have no need for them.

The extraction team was on the line. It was a go. We moved north in a line until we left the small group of houses behind once more, and then we turned west toward the beach. A lonely fisherman, old and withered, toyed with his nets. He saw us but pretended not to.

Humberto called his name.

"He is sick but you can go out with me tonight," the fisherman replied. "We can share the expense for the fuel. Do you have any money?" Those were the right words.

"No," replied Humberto. "But I have a radio and a good weather report."

We shook hands, and in thirty seconds we were on the boat, from there to a freighter that docked in Mexico six hours later. I was home for dinner the following day.

WHITE SHIRT LUNATICS

Making a drop from a cargo plane in the middle of the jungle and finding the payload later isn't a small feat. Rain, wind shear, thermal inversions, and other atmospheric phenomena simply add a level of difficulty to the operation that is almost impossible to anticipate.

Radio locators are great as long as the enemy is about two hundred miles away. Otherwise, the radio locator acts as a beacon for all to hear, not just the intended recipient. It wasn't uncommon for a group to arrive at the location of a drop to find enemy troops looting the cargo. Of course, the reception for the latecomers was always less than friendly.

After a few hit-and-miss drops in Honduras and Guatemala over a two-year period, we devised a clever way to receive drops. We assembled a strong weather and meteorology team. We convinced the Soviets to retask a satellite every time and we prayed for success. The novel variation in our approach was that we took delivery of our cargo at higher elevations and closer to mountainous terrain.

The strategy had two primary objectives: 1) to make it more difficult for the cargo plane to be hit by surface-to-air missiles during the drop, and 2) to make it more difficult for the enemy to reach the cargo in case they happened to be in the neighborhood. It worked . . . most of the time.

Our jungle triad had been operating in the area for two consecutive weeks. The weather was excellent, and we had been on top of a mesa monitoring the movements of an enemy patrol since the previous night.

The unit was composed of two dozen men, most of them young soldiers in the their teens and twenties. Their hesitation over the maneuvering and overall deployment denoted that they had assembled their unit recently and most surely they were right out of basic training.

We had received instructions to wait for a communication specialist who was going to assemble the satellite relay unit that was being dropped in a few hours. It appeared the Soviets were making a serious asset allocation in order to gather stronger data on air traffic and radio intercepts.

The multi-purpose station had been designed by the Soviets to handle a variety of tasks. It could scan two hundred thousand frequencies per second and record, collate, analyze, and rebroadcast to a low orbiting satellite to relay whatever information it gathered.

One of the problems with military intelligence in the former Eastern Bloc countries was the secretive and elitist nature of the work. Only a handful of government selected and vetted engineers even knew about the technology. That made testing, deployment, and actual use of the technology a long and painful process. Sometimes it took up to two years for the engineers to come around to install the devices. By then, the United States intelligence services had pictures of every screw that went into the device and knew how to neutralize it, rendering it worthless for the most part.

This time was no different. Our team had been waiting for instructions for two days. A local contact was inserting the specialist and was to bring him to us in order to gain some time. Once in place, we waited for the drop to retrieve the package. The four of us carried the component to an undisclosed location and assembled the unit there for installation

The shade was delicious. Early spring is always beautiful in Central America just before the rains come. The narrow neck of land allows for winds to crisscross the Isthmus bringing the ocean breeze to almost every corner of the land. Being at four thousand feet offered a magnificent view and a welcome rest from the jungle floor.

Vladimir had succumbed to the soft breeze and the shade. Humberto was scanning and recording radio traffic from the military unit below. Nothing to do but wait. The 80 mm scope mounted on the M-93 sniper rifle provided an excellent window into the world at the foothills. Suddenly an object jumped into the viewfinder. I swiveled the rifle back for a second look.

"Who are these lunatics?" I asked, shocked at what I was seeing.

In the jungle there are two basic rules. Disobey either of those and your minutes are counted. These rules are: 1) move slowly and pay attention. And 2) blend. Never call attention to yourself. Camouflage is critical to survival. Failure to disguise your presence can lead to starvation or extinction.

I wasn't sure yet what was coming down the trail a couple of miles away on a nearby hill, but it, or they, were ignoring these two rules at the same time—a deadly oversight.

"What is it?" Humberto asked, eagerly moving closer. "Let me see," he nudged at my shoulder.

"Hold on," I said, focusing on the objects. "Kids!" I exclaimed. "A couple of kids with white shirts and ties!" I couldn't believe my eyes.

Nobody I knew wore a tie unless you were going to be married or were dead in a coffin. Either way, out there in the jungle wearing a tie was like an Eskimo taking a T-shirt home from a vacation in Florida.

They weren't locals. They were too pale and their attire wasn't indigenous. They were skipping and jumping animatedly down the hill. I could see one laughing. They carried no weapons, although they both carried backpacks.

"Who are these people? Are they suicidal or what? There are soldiers in the valley below, less than two miles from them," I articulated.

"Let me see," Humberto insisted. "Where and what is it?" he asked while lying next to me and taking the scope off the rifle.

"A quarter of mile from the top of the hill, on the trail," I said.

He searched for a couple of seconds. "Ah, those are missionaries," he informed me, rolling away from the rifle and back to his shady spot uninterested.

I looked at him in confusion. "Who? What?"

"Missionaries, man. Brainwashed, Bible-carrying, God-talking, Yankee kids. They're from some cult and all they talk about is God and Jesus." To me, my grandmother's student, this stuff was fascinating, but my companion didn't seem to care.

"They're going to get fried in about an hour," I announced. "The soldiers are about two miles from them. They're toast."

"No they aren't," Humberto corrected me, still uninterested in the action. "They aren't game. They're all over, Lieutenant. No weapons, no money, just their Bibles and water. Either way, they're all kids and as far as I know they have always been around," he concluded, and with that he went back to his radio equipment.

Interesting, I thought. Who would, in their right mind, come into this godforsaken place, in the middle of a civil war, to talk about God? I kept looking through the scope. They had to be crazy or really brainwashed. I'd been around for a few months now and never seen them before. Apparently Humberto had. I was pleasantly surprised that I didn't know everything after all.

I followed them through the scope of the rifle. No doubt their current occupation made them happy. The odd pair kept talking nonstop and they were obviously very excited, walking and running, depending on the terrain. They arrived at the foothills and stopped, disappearing from view for thirty seconds. They reappeared, shoes in hand, past some bushes and hopped over the stones that dotted a small creek breaking through the path.

The soldiers at the base of the hill stopped their drill. They clumped in small groups pointing at the two white-shirted kids as they put their shoes back on their feet. They were so enthralled in their conversation that they failed to see they had become the object of significant attention.

They took a few minutes to drink out of plastic bottles without interrupting their seemingly interesting conversation. They headed south, away from the soldiers and toward our position.

I could see their flustered faces, freckles and all. A thousand questions raced through my mind. *What are these American kids doing here in the middle of the jungle amid warring clans who show so little concern for anyone, much less foreigners?* (And they were Americans, mind you.) *Don't they know death is being dispensed wholesale? What kind of mind control or psychological manipulation have they been subject to in order to come here?* The more I pondered, the less sense it all made.

As they turned away from me, I pulled down the rifle. I let my eyes trail them until they merged into the trees beyond. I resolved in my mind to brush the episode off as more evidence of American eccentricity. They built weapons to sell to the highest bidder, who frequently worked out to be their future enemy. They jumped in bed with the most unsavory characters on the planet, if convenient. And they sent children into war-torn countries to talk about God. They were just strange people.

The missionaries had gone about their business, but the memory of those white-shirted boys lingered for days.

ENTER THE JAGUAR
ONCE MORE

House cats are certainly not my favorite animals. They strike me as moody, cold, distant, and demanding. They shed, are finicky eaters, and don't herd, as if they are self-sufficient and don't owe loyalty to or need protection from anyone.

Big cats are a different story altogether. They're majestic and graceful animals. They move with dignity, style, and extreme athletic poise. The monarch of the Central American jungle is no doubt the jaguar: worshipped as a god by many cultures and feared to this day by everybody.

The sunset was approaching fast. We had been on the trail for two days in order to reach our intended theater of operations. Dressed in typical peasant attire: dirty, knee-length, khaki pants and a coarse faded shirts, pulling a tired mule, the three of us looked more like starving and overworked farmers on the verge of cardiac arrest than revolutionary warriors.

We arrived at our first way station and ate before sundown. We were late, so we decided to keep moving, hoping to reach the next little town and rest there in four hours. After swallowing the food that was offered, we picked up some weapons, left the mule behind, and pushed into the trail with only a flicker of light in the sky.

We felt secure in this area. It was rarely patrolled and we had plenty of friendlies to point out any Army units or paramilitary bands operating in the region. As far as intelligence was concerned, the coast was clear within the next ten to twelve miles all the way to Puerto Lempira, Honduras.

The two men and I were making small conversation and moving rather quickly. The feline roar sounded just a few yards away. The catcall of the jaguar is a hair-raising, blood-freezing roar that has to be experienced in order to accurately describe it. The cat was close to the trail, perhaps four to five miles, but its roar echoed within the canyon that surrounded the area. We had small weapons at hand, but the heavy artillery was hidden in the sacks on the mule. I held my breath instinctively, my right hand mechanically sliding into the grip of my weapon. We glided silently over the dry leaves and away from the trail, until we leaned against a large fallen tree on the edge of the path.

We blended into the jungle with ease. The monkeys disappeared high into the top of the trees in a mute, agile dance. Birds aren't on the jaguar's menu very often but they kept quiet all the same, just in case.

It was extremely strange that the cat had roared and given away his position, being so close to us. The wind had shifted. He was probably able to hear us but not able to pinpoint our position with his radar-like olfactory machine. This night, nature had dealt a card in our favor. I wondered what it was that had brought this unannounced visit, Was it the smell of our mule?

We waited behind the tree. The cat was there, no doubt. It was just a game for him, but one I could not afford to lose. For more than fifteen minutes, the noise of the nocturnal animals became subdued, as if they knew the stakes were high.

Suddenly, without warning and almost imperceptibly, the splendid feline jumped from a low branch onto the path. He'd been waiting there all along. By this time, only a glimmer of light filtered from the side of the trail, projecting the imposing silhouette of the jaguar. He stood there, unmoving, his fiery auburn eyes piercing the dimness of the evening. At the last minute, the wind shift had prevented the hunter from spotting the prey. He seemed like a statue, completely immobile, hoping for an inkling of where we were. Just like us, he was sure something was there, but he wasn't sure where.

In my mind I worded a prayer, a long one. Shooting the animal would bring the kind of attention we didn't need, having another ten miles to go to the nearest point of contact. On the other hand, I wasn't looking to engage in a hand-to-hand combat with a two hundred pound cat in the middle of the night. A small bite or a scratch can kill you in the jungle. Infection is almost inevitable and the kind of bacteria in the neighborhood was the sort you never want to be visited by.

After what seemed an eternity, the cat stepped sideways, eyes still nailed in our direction. In one second, he slunk into the dark. I took a deep breath. We all did. We waited a few more minutes as we pulled the night vision gear out of our packs. The jungle glittered right before my eyes, steaming with unseen energy and life. Most of what I could see were rodents and monkeys high up in the treetops, readying themselves for bed. The jaguar was gone.

I'd cross paths with the jaguar several times in years to come. But never again did I come so close as to be able to brush against his fur while still moving. In Central and South America, children and small herd animals frequently fall victim to the jaguar in communities deep in the jungle. Although a formidable hunter, humans aren't necessarily the prey of choice for these animals. Man, however, has hunted them to the brink of extinction.

We walked in silence for the next hour, Vladimir glancing nervously over his shoulders every other step, his hand gripped tight over the handle of his weapon. I brushed against him lightly.

"Are you okay, Vlad?" I asked, my voice low. I couldn't see his face very well in the darkness but his breathing sounded arduous.

"Crap, man. That was something I'd rather not deal with again," he replied, stretching his neck and turning to look back at the shadows on the trail.

"What, don't tell me you are allergic to cats now," I said, laughing a little. "I know you aren't afraid of men, so what's with the cat then?"

"Don't give me that. I heard you praying back there," replied Vladimir more loudly now, my humor lost in the exchange. "I hear you pray all the time, so don't tell me—" he stepped up the pace and pulled away from me.

Vlad never spoke again about the close encounter with the jaguar. Something had unnerved him; it rattled him like I had never seen before or ever again through many years of working together.

And yes, I prayed frequently. Often quietly, just a murmur, my face to the wind away from their eyes, but I prayed. They had their amulets and enchanted necklaces of colorful beads from their African gods. I had my prayers. I didn't know at the time if God indeed heard them but just in case, I prayed. Perhaps one day, He would hear and answer them like He heard my grandma's.

UNBREAKABLE

Insertion and extraction maneuvers are extremely hazardous in the jungle. Clearings and open spaces are great for helicopter landings. But they're also good for mine fields, RPG fire, and they offer a 360-degree small arms target during the operation.

Another factor that makes this kind of landing dangerous are shifting air currents. Thermal columns can cause an aircraft to violently drop a dozen feet within three or four seconds. A pilot will find himself landing much faster than he'd like, finding the ground a lot closer than he calculated.

The third and most worrisome is the RPG or SAM (surface-to-air missile) fire from the enemy on the ground. At close range, it's almost impossible to avoid being hit while trying to land the craft.

The wind and the rain can reduce visibility to about three hundred feet, which makes vertical sighting almost zero. Try landing a craft on a green carpet when you can't discern altitude. Depth perception is all but gone when the color scale is neutralized by the landscape and the rain.

Our twelve-man team had missed our primary LZ. The wind at twenty-five knots accompanied by strong rain made landing in the small valley a physical impossibility. We circled and flew low in the ridge between the mountains. We went due south for almost fifteen minutes until the rock outcrop broke. Then we turned west before heading back north on the other side of the mountain system.

This complicated everything. The change in LZ meant that now we had to climb the mountain four thousand feet in the rain and then descend while exposed on the west side of the mountain to reach our target. The mission was simple. There was a captain in the local military garrison who had arrived a few hours ago for a romantic rendezvous. We had collected the intelligence that led to the planning of the operation.

He came this way like clockwork every other week with a small detail, three or four men with side arms. The men would also be distracted, since they had been given license to infuse their blood with cheap sugarcane rum and indulge with local girls as well. We anticipated no resistance and a quiet extraction.

"Three minutes," announced the flight supervisor. His voice was barely audible over the roaring of the twin engines in the Mi-8T transport helicopter. I inspected my pack and weapons. I wasn't really looking forward to soaking for twelve hours. We'd have to climb and descend in one stretch in order to avoid missing the target. Although the target would, most likely, remain entangled in his romantic escapade for another day or so, time was of the essence. Most of the twelve men in the team I knew firsthand. A couple of last minute replacements due to illness were less familiar to me, but we had trained together on numerous occasions.

The mission commander, Lt. Colonel Montes, was a rugged and extremely smart operator. A veteran of the Special Forces, it was said he'd been demoted for shooting a General in the leg. Nobody dared ask him. Montes was four or five years away from retirement. They couldn't keep him in a desk job, so he ran special projects like this one, and others I knew nothing about since according to the officials they "never took place."

The Lt. Colonel was precise but flexible and creative, physically average, but capable of incredibly explosive strength. He inspired strong loyalty among his core unit and his leadership style was praised the world over in the Special Forces Core Development Center.

"One minute," screamed the flight supervisor, putting out one finger to signal. The lights inside the chopper turned red and everybody shifted on the hard plastic benches.

The chopper dropped into the small valley that was covered by chest-high grass. It began to hover twenty feet above ground and dropped the descent rope. One after another, all twelve members of the team slid down amid the propeller's wind and the exhaust fumes onto the green pasture. In less than a minute, the chopper was gone. After a couple of minutes of surveillance, we gathered for final inspection and instructions.

In five minutes, we had split into two groups of six and were climbing the mountain following two separate routes. The rain was light but persistent as usual. The soil was loose. The trails were gone, and moving up the hill with a ninety-pound pack in tow wasn't easy.

The mood was somber. This was going to take longer than expected. In fact, changing plans on the fly could jeopardize the mission. Twenty-four miles and ten hours of troop movement over steep terrain added a level of complexity to the operation that could destroy it. Lack of sleep, exposure, and the fatigue of the march could interfere with reflexes, precision, and muscle control. And we still had a mission to execute.

Coming down on the west side of the mountain was a bit easier but slower. Since we had to transit through exposed areas of terrain, by force, we planned our movements in pairs, to seek cover and observe. Night fell on us halfway down the mountain. We stumbled the rest of the way down, cursing in the dark. A few minutes later a small and fragile-looking old man joined our company. He was our local contact.

The town was small. The population was less than a thousand people, mostly farmers and their families. There was no electricity and the sparkling lights of candles and oil lamps glowed through the worn-out curtains in the windows.

The house where the target was expected to be was located at the north end of the town. We positioned ourselves and waited. The local contact pointed to the target, taking a leisurely stroll after dinner with his current love interest. It was possible that one or more of his associates were inside the house. Rather than risk a shoot-out that would attract undue attention, we planned to move on him while in the open and away from potential civilian casualties.

Why the overkill? It was quite a large team for an extraction that, for all practical purposes, appeared uncomplicated. After all, it was just one main target, three exhausted and chemically intoxicated hostiles in a more or less remote little village. I failed to see the need for a larger than usual operational detail.

The wind changed. The sweet, warm fragrance of the rain and tropical flowers made me nostalgic. I couldn't wait to go home. The change at the top hadn't been good for my unit. The emphasis had shifted, and resources and time were being devoted to issues and missions that, as far as I saw it, didn't correlate with the overall strategy.

I started to bite my nails in frustration. The door opened. A slightly overweight, balding man appeared, filling the entrance of the house. A cloud of smoke drifted away from him and his cigarette's fire dot glittered, illuminating his puffy face for a few seconds. He took a step forward and another silhouette joined him. This man was taller and much thinner. His yellow shirt blared with the light from inside the house. They spoke quietly and a few seconds later, started strolling toward us.

I jolted slightly when my silent communications link started to vibrate on my left arm, streaming real time orders from the commander a hundred yards away from me. I signaled my group silently to fall into position. Our job was to provide perimeter cover to those who were going to neutralize the "hostile," (you can guess what that meant), and momentarily incapacitate the target.

The road was deserted. A few minutes before, a small group of children had crossed from one end of the street to the other. They disappeared into a dimly lit house. No other movement was visible.

The team executed the maneuver with precision. I saw one flash in the dark, and it was over. One minute later, the silent communication link rapped again, announcing that the package was ready to be moved. I tapped the scout on the shoulder next to me, and we were gone.

We walked quickly over the soft sand. The air turned cooler and heavier with moisture. I hoped we could extract the same night. I wasn't looking forward to spending the night under a tropical storm. The plan was to move north along the mountain ridge and call the chopper.

When we were a few miles away from the town the wind was on our back keeping the noise level at a minimum, and all seemed to be going well. Then the advance team stopped and broke radio silence. Humberto came to me and whispered in my ear: "The eye in the sky says hostiles on our six, coming fast."

"Oh, freckles," I muttered. "How many?"

"Don't know, Lieutenant, twenty—maybe thirty."

"How far behind?" I asked, my pulse shifting gears.

"Two, two and a half hours tops," he said.

My earpiece came to life and I listened to the radio communication for a few seconds. I whispered a few instructions to Humberto and broke into a soft run to the front. I found Commander Montes huddled in a small group, reading a map under the blue light. He didn't waste any time, and spilled his orders without taking a breath.

"Lieutenant, I need you to split the team, take cover, and sever the arm of the incoming. We need time to reach the extraction point and deliver the package."

I remained quiet for a few seconds. Montes was a hard-case, motherless hyena but he was straight as an arrow. He hadn't know this was coming, but the idiots in operation planning had. That was why they had kept me out of the loop and brought Montes to command the operation in my backyard. That's why they had insisted on gathering intelligence from their own sources rather than mine. The operation was not done. Only phase one was complete; phase two was still in the works, and that carried the hallmark of trouble from where I stood. If I was right, we had a platoon crawling up our backs in one hour. Idiots! *Why do we keep listening to the drunken Russian intel? Yeah, they bring the hardware, but it'sour blood that gets spilled again and again in this jungle.* I felt my eyes getting hot, and there was a bitter taste in my mouth, but I had no time for anger.

I said, "Commander, you can keep four men, but I need the rest."

"Done," he said. He squeezed his radio microphone on his throat. "This is Alpha, on me."

The men moved quickly and converged on the commander. He dispensed orders nonstop for a few seconds. He signaled to four men who lifted the package from the ground, and they were gone.

The prospect was grim. I surveyed the group and calculated the odds. Darkness and surprise were on our side, but that was about it. I gestured to gather while someone opened a map.

I decided on a back trap ambush. We'd mine the front and sides of the road, stay at the rear, and wait on the side until they passed. We'd close behind them and when the mines began to cut off their advance line, they'd fall back and walk into the thick of the fire.

That would be enough to drop their count by 50 to 60 percent at least. They'd scatter, fearing they had encountered a superior force, and then they'd linger and regroup. It would take them two hours to figure out what had happened. We'd head west up the mountain, which they wouldn't expect us to do. If we were lucky, we'd all get to go home in one piece and on our own two feet.

An hour later the rumble of the fifty or so troops moving on the clay trail sounded. These were young, inexperienced soldiers who'd had little training. They were moving so quickly, in three disjointed rows, making such noise a train could have hit them and they wouldn't have noticed.

The U-shaped mine grid ripped at least twenty of them without warning. The rest hesitated in the middle of the trail and started running back. I don't know who opened fire first. A massive wave of lead swept across what was left of the enemy platoon. They fired back. Some of them did fire—not at us, but they fired as they ran into the trees, trying to escape. I manipulated the silent com-link and ordered my men to cease fire.

We didn't wait. A quick head count revealed that we were all in one piece, and then we were on the move again. The climb was silent but the mood was right. This was one of those rare nights when God had taken it upon Himself to spare all. The reasons were lost to our understanding. Most of the men had pagan beliefs and held on to the traditions of their parents. I'd seen the amulets, necklaces, the prepared powders, and the marks on their skin with the blood offering to the African saints. They didn't know God—not the God of my grandmother. And yet, it was clear that His hand had kept death away from us even if they were oblivious to that fact.

We reached the top and broke radio silence. The other group had reached the LZ for extraction and were due to be picked up in thirty minutes. As far as our group was concerned: "standby for instruction," the jargon went. That meant: "We have no clue; we're scratching our heads and trying to figure out what to do, so you start thinking too and suggest something. If not, you're in trouble." Sort of, anyway.

We were safe, for now. We had decimated the enemy platoon, hopefully taking the leadership in that snare. They wouldn't regroup until daybreak. It would take another two hours for reinforcements to arrive by truck. We'd be gone by then.

We reached the base of the mountain as the first light of dawn was spilling over the mountains in the east. It had been more than twenty-four hours since we had slept. We set a perimeter and rested for three hours. Then we moved north and hoped to get news of a location suitable for extraction.

Daytime movement is inherently dangerous, but we had no choice. With every passing hour, the enemy had more time to organize and develop a counteroffensive. The greater the distance between us and the enemy, the smaller the chance for another encounter.

By late afternoon it was obvious that the area was still compromised. The radio silence also meant that they had deployed active scanners to

122

try to pinpoint our location. Under the circumstances, I resolved to keep pushing north at a faster pace. We had to get out of the hot zone, or be stranded, going in circles for weeks until the enemy was convinced we were gone.

A day later we were completely exhausted and wrinkled as a dehydrated banana. Then the radio resuscitated. Good news. Twelve miles and six hours and we'd be in the clear. Anticipation hastened the pace and we made it to the location in record time. It was still early, but the sky was ominously gray. A light, moist wind lifted out of the east, and we waited.

Our lifeline, the radio, broke the slumber of the tired men. The "pelican" was fifteen minutes out. There was also the small matter of movement from unknown parties in the area. They weren't sure. It could be paramilitary, marijuana planters, illegal cattle hunters—who knew, but they were coming. We scanned the terrain with the binoculars. Nothing.

The roar of the helicopter appeared to come out of nowhere. It came in low from the other side of the mountain and dropped into the valley at the last minute. We lit the flares and they turned in our direction. We fanned out, and the chopper touched down in the middle.

One at a time, the men climbed up past the gunner and inside the aircraft. I jumped into the chopper and turned to look for the team sniper who threw his rifle at me as he slid headfirst into the belly of the mechanical bird. The pilot wasn't waiting. He jerked the craft off the ground hard on a side maneuver, and we were airborne. He flew following the contour of the terrain and barely above the treetops. Just when he was about to clear the valley, I heard it.

The brain is a remarkable organ. I guess life at home was rather mundane and deprived of sensorial stimulation. The loading noise of a helicopter could reach 200 decibels. It's practically impossible to hear anything inside a moving helicopter. But to this day, I believe I heard the incoming SAM rocket before it hit the tail rotor of the aircraft. The ear-piercing hissing sound of the projectile registered in my brain like nothing else I have since experienced.

The chopper shook violently, pitched the nose up, and then stalled. Smoke filled the craft and I felt the effect of gravity and a light sense of vertigo grip my stomach. The scene slowed down in my mind. I could see the panic in my companions' faces, the distant sounds of the yelling and screaming as the craft fell to the earth like a wounded bird. Time stopped.

I froze for a second, or a few seconds. *What happened? We've gone this far and now some are going to die. Not me, though.* For some inexplicable and morbid reason, I knew I wasn't going to die. I wasn't even afraid. I was in shock. Why now after we had made it this far?

I moved to the doorway and pushed myself out. The humid wind filled my nostrils and I abandoned any attempt to direct my fall. And then there was pain, sharp pain coming from everywhere. The encounter with the treetop was violent and sudden. It gripped my contorted body twenty or so feet from the ground. It held me firmly for a long time. I had no strength to break out of its clasp. So I hung there, my mind spent, my body numb.

An hour later, I managed to get free of the tree branches that had both saved and imprisoned me. Gasping in pain, I stumbled and slid down from the tree. A column of black smoke swiveled in the air toward the dark sky a few yards down the ravine. I made my way there, dreading what I'd find.

The wreckage was a charred, twisted jumble resting on a bed of scorched bushes. The bodies, in and out of the chassis, were a charcoal mass with barely recognizable forms. I approached and counted the cadavers. The fuselage was molten red in some parts. I needed to salvage something that would help me survive. I felt tears running down my face. It was a bitter, angry crying, one borne of frustration and impotence.

And then the rain came, hard and merciless. I sat there, broken and defeated. I knew the enemy was coming. They always swooped in over the ghastly findings like vultures celebrating their kill. I didn't care.

The downpour put out the fire. The wind scattered the smoke and the shadows at nightfall concealed the wreckage. I sobbed until I had no more tears. There, among the smoldering pieces of the helicopter and the bodies torn and burnt lay my friends Humberto and Vladimir. I thought about searching for their bodies to take a memento back to their families. A necklace or a picture, something to keep and to remind me of them. Unfortunately, I had no strength to do this.

A low howl broke through my slumber. I had fallen asleep. I stood up, agitated and frazzled. I waited. A few seconds later, it came again. I searched for it in the dark until I found the soldier. His leg was twisted in an unnatural angle. He wasn't going anywhere anytime soon.

It was our team sniper, a tall, agile kid from the Island's country-side mountains. We had trained together for this mission in the last few weeks. He wasn't much of a talker, but he had nerves of steel. According to the scores, he wasn't the best, but he had proved to be a fast thinker, able to improvise and anticipate. I especially admired how he was willing to be last to withdraw from the battlefield if his presence could save even one more life.

"Robi," I said while feeling the pulse on his neck.

"I'm in bad shape, Lieutenant," he replied, his voice faint and his face twisted by the pain. I smiled while I felt my pockets for a flashlight. I needed to check for head injuries. No luck with the flashlight.

I felt his leg for any exposed bones or lacerations. There were none. I looked back at the wreckage in the hope that something had survived. The crash box, I thought. In the cargo bin there was a waterproof and fireproof safe built in to store sensitive materials, small weapons, communication equipment, and the like.

I climbed into the chassis and traced the frame in the dark until I found it. The smell of burnt flesh and the bodies of my dead teammates made the task sad and horrible. I found the box and pried it open, cutting my fingers in the process. I found a small flashlight, a first aid kit, a radio, and a survival pack. I returned to my teammate. "Ensign," I said. "This is going to hurt. I have to reset the bone so it won't cut through the flesh. We'll fix you up back at the hospital, but this is the best I can do."

He looked at me and smiled. "More than it already hurts?" he asked with a naïve gleam on his face.

"Oh yeah. Think of it just like having a baby in about two seconds," I said, also smiling.

"Is it that bad?" The smile was gone from his face.

"It will pass before you know it." I kept smiling. "I want you to bite hard on the pouch. No need to call attention, right?" I said, handing him the pack I'd retrieved from the remains of the craft.

I sat on the ground and grabbed his left foot. I leveraged myself against his right leg and pulled and twisted. The bone cracked horribly. The soldier groaned almost inaudibly into the heavy canvas of the pack. Tears washed his face as he nodded. I bound his leg and injected some morphine, just enough to subdue the bulk of the pain.

"Morphine: a soldier's best friend," it's said. But I always wondered. The stuff is good. It's actually so good it's scary. It dulls the pain, robs you of your awareness, your memories, and your will to live. It has an almost demonic quality that ushers your brain into oblivion without remorse and leaves you wanting more. I'd had a brief encounter with morphine a few months earlier. I was almost disowned by my mother when, under the effect of it, I denied knowing her when she came to visit me at the Naval Hospital. That was a sad tale.

I helped my wounded comrade to his feet. We surveyed the dark remains of the craft and what was left of our unit. All bodies were accounted for. I looked with trepidation at the prospect of a funeral. I thought of the families, the half-truths, the classified information, and the inevitable slide into history. No one remembered the dead. There were no death benefits, no support, comfort, or care. Mothers were given a flag, a picture, and a medal. Except in the memory of friends and family, the life of a young soldier who fell in a strange land for a cause which he barely understood or could relate to was of no real consequence.

We limped our way up the ravine, sifting through the brush, trying to avoid leaving a trail. We found a broken branch suitable for a makeshift crutch and with it we were able to advance a bit faster to higher ground in order to use the radio. The enemy could come for the wreckage at any time. We had to move away from it—and fast—before daybreak.

It took until midday to reach a suitable elevation. We ate in silence without much to talk about. Robi hadn't complained once, but I could tell when the morphine started to wear off every four or five hours. His face became ashen and he began to sweat profusely. The pain must have been unbearable. He had multiple fractures and the bone was tearing at the flesh inside his leg, which had swollen to almost twice the normal size. He needed surgery to reduce the fracture. Otherwise, gangrene could set in and he'd die.

I knew they could trace the transmission, so we had to be quick. "Nest, this is traveler one—the bus wrecked. I have only one wounded traveler with me. Need new map and schedule to the next bus stop." I tried to use my most casual tone. It took three minutes for the reply to come back. They were stunned. After so many hours had passed from the time they'd picked up the "may day" from the chopper as it was going down, they had assumed that the whole unit was lost. They had probably picked up the location of it on the infrared. A fireball in the middle of the jungle at nighttime is hard to miss.

"Traveler, this is camp. Do you have your old map?" came the response. It was Commander Montes. I relaxed a little. I knew he'd do whatever it took to extract us stranded soldiers. That wasn't always true for some of the others, especially the Soviet advisors for whom we were all expendable assets.

I responded quickly, "Yes I do. I'm concerned about the other survey team. We want to win the competition and finish before they can reach our location." The exchange was cryptic but for him transparent: We possibly had people on our tail and needed a pickup location yesterday.

"We understand. Standby, traveler," he replied.

More minutes. I took a deep breath and looked at Robi. He seemed lost in thought. He was calm and in no apparent distress. I loosened the bandages a bit since the leg kept swelling. If we could extract in twelve hours or so, they could probably save his leg. It was doubtful he could deploy again. That leg most likely would never fully heal and, for a sniper, that was a career-ending injury.

"Traveler, you need to move to sector HF-76 to check the bird nests there and wait till sundown to catch a specimen. Can you make it?" He sounded worried. He'd never lost so many men in one operation. It was eating him up so much that I knew he'd come himself to take us home if he had to.

"You ready?" I asked my wounded companion. He nodded. And with that we were on the limp again. We made our way slowly up the hill and took regular stops to give him time to rest a little and to check behind us. If we had somebody tailing us, I'd have to die with him or leave him behind. We had no weapons to speak of with which to mount a defense. *Some choice I have,* I thought to myself.

We reached the extraction point in late afternoon and radioed our position. To our surprise Montes had estimated our travel time with pinpoint accuracy. He was already in the air and circling; his chopper was there in five minutes. The medics jumped out and tended to my companion. Other than my bloodied hands, I was okay.

I slept for two solid hours in the chopper. I hadn't realized that I'd been awake for almost thirty-six hours. In the base in Nicaragua, I took a shower and crashed. Usually the after action review team was eager to ask questions. Commander Montes kept them away from me until I'd awakened ten hours later.

Is the Lord My Shepherd?

I went home five days after the "successful" extraction in which most of my unit was killed. I didn't go to the funerals. I visited Humberto and Vladimir's parents. I told them of the crash. I'd known them for a long time, so I figured I owed them that much.

Sleep eluded me for weeks. I felt tired, sad, frustrated, and confused all at the same time. I spent most of my time reading. By then I'd gotten hooked on Hemingway. I'd read *Farewell to Arms* a year or so before. I had resolved that I would read it in the original language (English). Dictionary in hand, I took on *For Whom the Bells Tolls*, and *The Old Man and the Sea*. I liked Papa Hemingway's straightforward prose, unvarnished descriptions, and stark grade-level style. It was simple and straight to the brain. I found refuge there; reading kept me from thinking, from remembering.

Grandma was the most empathic psychologist I'd ever known. She smiled, comforted, supported, invited, and encouraged but never pushed. She waited for me to tell her. I wanted to regurgitate all the nauseating memories and despair. My friends kept dying, and I felt helpless to stop the loss.

One night, almost one month after I had been home, I had finished my dinner and readied myself to do a little more reading. Grandma went out of her way to spoil me whenever I returned from deployment. Caramel custard is my absolute favorite dessert. She placed a healthy portion of it before me and sat down across from me. Her old battered Bible rested on the table next to her. We had been reading a little before dinner.

I confided in her about the loss of my friends. How, for some unknown reason, only another teammate and I had survived the crash. How it was difficult to explain to others what had transpired and how I dreaded the way they looked at us now.

She shrugged her shoulders. As far as Grandma was concerned, nothing is left to chance. "Only fools believe in coincidences, my son," she said time and again. "Life is a collection of connected events separated only by time and place. Sometimes we're aware of it; sometimes we're not." She said she had learned that from Isaiah.

We read chapter 28. There the prophet talks about a farmer planting different kinds of plants in different parts of the field, caring for them, and harvesting them in different ways. Of course, I failed to see the linkage between the farmer, the crops, my fellow soldiers, and me. Since Grandma could read my mind, she jumped right ahead with the explanation.

"It's us, son," she said. "Some people were born in Germany, or in London, or in New York, while others were born in the North Pole, and in Africa, and in the Amazon, or some Island in the middle of the ocean." She smiled. I raised my eyebrows. I thought it was a stretch but I listened.

"Son, do you believe God doesn't know where you are? He put you here! Why? Well, only He knows. But rest assured that you'll live out your life according to God's plan and He will take care of the rest."

I pondered her words while savoring my dessert. I contemplated the fact that God could know every living thing and its exact position on the planet. It was really not hard to imagine. A satellite can track hundreds of thousands of signals simultaneously. According to Grandma, God could do unimaginable things simply because He knew how.

"Everything we call knowledge belongs to Him. He created all things, so we don't discover anything. We simply become aware of it and collect applause and recognition, but it's all vanity. It's His," I'd heard her say countless times.

"So Abuela, God preserved me . . . for what?" I asked, still in a bit of a fog about the scripture.

"We don't know right this moment, but you will. He will reveal his purpose for you at some point in time," she stated.

"In the meantime, I'm unbreakable," I said humorously, but looking for corroboration.

Her brow furrowed. "Don't push it. As long as you don't expose yourself unnecessarily and you take every measure to protect your life, God will do the rest."

I reflected once more and thought about the faces of those that were no longer living. They had known no God, at least not the one we were talking about.

"What about those who died without even hearing about our God? Maybe in Australia somewhere?" *Abuela*, I thought, *I gotcha*. "What about knowing about Jesus and baptism?" I asked, feeling pretty strongly about my doctrinal position.

She lifted her right index finger. That meant, "I'm on it."

I started to savor my caramel custard dessert. I craved it every day while away. *If this is dope*, I thought, *I am certainly in trouble*. Grandma started to fan her old Bible and mumble a bit until she found what she was looking for.

"Read," she said, pointing to a passage in 1 Peter.

I read to myself for a minute. I heard ball bearings screeching in my head.

"Aloud," she demanded.

> Who shall give account to him that is ready to judge the quick and the dead.
> For for this cause was the gospel preached also to them that are dead, that they might be judged according to men in the flesh, but live according to God in the spirit. (1 Peter 4:5–6)

"Now, where does this come from?" I said, just about ready to jump out of my skin with the exhilaration of having stumbled onto gold.

She just smiled. "Death is just another way station," she explained. "Just because somebody isn't here in the body doesn't mean they cease to exist. There are millions of people that have died and will still die without knowing God and understanding what Jesus Christ did for them." She left the table for a minute to bring two glasses of cold water.

"If He didn't secure a way for all people," she emphasized the phrase, "He wouldn't be a fair and just God."

That was a revelation as far as I was concerned. This was unheard of. Popular wisdom pointed to a world of the dead where the past and the future did not intersect. Also, most people believed that once you were dead, you were done. So, if you lived all your life in the middle of the Amazon and never heard about God, well, tough luck. You got to go to a working-class-heaven neighborhood, not to the mansions prepared for the chosen ones.

"Abuela, tell me somebody else in the world knows these things," I pleaded with her.

I loved Grandma, but she was speaking and opening my mind to things I'd never heard before. Things found in the Bible only after years of reading it over and over again. Besides, I reasoned, truth has to be verified independently. In other words, if graduate school was worth anything, I had to assume that if Grandma was right, there had to be others who believed the same thing and had arrived at the same conclusions.

"I'm sure there are others. After all, it's in the Bible," she said, without losing her smile, eyes fixed on mine, waiting for my reaction.

I pulled the Bible from the table and leaned back on my chair. I had to read that passage a few more times, perhaps the whole chapter. What she said made perfect sense but it was so far removed from any reasoning I'd heard from her before. Even in the face of this evidence, I hesitated.

If I followed the scripture correctly, then my dead friends would have a chance to hear about God, even after death. In itself, that was comforting and merciful. I could appreciate how that made a difference. Some of these young soldiers didn't know anything but the traditions they inherited from their parents. If in fact God had a hand in everything, He knew what to do, and how and where to reach my dead friends with his message. It was all part of the equation, I reasoned.

I got up and kissed her on the forehead. She smiled while stroking my arm. I left feeling lighter, leaving an immense weight at the dinner table.

Slowly, as life imposed increasingly more difficult emotional challenges on me, my mind also began to awaken to her teachings.

Military existence, after all, was far from what I had envisioned. There was no automobile, no personal driver, no vacation home, and no expense account. My choices were limited. I had to endure my four-year commitment in order to finish my career and earn the privilege of a graduate degree.

The realities of communism and the so-called "politics" seemed more like stone-age aberrations than a twentieth-century exercise. Time would show me that all I held to be true about our political system and form of government was nothing but a lie. "Philosophy," Grandma used to say, "is nothing but the well-intended dreams of those who fantasize, while imposing it on unsuspecting others."

For the years of indoctrination, fear, and social intimidation that I endured, my brain managed to keep feeding itself and developing at least an average intellect. I kept looking at the horizon and whatever was beyond the fence. I developed an awareness of the fact that there was more than what was being taught in the surrounding social environment.

FEAR THE LIVING
MORE THAN THE DEAD

Superstition is rampant in Cuba. Five hundred years of ancient religious history and, more recently, four or so decades of total absence of religion make for an interesting collage.

Traditional religion, more specifically, the "inherited" European traditions, were dead to my generation. I remember hearing, though I have no personal knowledge in that regard, that there were groups of the Watch Tower Society, better known as Jehovah's Witnesses, in Cuba. There were also small congregations of Baptist denominations but none of any real significance.

Their lack of relevance relates to the openly declared hostility of the government toward religion, at least until recent times. Communist governments assert that "religion is the drug for the nations." That bold statement stems from the fact that most Christian-oriented religions don't advocate violence, but rather obedience to the rule of law and government.

Communism rose from a peasant revolt in Russia, which deposed the monarchy and gave way to the most repressive and bloody political struggle the world has ever seen. The Bolshevik revolution of 1905 was the birth canal for Stalin and his cohorts. Although exact figures are impossible to obtain, the Parliamentary Assembly of the European Council estimates that during the purges and starvation in concentration camps, twenty million people died in the former USSR.

Christians in the twentieth century came to understand the errors of their past (read: the *Inquisition*). The shedding of blood violates one of the principle tenets of their religion. Revolutions by their definition require a strong hand, a willing heart, and a zeal for the cause. All this in order to enforce the credo—the ends justify the means—to intimidate, imprison, or subdue by any means necessary.

Church-going people, life-loving people, faithful people were useless to the Communists. Thus, anybody that openly acknowledged being a Christian was subject to the most severe "social punishment." The person was immediately branded as "corrupted" by foreign ideologies—an untrustworthy element by decree, not suitable for positions of responsibility in a place of employment, and a candidate for immediate demotion to day laborer, regardless of academic credentials. For most anyone, religious affiliation was a social and professional death sentence.

Interestingly enough, the practice of ancestral African rites and ceremonies—as long as they were not done in public—was condoned and generally accepted as a fact of life. It was a loud secret that most people used such traditions and practices in order to deal with everyday issues.

According to those traditions, sacrifices and offerings were made to appease the gods. The ritual would serve as a way to change the gods' moods and dispositions, allowing the practitioner to ask them to interfere with enemies and rivals of all kinds and, of course, to discern the future.

That was acceptable, primarily because these deities were also warrior entities capable of great feats of violence. In certain occasions and under determined circumstances they were even sought in order to take somebody's life through diverse magical ways.

As truly superstitious people, Cubans commonly believed in ghosts, apparitions, hauntings, and the like. Invocation of familiar spirits was an everyday affair but also, curiously, most people had a tremendous fear of physical contact or experience with the dead. All things associated with death, dying, or the perceived proximity of it were anathema for the Island folk.

Grandma's perception of it was most unusual. "Let the dead stay cold and for the living, courage to be bold," she used to say, implying that it took hard work, courage, and determination to be alive and to remain so. The dead had nothing to offer physically and fell either in God's or the devil's domain. If the person had been good, we should remember his legacy and how his life had impacted other people. If he was bad, well, it was perhaps better that he stay dead and not bother the living. Because she taught me when I was a child, Grandma made her ideas quite simple to grasp: honor the memory of the good and don't care about the bad. I had no fear of death in general. The urban legends always struck me as lacking imagination.

Grandma once suggested that if they started putting people to death for doing witchcraft, like in the time of Moses, most of the Island would be deserted. She pointed to the Bible and the fact that such practices were "an abomination before the Lord." The issue was settled for me.

El Golfo de Fonseca is a small horseshoe bay in the Pacific that leads to three Central American countries: El Salvador, Honduras, and Nicaragua. Some small wars have been fought since the early twentieth century as a consequence of the proximity of the three borders.

It's quite a popular port, with numerous freighters and small cargo ships crisscrossing the bay and the surrounding areas. It has also been utilized successfully for several years by drug traffickers, gunrunners, knockoff manufacturers, and mercenaries, for precisely the same reasons.

Entering any of those countries through this port facility was, at the time, the preferred and less complicated route for infiltration. The Caribbean side catered to the international tourist class; it was the shorter way to the continental US, with lots of satellite and coast guard activity. It enjoyed much greater scrutiny, and was notorious for fierce, unpredictable weather.

To say that I objected to my next mission was an understatement. I protested strongly when I became aware of the fact that the high command had planned a mission with one of the legs—the extraction—through the Atlantic coast. The argument with the planning group lasted well into the night but, once more, the Soviets had something to say in the matter. A communications specialist was supposed to connect with us once we were on the ground, and we were to position him at a location where satellite relay station equipment had been dropped a number of weeks before. Not only were these "babysitting" arrangements demoralizing to the unit, they also created unnecessary hazards. The civilians in our charge were often undisciplined, careless, noisy, and stuck up beyond measure.

This time we were on a delivery mission and prisoner exchange. We were returning a "guest" that had spent a few weeks in training in Cuba. Castro was the sponsor of revolutions, upheavals, and revolts in the region. Sponsorship meant anything and everything for those guerrilla fighters: military and political training, medical care, vacation time, detox, you name it, and rest assured, Castro provided.

Our group was to land on the west coast of Nicaragua and move quickly into El Salvador by boat. Then we would go afloat again on the Pacific side going south into Nicaragua and fly northeast to the border with Honduras. We would then pick up the Soviet engineer, and take him to the location across into Honduras for the installation. It was up to us to keep him alive and away from mosquito bites and those kinds of dangers for thirty-six to forty hours until the installation was complete.

There were reasons why the mission was structured that way. Only years of experience and high-level mental gymnastics taught me to develop the telescopic eyesight required to see beyond the obvious.

Nicaragua was friendly territory. Since 1979, the Sandinistas, sponsored by Cuba, had maintained a quasi-Communist ala-Cuban government. Castro had poured millions of Soviet dollars into Nicaragua. The Cubans ran the health care, fishing, mining, communications, and just about all critical government functions. Language and history made for very good bedfellows. For the most part, Cubans were revered in Nicaragua.

We picked up the specialist and proceeded across the border into hostile terrain. The man, whom we called Vasili, was a nuisance. He spoke nonstop, complaining about the food, the rain, the bugs, the clothing, and just about everything under the sun. I intervened a couple of times in order to avoid him "having an accident" with a firearm held by one of the soldiers.

Military intelligence is dead without ground operators. It is indispensable to have friendlies in hostile territory and we had plenty of sympathizers. We arrived at nightfall at a remote enclave in the mountains. Radio contact advised that all was well, and we approached the village without concerns. We almost had to gag our guest; he appeared to be manic and talked at an inhuman speed.

We greeted our host, Ramiro, at his barn. He escorted us to his house where we washed, changed, and sat down for a midnight meal. Things got interesting from that point on.

"Ramiro, how is the weather these days?" I asked, after loosing myself from his asphyxiating bear hug.

"All is well, my boy. Nobody bothers us out here in the mountains. Besides, we can see the soldiers coming two days before they get here," he said, laughing contagiously. We all laughed with him.

"I can see you brought the shrimp boy with you," he noted, pointing to the pink-faced Soviet engineer combing his hair at the mirror in the humble living room.

Yeah, that's him," I said, making a face and mimicking his less than masculine gestures. Laughter erupted again.

"Smells delicious," said Vasili, the Soviet engineer, walking into the dining room. "What's for dinner?" he asked, sitting at the long table.

His Spanish was horrible but understandable. His English was impeccable, however. He carried a Canadian passport.

"Guisado de Garrobo," Ramiro announced.

"That sounds delicious," Vasili said in the midst of ill-concealed laughter. "What, what did I say?" he asked. He found out soon.

Ramiro's wife and oldest daughter served the meal. They were kind but rough women. Their beauty was certainly deeper than the skin— much deeper. They had a meager existence, no luxuries, no indulgences, and constant anxiety. Civil war had robbed them of their best years and the future didn't look any more promising.

The meal was excellent, as usual. Vasili couldn't stop extolling the taste and exquisite smell of it. Almost at the end, he queried again about the meal.

"Ramiro, show him," I said, smiling.

He got up from the table and returned with the head and tail of the garrobo. It's a very large green lizard, indigenous to the region, and a local delicacy.

Vasili shot out of the room, vomit hurling from his mouth. That was a prelude of things to come for the next two days. The upside was Vasili didn't speak another word to us until we were ready to leave.

The next morning we were on the mountain trail before daybreak. Vasili, dehydrated and sleep-deprived, dragged himself at the tail end of the group. He looked on the verge of collapsing but refused any medication. *Spiteful little weasel*, I thought.

The trip to the mesa where the station was to be installed was secured by friendlies, and we made contact without incident. Vasili got to work and for the next two days, I slept most of the time.

Military intelligence had invested heavily in electronic surveillance, a measure that I judged misguided and shortsighted. Eyes on the ground had always provided greater advanced warning and more accurate information than all the hardware the Soviet GRU or "Main Intelligence Directorate" had sent to the region. The shelf life of the equipment was short due to hazards. And since the technology was "bleeding edge," no one could fix it once it went down. Inserting a specialist was always a cumbersome enterprise.

I had a chance to recover from the exhausting pace of the previous two days. I saw the young guerrilleros play soccer and wrestle each other over the soft, moist grass. A moment of carefree play; perhaps their last. Many of them wouldn't live to be thirty. Illness, malnutrition, and combat wounds would most likely cut their lives short. Most would never marry, have children, or know love. In fact, a whole generation of orphans had grown to become an army without a cause or purpose after a decade of civil war.

They looked upon us Cuban soldiers with admiration bordering on awe and wonder. They always compared their meager uniforms and equipment with our first-class weaponry and field tools. They were particularly impressed with our communication gear and medical supplies. For the guerrilleros, a skin lesion could mean septic shock and death in hours. A snakebite was always fatal due to lack of basic anti-venom serum or epinephrine.

Invariably, in the outskirts of every small enclave in the mountains, in the prairies, or on the edge of the jungle there were cemeteries, most filled with small, poorly marked graves of children. Insect bites, tooth abscesses, infected wounds, or the common cold killed three out of every five children in the region.

A subtle and effective way of securing cooperation and intelligence in the area of operations was to share medical supplies and expertise with the natives. A few tablets of penicillin, some antiseptic solution, and some gauze made the difference between life and death. Small ambulatory surgery to extract an infected tooth or a deep-set thorn was seen as a heaven-inspired miracle.

We fed Vasili an antihemetic in his fruit juice. It wasn't an act of kindness; I was just trying to keep the little weasel alive. He looked like a Renaissance painting of a plague-infected peasant from the European countryside. He stumbled frequently; his speech became slurred and incoherent. We had to do something, otherwise our Soviet comrades would insist on having our skin for a souvenir. We weren't on the best of terms anyhow.

We retraced our steps almost to the border crossing. There Vasili joined a group of entomologists, traveling north with them to fly out through Canada. We said our good-byes as a matter of protocol. *He'll have his prayers answered if he never sees me again*, I thought as I smiled from the look Vasili gave me the feeling was mutual.

The weather turned foul as we approached the Atlantic coast. The wind seized the top of the trees and ripped the high branches and leaves with fury. We found a partially exposed pre-Columbian ruin to hide from the storm. I felt uneasy about the extraction. We had no instructions about exactly how and when it would take place. We'd have to wait about six miles from the coast until the signal came and then move to the coast to catch the ride. Improvisation is the essence of jazz, but it didn't play well with me when it came to military operations. It always spelled disaster.

In the darkness of the earth-covered building, I meditated. Hundreds of these massive temples and buildings are spread over the continent. They are the vestige of a superior civilization that lived and died just a few generations before the great white hunter stepped onto these lands. If only Atahualpa had had gunpowder, our history would have been written in Quiche instead of Spanish.

From the ruins it is obvious that warfare was part of their existence. The murals and wall carvings demonstrated the constant upheaval they endured. Nevertheless, they managed to build cities that rivaled the existing modern ones. They built dams and irrigation canals that moved water across dozens of miles, sometimes defying gravity. They had knowledge of astronomy and astrophysics that advanced beyond that of the Europeans by five hundred years.

But they are no longer. All we have is the carved walls and a handful of historical accounts. We're not even sure we understand the pictography they used as a language.

Outside, the water fell with violence, pushed by the relentless wind. I tried to sleep but I felt restless with anticipation. The uncertainty of the finale wouldn't let me rest. I had broken, interrupted dreams and finally crawled deeper into the ruin to examine the maps with my flashlight. I returned to the watch post before dawn. It was still raining and the wind hadn't abated. The ominous reddish-gray sky wasn't inviting, but we had to move to stay on schedule.

The march was slow. The sluggish soil, the knee-deep pools of water, the fallen trees, and the thin, relentless rain made movement strenuous. I remained in the front most of the way, thus forcing them to keep my pace. I wanted to leave the jungle quickly, at least for a few days.

We moved on to the edge of the wetlands. The unusually high tide had raised the water level; the runoff from the high lands had colored the water maroon red. We were two miles farther inland than we should have been. Passage to the coast seemed almost impossible in the time allowed to arrive at the extraction point.

We gathered and studied the maps for a while. Rolando, a tall, husky soldier, was the group's expert navigator. He'd memorized every mountain, river, cove, and island south of Belize to the Panama Canal.

By his estimation, we were a notch over two miles from the coast, but about two miles south of the extraction point. We were off course and dangerously late for the pick up. Experience pointed to a delayed extraction, which, under the circumstances, increased the risk of unintentional contact with locals or military patrols.

We headed north as fast as humanly possible over the slippery, soggy mulch, but it wasn't fast enough. The light was fading and with it my confidence in the success of the extraction. We reached the coordinates and searched for clues as to the location of the makeshift cave where the dive equipment was stored. We geared up in silence, the sound of the restless ocean pounding in my ears. I felt the tension moving to my throat, constricting my vocal cords.

We reached the shore and the green wall of mangroves growing in the shallows. We had radioed several times en route with no response. That could mean many things, none of them good, but then again, it could simply mean radio trouble—unlikely.

The wind seemed to gain speed, and the waves doubled in size. Eric kept his eyes glued to the binoculars scouting the horizon, and especially the peninsula on the north side.

"You have to be kidding me," he said sarcastically, handing the binoculars to me.

"Geez," I exclaimed, slamming the optical equipment against the soft bark of the mangroves.

The craft making its way south of us seemed in serious danger. It kept a precarious balancing act over the twelve-foot waves of the agitated ocean. *How is it going to hold another three thousand pounds of additional net weight?* I cursed quietly at everyone I suspected was in the ops room right now getting the play-by-play and awaiting for news.

The radio operator attempted to raise the boat once more without results. I knew this man well. He was an able fisherman and a faithful collaborator with the revolutionaries. Although he'd never attended a day of school in his life, he was careful, methodical, and punctual. Now, why was he late? Why had he failed to make radio contact with us? And why was he coming on a craft way too small for the extraction? *Last minute orders and poorly planned operations*, I figured. As a last precaution, light signals were offered to the incoming craft and he responded appropriately.

He headed straight for us. There was just a sliver of light in the sky. I signaled, and we were all swimming with ninety pounds of gear in tow. The current was strong and the waves merciless. The single boat light appearing and disappearing in the waves was the only visible object apart from the twelve shadows fighting to reach it.

Eric was the first to climb on board and drag his pack on. The kid was a fish. He didn't know his father, so we speculated his mother had had an affair with a shark. He could dive deeper, and swim faster and longer than anybody I knew. He held all the swimming records in the Naval Academy and in the Naval Special Warfare Training Center.

I saw a few more men climb onto the boat before I turned and saw a shimmer several feet behind me. I pushed until I reached the rope dangling on the side of the craft, then pulled my pack. A hand hauled the pack up, and a couple of seconds later I was bouncing like a drunk on the small vessel.

It took almost twenty more minutes to recover the last diver. The fisherman maneuvered the boat out of the small bay and into deeper water. No lights, no equipment, nothing but his many years at sea and his instinct. They called him Genaro, although I doubt it was his real name. I'd seen his fragile house in Pranza, at the edge of the river upstream. I'd had meals with him and had learned of his dead family. His two daughters were all he had left.

Men like Genaro didn't like war. They preferred the gentle and docile existence of their ancestors, living off the land in peace. It wasn't to be so for Genaro.

For centuries, agriculture was a necessary activity in order to exist. The twentieth century brought industrial farming to the continent. Suddenly, whole communities were uprooted from the lands they had occupied for thousands of years to give way to "export crops." Millions of acres of virgin forestlands were burned to accommodate off-season fruits for export.

Land barons pushed millions of peasants at gunpoint into the mountains, and built dams that dried up their artesian wells and natural fisheries. The scene repeated itself again and again in almost every Central American country.

As usual, guns mediated economic strife at the multinational level. When the nationalist governments attempted to reshape the business of agriculture, all of a sudden what had been a commercial issue became a political one, and one of such national interest it precipitated United States congressional attention. About a minute later, military aid and logistical support were flowing into these regions to combat the "radicals."

Of course, every action is followed by a proportioned reaction in the opposite direction. The Cubans—supported by the Soviets—saw an opportunity to rekindle the smoldering embers of revolution. They were certainly master agitators, I had to admit. Hungry, destitute, illiterate people make excellent fighters. Thus the recipe for the longest, most violent and bloody conflict in the world (without war being declared, by the way), was ready.

The wind gained five knots within one hour and the sky closed in on us—pitch black and no hope for change. We scrambled to secure the gear we had brought on board. The vessel bounced wildly as the waves toyed with it. Unexpectedly, the wave picked up the boat and pushed it from the starboard side for what seemed an eternity. I grabbed my pack instinctively. We were capsizing—there was nothing we could do. The small deck filled with water. I heard shouting and commotion before I went under.

The small vessel tilted on the forward end, its engine squealing like a wounded animal for a few seconds before the waves drowned its cry. I pulled my pack and searched for my fins strapped on the side. The roaring of the waves was deafening. Visibility was near zero. I thought I heard yelling but nothing concrete. Then the night swallowed me up.

Swimming in twenty-foot waves is almost impossible, especially while dragging a ninety-pound pack with weapons and survival gear. It's a true feat of endurance to tread water for six hours. I was lost in complete darkness, alone all night.

I tried flashing a light in all directions but received no response. I had radio equipment in my bag but it was in a waterproof bladder that I dared not touch. The radio set around my neck and strapped to my waist was short range and only effective if others were in my line of sight. It was completely useless in the middle of the ocean.

Men are mostly emotionally handicapped. We either laugh or rage about an issue. These responses are of course socially acquired. Middle range emotions are hard to handle and almost impossible to express. But alone, in the dark and almost totally dependent on God for survival, the defenses go down.

I cried, yelled, and thrashed at the water in frustration. People were about to die or were perhaps already dead. Again, somebody's son, brother, or husband wouldn't return and we had only the most ridiculous explanation as a justification. Once more I had the macabre honor of presenting a family with medals, certificates, and condolences. It was turning into a routine assignment.

But the core of my bitterness and anger rested on the fact that hours before my higher awareness had pointed to a disaster waiting to happen. I knew that too many things had gone wrong. The timing was skewed. Everything was flowing wrong, but I hadn't been afraid. Yes, I had worried; I'd had a sense of urgency and a nagging discomfort. But fear didn't enter into the equation.

Was it that I no longer cared if I lived or died? Was I so tired, apathetic about my life, my task, and those around me that I welcomed danger and a brush with death as if they were small things? *What would Grandma say if she heard me?*

I tried searching in my tired mind for the scriptures. *Which scripture would Grandma read to me now if she were here? Something about total despair,* I thought. I wasn't sure if I'd done something to deserve my current situation, but why had God chosen to exact His punishment in this fashion? Would other people die just so that I would think about my life and what I was doing wrong? It didn't make sense, but I had no better explanation.

I screamed at God in the dark until my voice failed. Short of cursing Him, just in case, I argued and contended with Him about my current state of affairs and the fate of my men. Of course there was no answer. I remembered Grandma telling me that He no longer gives interviews. "Well, that is wrong," I screamed. "How are we supposed to make sense of anything?"

"Son," Grandma had said, "in this life God has set it up in a way that we must be tested and proven through life's struggles and then the lesson becomes apparent."

I could see her smile as she made that point. "So, my child, concern yourself with always doing the right thing and not with hiding from trouble, for trouble will find you," she had explained with academic certainty.

Had I done the right thing through the course of the mission? I had been concerned about the rain, about being late, about the flooded marshes and not reaching the extraction point in time, about the radio silence, and about the wrong boat. Talking too much robs men of their confidence, and I wasn't sure what else I could have done.

I drifted and treaded water until daybreak. By then the waves and the wind had begun to subside. My lips were cracked and my throat burned from thirst. As the morning lights pushed between the clouds, I could see the contour of a landmass vaguely in the horizon. It had to be four or five miles away. I also saw what I thought was a body floating a hundred yards away. I yelled as he reacted and waved. We both started swimming.

The soldier had cut his face in several places. It occurred to me that I could be hurt too. Salt water is loaded with iodine and other compounds that cauterize wounds and keep them from hurting. We embraced.

"You look like crap, Marin," I said, trying not to laugh. My lips were broken by dehydration and the many hours in the water.

"You probably wouldn't qualify for a beauty contest either, Lieutenant," he said, returning the joke. His face was bruised and the wound in his forehead and on the hairline over his right ear would require medical attention as soon as we left the water.

"Have you seen anybody else?" I asked, fearing the response.

"There's a body about two hundred yards south," he said, pointing in the general direction; but I couldn't see anything.

"Let's go—you lead," I said as we began to swim in that direction.

A few minutes later we saw the body. I couldn't tell, nor did I care to anticipate who it was. He was floating on his back. We called—out of habit. Wounded or scared soldiers react in unpredictable ways.

"Sailor," I yelled. No response. We circled around and faced him. His eyes were open, frozen in a flat, lifeless state. No vital signs were present. I looked at my companion, and he nodded in agreement. He pulled his knife and made a small incision in the scalp of the inert sailor. No bleeding—no corneal response to pain.

We tied him up and resorted to pulling him as we swam toward land. An hour or so later we found a second body. We tied him up as well and continued to tow them in tandem until we were a mile from the coast. The sun was climbing fast. The surf pulled back at noonday but the riptide kept pulling us down south.

We saw a low reef barely peeking out of the water. If anything, it could provide a place to rest, dry up, and eat something. We now had four packs loaded with weapons, ammunitions, and supplies. If we managed to stay alive long enough to reach the shore, we had a chance.

As we approached the rock, the coastline also became visible. A small group had gathered. We thought they could be fishermen or just local folks. Most likely they had found more bodies or part of the wreckage. Whatever it was, we couldn't afford to give away our position.

We reached the rock that was barely a small pinnacle of a reef out of the water, but we knew it could reach down several hundred feet. It was slippery, and had few suitable surfaces to hold on to. I searched my pockets for a cam to anchor our contingent of the living and the dead to the rock. The current was fairly strong. We secured ourselves and waited, the sun burning our faces.

For two hours, the group on shore toiled about. We couldn't see what occupied them without exposing ourselves too much. Once anchored, we were able to rummage though the packs for food and drink. Never did dehydrated protein tablets taste so good.

Until nightfall I stared at my dead comrades. Out there in the ocean, death didn't seem so grotesque. It wasn't the fear-inspiring "lady in black" of the mystery novels. These were my friends and I'd been with them in their last moments alive. They had waged a struggle with the elements and lost a good fight. They seemed thoughtful, absorbed in memories of better times, better places in another life. I never thought about death and dying the same way after that.

As far as the living were concerned, Marin and I talked about the future. There's nothing to dispel fear like an exercise in life-affirming tasks, and visualizing things to come ranks top on the list. We talked about what we'd do after we were done in this business. We discussed the trivial: more school, work, recognition, respect, love, family, all the while glancing at our dead friends.

As the shadows pushed the sunlight behind the western horizon, the locals moved inland, away from the shoreline. After a while, we cut ourselves loose from the rock that had offered us shelter and rest for so many hours. The waves were also tired, showing a more gentle side and providing an easier swim. We reached the coast in less than an hour. My companion went ashore before me while I waited in the surf, holding on to our two dead teammates. We didn't need any more surprises.

He signaled to me with his flashlight, and as I struggled with my cargo he came back into the water to help me. On the edge of the surge, we lifted the bodies and carried them onto the sand dunes a few yards away. We returned for the packs a few minutes later.

As he performed a salvage operation on the packs to see what we should carry with us, I worked the radio behind some bushes. Different frequencies, different calls—and then we waited.

We were a few miles away from the Nicaraguan border but the closer we got to it, the more complicated it became. Almost at midnight the response came. The report wasn't encouraging. It was four survivors out of eight and the two bodies. We waited for instructions.

The rest was easy in contrast. We stripped the bodies to their underwear and buried their gear a hundred feet away. They were recovered the same night by local friendlies. But first, a small boat came for us.

The squalid fisherman didn't utter a word. He offered a toothless smile as we climbed on board and cranked the engine nonstop until the delta of the Rio Coco. We reached the base a little after midnight. Going home a week later on a nonstop flight wasn't a trip that I anticipated like I might have before this last tragedy. I wasn't looking forward to another host of funerals and empty coffins. Even more difficult, how could I withstand the inquisitive, reproachful gaze of a mother who had lost her son? What do you say to a mother who cannot be comforted? What explanation could I offer for why her son was dead and I was not? Why was I left to bear the responsibility of explaining?

I resorted to avoiding all. I cried and yelled to the wind while walking on the shoreline at nighttime. Why? It seemed to me as if God had embarked on a crusade against my friends and comrades. Now their families hated or feared me. It seemed death followed me, brushing against me but never managing to hold me.

I felt confused. It couldn't be; Grandma's God was benevolent. He was merciful, kind, forgiving. But why keep me? Why, when death and destruction were being dispensed was my portion withheld?

I didn't know what to think. My soul hurt and my mind couldn't rest. And when I could rest, my dreams were filled with faces of those who were no longer among the living. I came to hate my bed.

EMERALD CITY

Colombia is, in my estimation, one of the most beautiful countries in the world. It has thousands of plant and animal species; ocean-like rivers with small pink dolphins that are found nowhere else on the planet. It has birds and flowers of astonishing colors and beauty, some of the tallest trees in the world, and enviable natural resources. The running joke amongst Colombians is that the punishment to the land was the people.

The country had more deaths per capita than Beirut and there was no war to account for it. A political battle in the mid-fifties had left forty thousand dead in one month all on account of an election dispute.

On the other hand, Colombia produces one-third of all the emeralds commercialized in the world every year. Something like 60 percent of all the flowers sold by lunchtime in the United States arrive airborne from Colombia the night before. And let's not talk about Juan Valdez and his famed mountain coffee.

The genetic mixture of indigenous people, imported African slaves, deported Spaniards, greedy Portuguese, German refugees, Dutch pirates, and French corsairs make for some of the most beautiful people on the planet. Of all the places I've found myself traveling in, Colombia has to be the most hypnotic one. If nobody was shooting at you or no animal was trying to eat you, you would want to stay always—and gladly.

In Colombia, you can drive a short distance and find yourself in the balmy water of the coast, east or west. Another short drive and you can get lost in the Amazon. Be it dry, rocky, tundra-like landscape, the cold highlands, or the tropical surf of the Atlantic, in that country, nature abundantly exceeds itself.

Since the sixties, Cuba has provided logistical and every other kind of support to the FARC—the Revolutionary Colombian Armed Forces. They're a ragtag guerrilla group that has been scavenging in the jungles of the country for close to forty years now. Several generations of guerrilleros have come and gone. Most of the leaders, almost without exception, have found their way to Cuba for training and development, counseling, medical care, vacation, drug treatment, plastic surgery, or whatever else was necessary. These days they have diversified into drug trafficking, kidnapping, extortion, gun-running, and other not-so-revolutionary kinds of activities.

The emerald trade surpasses that of the famed cocaine trade. But CNN and their cohorts aren't interested in any of the other many values and beauties of that nation in the basin of the Amazon. It's never mentioned that Colombia prints more books per year than any other Latin American country. Or that the University of Los Andes is one of the largest and oldest higher education facilities on the continent. Colombians are quite a sophisticated people. Some of the most intellectually stimulating conversations I have had in years past took place with my friends and associates in Colombia. Emerald Street is a long, colorful street in Cali, Colombia. It begins with makeshift sidewalk stands where vociferous, musically inclined vendors fan their wares. Items vary from hair-thin gold-plated chains to low grade, bug-size, poorly cut emeralds.

The street's landscape mutates slowly along the mile-long stretch. Small stores with carefully arranged displays and friendly attendants are next. Finally, the roaring of helicopter fan blades fills the air. Here you find stores with solid gold door handles, mirror-like polished floors, and beautiful miniskirt-wearing attendants. Bodyguards carrying semi-automatic weapons escort three-piece suit types with cash-stuffed suitcases in hand. The whole scene is better choreographed than a Bond movie. And by the way, robberies in the neighborhood are unheard of. Thieves are at the bottom of the social scale, but there's no evidence that they're suicidal. The life expectancy of anyone crazy enough to try a heist in those parts is one hour.

Emeralds are just like currency. Land, guns, cars, planes, or any other kind of material goods or services are traded worldwide for those precious green stones.

Emerald fields are protected and marked with twenty-foot tall electric fences, attack dogs, motion sensors, and every other security gadget money can buy—and let's not forget heavily armed men. The signs that hang over the fences illustrate the extremes that people will go to in order to protect their property and the stones laying on the topsoil: "Trespassers will certainly be shot dead."

Carrying large quantities of cash in the Amazon is definitely hazardous to your health. In contrast, emeralds, especially if they're uncut, are much easier to conceal, transport, and keep from prying eyes. Supplying weapons and other staples to Colombian and Peruvian guerrilla fighters was quite tricky. Not only has the CIA, the DEA, and every other alphabet letter agency had carte blanche in Colombia since the eighties, but also the Pacific Fleet has always had vessels in Panama. They go on deepwater patrol, making any approach to the coast of Panama or Colombia almost impossible.

My two companions and I arrived on a cruise ship via Jamaica into Panama. We made our way south to the border. The road ended there and with it law and order. We ventured into the jungle with the host of peasants that traveled across to trade. The border was brewing with refugees from Colombia, Peru, Bolivia, and Brazil. It wasn't surprising that they became the targets of local police, paramilitary groups from both sides, and of course the local crooks.

After making contact in the town of Nazareth on the Panamanian side, we waited for nightfall in order to move across into Colombia. Friday nights were always charged with the intoxicated energy of the lonely, the insecure, and the greedy. It seemed everyone felt as if the end of the week brought a new lease on life and another opportunity to soothe whatever ailed them.

We made our way into Colombia without a hiccup and boarded a freighter headed down south into Buenaventura; from there we traveled south and east over the mountains. My two other team members were well-versed in the region. In fact, one of them had lived in Venezuela for fifteen years prior to moving with his parents to Cuba as a young man.

The vehicle that made the dangerous trip over the mountains was considered a hazard—in any other country it would have been a clear and present danger. But in Colombia, not catching the "bus" meant not going anywhere. So we joined the chickens, pigs, small goats, and other animals, as well as their owners in the foul-smelling deathtrap on wheels.

I made small talk with the locals because it helped me to blend in and people assumed that I belonged. It also provided me with bits and pieces of valuable local intelligence information. My alias was as an academic bum who went from university to university, and took more trips and sabbaticals than Leonardo da Vinci.

Our cargo consisted of ropes, digging kits, copies of maps, camping gear, and a collection of rock specimens. We carried nothing of interest since all our supplies were locally purchased in Panama.

The rain came and went, but inside the bus it always rained. The air was thick with humidity and a thousand smells assaulted the senses relentlessly. The green surrounding us from every direction was intoxicating, intense. It seems like in the Amazon, plants compete for every available inch of soil. A rock here and there shares its nakedness with the passerby, but the ground remains hidden from view.

The bus slowed down considerably. A certain anxiety was evident in the driver and those seated in the front. They had been talking animatedly and continually, almost from the start of the trip. Suddenly their tone and demeanor changed.

Roberto, one of my companions and our field lab specialist, had grown up in the outskirts of Habana. He had no father, and the woman whom he had thought to be his mother had turned out to be his grandmother. He also had a deaf mute twin brother. They could read each other's minds, almost, and Roberto could read lips even a couple of miles away with the help of binoculars. Grasping the crux of the exchange in the front of the bus was a school game for him.

"The driver saw armed people on the side of the road hiding a couple of kilometers back," he said, his eyes on the inaudible conversation of the driver and those around him.

My other companion scrutinized some of the maps we carried. They looked ordinary to the casual observer, but under the right light they revealed details not visible to the naked eye. They were also printed on special paper and some of the rich detail on them didn't appear in any Central American maps ever printed.

"We could get out here," C.T., our other companion said. That was his nickname. He never said why or how he came up with it. I even tried perusing his file once, but there was nothing to explain it.

Hidden armed men on the side of the road meant only one thing: ambush ahead. They had to be the lookout for the group that forced the bus to stop. And stop it they planned to do, by any means necessary. The barrier of choice was trees or other vehicles.

Our options were limited. We either had to get out of the bus and make our way on foot across the mountain, or risk being robbed. After a brief conversation, the decision was made: the mountain it was. I moved to the front of the bus and spoke to the driver.

The man was razor thin, with deep wrinkle grooves that hid his eyes. He was sweating profusely and kept wiping himself down with a dirty rag he kept over his shoulder. He was scrutinizing the road through the huge mirrors on the side of the bus.

"I want you to stop the bus," I said, grabbing his left shoulder. He opened his eyes wider.

"What? Now?" the driver answered. "It's dangerous. You don't know what you're doing," he stammered.

I squeezed his shoulder a bit harder. "Stop the bus now," I repeated firmly in his ear.

He brought the bus to a stop. The chorus inside the bus went into crescendo. People could sense that something was wrong. Some even knew. They started to conceal their valuables on their children's bodies and in their shoes.

We jumped out before the bus came to a full stop and stood by the edge of the roadway as the old battered truck continued sliding down the hill. Fear had gripped the hearts of the people inside it. Their tense, labored breathing spoke of anticipation.

We crossed the road and made our way east into the jungle. I saw the glimmer of an oncoming vehicle far away in the distance and tension rose in the pit of my stomach. We left the road behind and traveled southeast into the thick forest. It was like sinking into a steam bath with nature dominating the airwaves in stereo sound.

After a few minutes, we stopped to get our bearings. C.T. spread a map on top of his pack and I pointed a small flashlight at it. We were about five thousand feet above sea level and the road would continue to climb for several thousand more feet as it made its way south. To walk the distance was impossible. We walked in the same direction, parallel to the road but under the cover of the jungle. After we could ascertain that it was safe, we'd return to the road and try to hitch our way south.

It was slow going over the forest's soggy, slippery ground. In the late afternoon, a light vapor hung over the jungle floor. I was completely wet and had no hope of drying any time soon. We spoke very little, though, and we worried about the fact that all we had in terms of weapons were small hunting knives. If we had to face armed opponents, it would need to be up close in hand-to-hand combat.

C.T. had excellent hand-to-hand skills and the flexibility of a cat. Roberto could handle himself well but was more restrained. I'd seen him in combat situations and his strikes were measured and precise, with no energy wasted. If I had to guess, I'd say he was trying to avoid killing with his hands. That wasn't always possible in the heat of battle. Restraint could give the opponent the edge he needed to respond; the outcome could be disastrous.

"I heard something a few minutes ago when the wind changed," Roberto said. He could hear the ants crawl, and if he said he heard something, I knew he hadn't imagined it—we had company, and it was close.

No doubt it was the people in the car I had seen as we were going into the jungle. When bandits were going to hit a transport, they ensured that no troops or police were coming from behind. They kept an eye on their rear by allowing for a car to fall back and travel slowly, warning them via radio of any activity coming to them. When they saw us get out in the middle of nowhere, it would have been safe to assume that we *really* didn't want to get robbed. Most people traveling in those desolate places accepted it as a fact of life and a normal hazard to get assaulted on the road. Our resistance to what others may have perceived as somewhat trivial would have inevitably caught their interest.

We stopped and planned. We had no idea how many banditos were lurking out there, but they were most certainly armed. In all likelihood, they had split: two in the car, two behind us in the jungle. If that were the case, then it was a manageable situation. We waited, resting against the moist bark of some massive nut trees that grew in a cluster. Some of them were perhaps two thousand years old. I marveled that they had seen so much.

The crackling of a radio interrupted my thoughts. I peered through the bushes intently. I could feel my pulse quickening and my breathing becoming deeper, fuller. Light was beginning to fade, and in the jungle movement was the only telltale sign left.

I could see them. Two men walking side by side, their eyes on the ground following our tracks. They were clad in dark green uniforms with no discernible insignia or markings. Either they were freelancers or they were paramilitary—hired guns that occasionally terrorized the population when their overlord got himself killed, and they found themselves unemployed.

I signaled to Roberto to wait. He was the distraction while C.T. and I faced them. I waited until they were fifteen feet away from us and then came out from behind the trees holding my pack.

"Good evening, friends," I said smiling. The startled men lifted their guns, pointing them at us. C.T. had this dumb "I shouldn't be here, I don't know what's going on" look on his face that I found amusing. Especially since he was about to jump on them and shred them to pieces. It was his "emotional camouflage" as he called it. A neat act of concealment that worked very well, I must confess.

"You scared us. We weren't sure who was coming," I said, insinuating a bit of nervousness. The man pointing at me was massive. His bovine look reminded me of the bull from the Looney Tunes cartoons. Both eyebrows joined on his forehead, creating a menacing look. His shadowy, small, dark eyes danced nervously, and he licked his lips continually. He was a novice; his uncertainty couldn't lie. I relaxed a little.

The man pointing a modified R15 rifle at C.T. wasn't a soldier either. He was holding the rifle wrong, and his posture denoted no military training. But he was a killer. He had the cold confidence of someone who had pulled the trigger one too many times. He didn't rush; there was no discernible anxiety or fear. He worried me a little.

"Where are you going?" he yelled, raising the weapon. I searched in my shirt pocket as I took a couple of small steps forward.

"We're looking for Pastizales, close to Mocoa. The rest of our group is there. We're from Universidad de Antioquia on a mineralogical research trip," I said showing him my hand-drawn map and notes.

He closed the distance and stretched his hand to grab the paper. He glanced at it and returned to me. *Yes, I can handle this bushy-eyed giant,* I thought.

"What's in your pack?" he asked, all business now.

"Well, a couple of shirts and pants, shorts, some hand digging tools, some papers—nothing much. We should be here only four days," I said, trying to justify my meager possessions. *Nothing you would be interested in,* I almost said.

"What is that bundle?" he said, pointing to a small canvas wrapping. That bundle was the reason we had gotten off the bus. The dirty canvas bundle contained half a million dollars in uncut emeralds. But with a little creativity and some oil-based paint most people now wouldn't be able to distinguish them from garden-variety stones.

"These are rock samples we collected near Guapi yesterday. They look interesting—volcanic probably," I said, trying my best scholarly mannerisms.

He wasn't impressed, but his companion, the killer, was. He approached slowly, eyes on the stones resting on the ground over the square piece of stained canvas. He squatted and inspected the stones for a few seconds, then placed them on the ground again. His grip on the rifle tightened, he swallowed hard but didn't look at me. This was a very cool customer. He knew about the stones. The charade was over.

I nodded to C.T., who took two steps and motioned as if he was offering his pack for inspection.

"I have a few more rocks and an old radio, but that's about it," he said while starting to open his pack.

"Roberto," I called and he stepped out of the trees. But the killer bandit didn't waste time. He swung the rifle toward C.T., but my mate was ready. In one smooth motion, he blocked the movement of the weapon's barrel. The gun went off once. He pulled the man toward him hard, striking him with vicious force in the face with his forehead. The bandit let go of the trigger guard to grasp his bloody face. C.T. yanked the weapon from his shoulder, spinning it around and pressing it against the bandit's stomach. A stifled single shot tore against the bandit's insides and propelled his body against the trees. It all took two seconds.

The giant in front of me had half a second to react. He started to raise his weapon as I stepped to the left and away from the tip of the barrel. I pressed it down hard. Not hard enough, however. It went off as I was holding the barrel with my right hand.

I jumped and struck him square in the face with the edge of my fist. He stumbled back and the barrel of the gun got away from my bloody hand. The gun went off again, and this time I felt fire burning between my legs. I moved sideways, searching for cover behind a tree. He fell backwards and struggled to get upright. C.T. fired at his center mass—one, two, pause. Three shots and the big bandit went down.

I surveyed the scene for a second and exhaled. My hand started to burn. My index finger was missing a piece and I was bleeding heavily—a wave of panic swept over me. C.T. ran toward me, and I could see Roberto rushing my way from the opposite side.

I unfastened my pants and choked. My underwear was covered in blood, but I still felt no pain. The most horrible thoughts and images raced through my mind in a split second. Forget the teasing of my comrades about being DIA (disabled in action) and not being able to show my scars with pride. *What—no wife, no children?* The thought was terrifying.

I pulled my blood-soaked underwear down and sighed as a ton of bricks fell off my shoulders. It was all there. *Yes! There will be a wife and children in my future, if I can manage to keep dodging bullets.* The round has burned a trail between my genitals and my leg, missing the femoral artery by a fraction of an inch.

Roberto went to work right away. He sprayed a wide area of ground with his insect repellent bottle, then spread a small blanket on the ground where I laid naked from the waist down. For a casual observer the scene would have looked beyond bizarre.

The double bottom of the bag contained the first aid kit and a few other small survival tools. Since there was no anesthesia, the pain was excruciating. But the thought that I was saving my genitalia, and thus my chances to contribute to the genetic pool of the earth, was comforting. I did my fair share of groaning and moaning, but I endured the pain.

After almost an hour of field surgery, they buried my bloody clothing and scavenged the dead bandits for any useful items. My finger was still in pretty bad shape, but there was little we could do beyond a penicillin shot. I needed a doctor.

However, there I was again, defying death and overcoming incredible odds. One tenth of an inch more to the right and my femoral vein would have been severed. In the jungle, such an injury would have been fatal. One more time, I felt that I'd been spared, preserved for some obscure reason. Those around me intuitively knew that certainly luck seemed to smile on me rather consistently. As far as I was concerned, luck had nothing to do with it.

They carried me down the hill slowly and onto the edge of the road. I remained hidden in the growth while Roberto came to check on me from time to time. I felt the fever beginning to overcome my will to stay awake. Shivers ran up and down my back almost constantly. Superficial gunshots rarely kill anybody, but infection does most of the time. The natural environment we were in was boiling with pathogens that could infect an insignificant wound in a matter of hours.

They managed to get me into the back of a fruit and vegetables truck. I could hear others' voices but the conversation was unintelligible to me. I drifted in and out of consciousness during the trip. At some point, we got off the truck and rested against an abandoned shack. Roberto gave me another dose of antibiotics and analgesics. A few minutes later I began to feel somewhat better. Walking was still difficult and my right index finger throbbed like it had grown its own heart.

A few minutes later a tiny man appeared with a horse and a wooden wagon loaded with wheat. We boarded it, and I lost track of time once more. I awoke in a small house, sparsely furnished. I was swinging slowly in a hammock, my left foot brushing against the smooth dirt floor. I got up slowly. Pain as sharp as a stab wound ran from my crotch into my stomach. I dragged my feet to the small window from where I saw my colleagues talking quietly to a tiny man.

"Roberto," I called, my voice as faint as a child's.

He turned and reached the window in four strides. He smiled. "Are you growing boobs yet?" he asked, smiling. The comedian doctor on a skid—I had to ignore him or he'd never stop. "Since your boy equipment is gone, I'm waiting for your transformation."

I cracked a painful smile onto my face. It was enough. "I need a doctor. Penicillin isn't going to work for long. I need a wide spectrum antibiotic and more analgesics," I said, almost without breathing. The fever was returning.

"I can go with Cristobal down to—"

I interrupted him with my hand. "No, don't go calling attention to yourself in a strange town seeking medicine. We'll have soldiers or worse here within the hour. Just get the doctor."

He nodded, looked at his watch, and stepped outside the rustic house we occupied.

C.T. walked through the door a couple of minutes later. I was beginning to drift away again. He was carrying some papers.

"I told them what happened," he said, making the "OK" sign. That meant we had to get together and get our story straight before the command interviewed me or we'd be in trouble. I was never sure if I was a poor observer, or if C.T. had a vivid imagination.

"And?" I asked, prompting him to elaborate.

"Can you believe the idiots? They asked me about the stones before they asked about you!" he exclaimed, raising his hands, shoulders, and eyebrows in his unnatural signature gesture.

I smirked. It was typical, and I wasn't surprised. After all, we were expendable and of not much value in the large scheme of things. He continued talking while shuffling through his papers.

"They said that we could rest here until you're fit to move. They'll arrange for the extraction but we have to go back to the coast to get a ride north."

I figured I'd be out of commission for two weeks, maybe three. As long as we could stay undetected for that long, we'd be okay. It would take them just as long to ready another team and transport them to the infiltration point. Accounting for four to six days while they made their way to our location, I figured we might as well take a vacation and get better.

I was worried about my index finger—the trigger finger. I hoped the missing piece of flesh didn't include the tendon.

The squeaky sound of the wagon wheels signaled the approach of someone. I hobbled to the field packs against the corner and retrieved a handgun. I peeked through the window and saw Roberto driving the wagon and a balding middle-aged man next to him. The wagon pulled up to the door of the hut, and the bulky, bald man walked in. I put the gun away in my pack and went to the hammock.

"So where is my patient?" said the country doctor in a patronizing tone. I disliked him immediately.

I started to unwrap my finger. The doctor tried to take over the simple task, but I resisted. He tapped impatiently on the dirt floor with his shiny high boots. He smelled of cigars and of Colombian Aguardiente, an anise-flavored sugarcane rum favored in the country. His eyes were glassy and his speech a bit too slurred to be normal.

"Doctor," I said dryly, "all I need is some wide spectrum antibiotics, clean bandages, and analgesics. We can take care of the rest." I showed him my finger.

"It's clean; no infection there," he said, poking the edge of the wound.

I started to unzip my pants and he got tense. Undoing the bandages from my in-between-the-legs wound was tricky and quite painful. He pulled a small flashlight from his discolored, worn case.

"Don't touch it," I warned. I had no idea where he'd been before he got here. I couldn't risk an infection, not here.

"Who did the stitching?" he queried while inspecting the injury.

"My friend outside. He dropped out of nursing school," I said evasively.

"It's very good, quite good actually," he marveled.

He sat at the crude dinner table and opened his bag while I placed new bandages on the wound and pulled my pants up. He spoke to himself between his teeth for a minute and turned to me. Roberto and C.T. had joined us by then.

"OK, engineers. Try not to get robbed anymore, and especially avoid getting shot," he laughed at his own stupid humor until he realized that no one else was laughing.

"Here are six dosages of antibiotics and some analgesic, clean bandages, and disinfecting solution. Use it once or twice a day for a week. It should dry up by then. "His prescription sounded like a bad sermon. I was glad when I didn't have to smell his alcohol-loaded breath another second. Cristobal drove the doctor back to whatever bar he found him in and retuned an hour later with ready-made dinner.

During the next two weeks we communicated daily with our liaison in Venezuela. Back at the Island they were eager for us to complete the mission. We did . . . four weeks later.

It was five years before I returned to Colombia again. But in spite of this troubled trip and close encounter with death, I am still in love with the beautiful country.

Coming home weeks later, I pondered what had transpired. Although no doubt, I'd successfully negotiated the skirmish, I was still uneasy. Injury and my hurt pride aside, I hadn't been able to stop thinking about my own vulnerability.

Grandma saw my nipped finger phalanx. I dared not talk about my other injury. She offered her motherly concern, but that was it. She didn't seem to fear or be alarmed at all. We talked about the weather in the Amazon basin, the animals, and the exotic food I tried this time around. Our conversation remained fairly benign until I changed subjects.

"Abuela, in the Bible, fathers gave their sons blessings and things like that. What was that all about?" I asked, more or less pretending to be distracted by the condensation on my cold glass of lemonade.

Grandma thought for a while. Precision was her game, and a master she was. She was pulling words into a straight line.

"Well son, in the old days, there were men that spoke with God. Because they had a very close relationship with God and went to Him for all their needs, I guess they felt blessed. They in turn passed those blessings and goodwill to their sons and daughters. It seemed that God had given them the right to do so."

She got up and returned, Bible in hand. I knew she'd be able to explain it. I had this nagging idea in some dark corner of my mind that needed light. Out there in the jungle I had felt naked, exposed, as if I needed better protection. *But where to get it? Was it enough to pray to Grandma's God for it? He could give it to me, of course. He could make me unbreakable if He chose to, but would He?*

"The blessings come from God and not of men. You can't say you bless somebody if God hasn't given you permission to do so by His own mouth," she explained, a curious look in her soft blue eyes.

> Now the Lord had said unto Abram, Get thee out of thy country, and from thy kindred, and from thy father's house, unto a land that I will shew thee:
> And I will make of thee a great nation, and I will bless thee, and make thy name great; and thou shalt be a blessing:
> And I will bless them that bless thee, and curse him that curseth thee: and in thee shall all families of the earth be blessed. (Genesis 12:1–3)

"In the Bible, Abraham receives a blessing from God and he is told that he, in turn, will bless all the families of the world. I don't understand that, by the way, but if God says that, it's certainly true," she concluded.

She offered a simple statement of truth. She had no issue with things she couldn't fully comprehend. In her book, men needed a lifetime and then became just like God to understand His mind and all his mysteries. "Maybe when we're in heaven," she said in that regard.

She let me brew over her last statement for a minute or so. She had her Bible ready once more.

> And he came near, and kissed him: and he smelled the smell of his raiment, and blessed him, and said, See, the smell of my son is as the smell of a field which the Lord hath blessed:

Therefore God give thee of the dew of heaven, and the fatness of the earth, and plenty of corn and wine:

Let people serve thee, and nations bow down to thee: be Lord over thy brethren, and let thy mother's sons bow down to thee: cursed be every one that curseth thee, and blessed be he that blesseth thee. (Genesis 27:27–29)

"Jacob is getting a blessing from his father because God had blessed his father Isaac all the days of his life, and He told him so. It couldn't be any other way, son. The blessing has to come from God."

"So, Abuela, can you bless me?" I asked, rather slowly.

She smiled and slid into heartfelt laughter. She dipped her finger in her glass of water and sprinkled my face, teasing me. I smiled, though I was still a bit confused.

"No, son, I can't," she said, now more composed.

"But Abuela, you always say how much the Lord has blessed you. Aren't all of these blessings from God?" I contended, following the logic of the argument.

"Now, that's a very good point, son, but I don't think it holds water," she said, shifting a bit on her chair and drawing closer to me. "I'll let you in on a secret," she said in her best conspiratorial tone. *This is getting good*, I thought. "I know that God is there, here, everywhere, and I'll tell you more. He took Jesus back into heaven—He is also there," she said without blinking. She held my hand. "I've felt His presence, His Spirit, or whatever it is He sends to the earth so we know that He still exists," she said. I felt goose bumps on my back. "Son, I've pleaded with Him in the night for something, and in the morning it's done. I've prayed to Him so that someone may be healed and go back to work to support his family and He has done it. I've prayed that a woman wouldn't die in labor, for she had many other small children who would be left helpless. And she lived, even when the good-for-nothing doctor that came here said she was going to die," she said, her pitch going up a notch as she closed.

I sat there, engrossed. I had a pretty precise idea of whom she was talking about. I had heard adults talking to Grandma at home about "so-and-so" being ill and the like. I'd seen Grandma's concern for the sick and those who had very little. But that she'd asked God to heal them, and it had been done? Now, *that* was earth-shattering.

She looked out the window, trying to hide the tears in her eyes.

"But," she added, "I don't think I can bless anybody. God hasn't told me that I can do so. His blessings for my family and me I've sought on my own. I think all people have the same privilege." She read the passage again where God tells Abraham that because of his obedience He will bless him and his family.

"The fact is, God will bless everyone if they do things His way, period. Now, these are individual blessings given to each of us. It isn't an acknowledgement, not an indication that suddenly you have permission to start dispensing blessings." She suspended the statement in midair, looked at me, and smiled. "Not even if you ask me, son. It just can't be done that way," she concluded.

"So, let me get this straight," I said, trying to press my point by a summation of the argument. "You can't give me a blessing because God has not given you permission to share yours around. But you can pray to God, and He will bless somebody in your behalf?" It sounded like a very good line of reasoning.

"Yes, that's right, Son. I can ask God all day long to have mercy and compassion with somebody, to heal somebody, or to spare somebody's life. And if it's His will, He does His work, and everything turns out okay." She swallowed some cold lemonade quickly.

"It is His doing and His will, because we're His children," she continued. "I have absolute faith that He can do what we call miracles and, depending on the circumstances, He absolutely will. Incidentally, the 'so-called' miracles are just a display of how smart He is. The secret is that He knows stuff we don't. That's why He is the best doctor, the best engineer, and the best fisherman," she said, almost savoring her own words. It was a treat for her that I asked these questions.

"The most I can do, son, is ask God to have mercy, to be kind, or to provide for somebody. The rest is up to Him," she said, swiping the table with her hand emphatically.

"So, can you ask Him for me to be safe and that nothing really bad will happen to me?" I asked, not sure of what answer I'd get.

"I have for years, son. Day and night since you went into the army," she said.

Grandma never made a distinction between the navy and the army, since I only "traveled" at times on a boat and most of what I did wasn't actually on the water, I was more a soldier than a sailor, she said.

"Have you prayed while you've been out there?" she asked. It wasn't a rhetorical question.

"The truth, Abuela? Not as much as I should," I said, feeling my face getting hot.

"And why not? I've taught you to pray since you were little," she said, genuine surprise now in her voice.

I bowed my head trying to hide. "It feels strange, Abuela," I said. It was a lame excuse, and I realized that as soon as the words came out of my mouth.

"Son, He is our Father, He knows everything in our hearts and sees everything we go through. It costs you nothing and it preserves your life every minute. I can pray for you until I die, but you should ask for His favor with your own voice. It's a sign that you believe in Him. You should try it," she said with a tender, encouraging smile dancing on her face. "Son, don't be like the rest of the people. They have heard of God, but they don't know Him. Get on your knees and pray for your own life and the lives of those you work with. Many mention "god" in every other sentence but it isn't my God they're talking about. So, whatever they say means nothing."

There was no doubt, no trepidation in her words. They were uttered with absolute conviction. There was no room for doubt, and I believed her. I believed that, in fact, God was there and could protect me at all times. Well, maybe just most times.

"Abuela, you know what I do. How can God protect me at all times?" came my question, and I wasn't being philosophical.

She flipped though the pages of her faded Bible again and read for me.

> The Lord is my rock, and my fortress, and my deliverer; my God, my strength, in whom I will trust; my buckler, and the horn of my salvation, and my high tower.

She paused, for effect or in kindness to save my brain, I wasn't sure.

> He sent from above, he took me, he drew me out of many waters.
> He delivered me from my strong enemy, and from them which hated me: for they were too strong for me.
> They prevented me in the day of my calamity: but the Lord was my stay.
> He brought me forth also into a large place; he delivered me, because he delighted in me.
> The Lord rewarded me according to my righteousness; according to the cleanness of my hands hath he recompensed me.

For I have kept the ways of the Lord, and have not wickedly departed from my God. (Psalm 18:2, 16–21)

"Son, if you believe that the things written in the Bible are true then you have to believe that He can do everything it says here," she stressed emphatically pointing to the Bible on the table.

"I tell you today, that if you believe that there is a God and that we're subject to Him, even for the air we breathe, and you commend your life to Him, He will preserve you."

I nodded quietly, the resolve to test Grandma's theory beginning to take shape in my mind.

"Now, don't do stupid things, you hear?" she said pointing her finger at me. "If you don't risk your life unnecessarily and do these things, He will preserve you and snatch you from the edge of hell if you happen to stumble onto such a place on the earth."

I thought about it. I thought about it all night, actually. On the one hand, the prayers of my grandmother were, most certainly, instrumental in my safety. And on the other hand, from now on, I could go directly to Him and ask for my own security.

I felt an out of the ordinary need to visualize a prayer. "Can I walk, Abuela, while I pray?" I asked her, thinking of my environment while away from home.

"Sure thing," she said. "Actually, you don't have to pray out loud if you think you can't. God knows your thoughts and your intentions before they come to your mind." Her face shone, and I knew it pleased her to give me such insights, that I had such curiosity.

That night, I prayed to the God of my grandmother for the first time in a long time. I told Him of my fear, of my uncertainty, and my nightmares. I told Him about my experiences and my desire to finish the war—to come home for good.

A wave of emotion swept over me, making me shrink on the floor of my room in tears. I never told my grandmother about it. I didn't know what to make of it. The intensity of the experience scared me, but comforted me as well. From that day, I offered a prayer in my heart every night.

A Tool in His Hands

Life in the military had little to offer the common soldier. By Cuban standards, officers enjoyed a larger menu of options, both professional and personal. They received, on the average, larger compensations, better working conditions, and additional subsidies for food, clothing, and domestic appliances. They also had slightly better access to housing and preferential medical care.

For those in deployment, conditions were extremely hazardous. Without independent press and reporting, without external oversight, and with being anchored in a hermetic system, whatever really happened was never known. It is estimated that one million Cuban soldiers have lost their lives in foreign wars since 1959, yet there has never been a single documentary, report, or newscast about it on national television.

Although Africa wasn't my theater of operations, I had the opportunity to travel to Angola, Mozambique, Ethiopia, Congo, and Guinea Bissau. There I saw soldiers who were very poorly trained for the environment they had to operate in. Cuba has no deserts or places to train prior to deployment. I saw ill-equipped units with insufficient provisions, and worse, no real intelligence.

Since military service is compulsory for the most part, there's a never-ending supply of young men getting ready in boot camp. Many of them eventually succumb to a war fueled by strange ideologies or to diseases unheard of in our small island.

Cuban soldiers armed with Soviet-made weapons and equipment shed their blood in the middle of African ancestral tribal wars for three decades. Many of my classmates died in Africa. Not even their remains were brought back home.

In Central and South America, the story was much the same. Other than Nicaragua, revolutionary ideals and forms of government haven't prospered in Central and South America to this day. Our involvement was limited to training and logistical support in the region.

The crumbling of the Soviet Union and its geopolitical sphere of influence brought the end of large-scale support for those operations. The shift was seen almost immediately. Guerrilla groups disbanded and fused back into the population, unable to support themselves in the mountains. Overall, operation dropped by 80 percent within six months.

The institutional governments and military forces in the service of those governments also saw themselves cut off from the CIA supply pipeline. War was over, although the roots of the conflict persisted. Specially trained counter-insurgency military units lost all operational cohesion, fragmented, and then turned to their own devices.

Strongly armed but without visible targets, those units embarked on private operations to support their own illegal enterprises. Frequently, civilians in isolated population groups became the casualties of the process. There was no particular reason; they were just in the way.

CIA and other United States intelligence officers always operate from inside the United States Embassy in every country. It isn't a secret to anyone. It provides the officer with strong credibility, excellent cover, and immunity. At the same time, they become untouchables.

It's quite a sick game. They knew that we knew. But they pretended that they didn't know that we knew. And we did the same. We went to the same parties, patronized the same restaurants, and enjoyed the same coastal resorts. There was ample opportunity to mingle, buy each other drinks, and chat casually.

In time, zeal gives way to clarity and insight. Casual acquaintance gives way to professional admiration and understanding. Politics is the observable social behavior of those in government. Nothing else.

Rogue military units began at an alarming scale to traffic in women, children, weapons, drugs, or whatever happened to be in the market that week. Because military alliances are fragile, obtaining intelligence from active members of these units was just a manner of money.

C4 is the most coveted substance in the world. It has a higher price per gram than gold in the arms market. Because there are only a handful of companies that manufacture this high-density explosive compound, supply is always quite limited.

When one hundred pounds of C4 showed up in a remote landing strip in Guatemala, alarm bells went off, thunderously. Contrary to protocol, I withheld the information from the wire and decided to make some inquiries of my own.

Jeff Patterson was a station analyst in Guatemala. He was a young, clean cut, Ivy League graduate in political sciences, and a soccer fan. He was married to an "imported Guatemalan." She was the daughter of a retail chain potentate who had gone north to school. Jeff was wired at both ends.

He was friendly and amicable, a pragmatist and, as far as I was concerned, very smart. That made him approachable for interesting conversation. I waited until Saturday for the local prep school soccer match where his adolescent brother-in-law played. At halftime, I waited for him near the concession stands.

"Jeff!" I shouted, waving. He had only one security detail agent with him, but the situation seemed non-threatening—I had both hands busy with drinks.

"It's Daniel, from Pittsburgh," I said, using the alias I'd used when we met for the first time. I moved a bit closer, smiling still. "Don't you remember? We took that class together . . ." I was almost next to him now. "The class in the School of the Americas," I said in a more subdued tone, but my face kept its smiling mask. He wasn't smiling back.

The School of the Americas was a special military school for counter-insurgency that unfortunately had trained some of the most brutal paramilitary groups and officers in the continent.

I pointed with one drink-filled hand to a corner of the busy hallway. "Sorry to disturb you, but if you have a minute I'll make it worth your while."

Jeff hesitated for a second, and the security made a gesture as if he was going to end the conversation. "No, it's okay," he said walking toward a less crowded part of the food court.

"How can I help you . . . Daniel?" he asked, accentuating the name.

"There are about one hundred pounds of C4 on a landing strip two hours away, near Zacapa. Did you . . . lose them?" I slowed down the phrasing. His eyes opened a fraction. I knew I had his attention, so it was time to give him a token of trust.

"My name is Leo," I said offering yet another alias, but this time one he might actually recognize. "I was a friend of David's. I'm sorry about him." I offered my sympathy with sincerity. David was his pilot and well-known "go-between" since he was a native. He flew children out of the mountains to hospitals in the city. I had often passed along vital information to him about a potential kidnapping. He always appreciated the tip. His plane had gone down in the middle of the jungle a few weeks prior. It was unclear at that point what had happened.

"Let's go to my car," he said, starting to walk.

"No," I said. "The game is about to begin. Look, if it's lost then you better go get it before somebody else finds it. I don't like messy houses, so we could offer to clean it up, but it will take me a couple of days."

"Where did you find it, specifically?" he asked

"The old quarry. Everybody knows where that place is. Please have them pick it up by sundown. You have what—six hours?" I started to walk back to the bleachers, my steps echoing across the hollow walkway.

"Leo," he called. "Why?" he asked.

"We all want a safe neighborhood," I said as I drifted into the crowd.

Intelligence reports showed a huge explosion in an abandoned mine southeast of Guatemala City that night. The explosion was felt twenty miles away. Not a whisper was heard in the local news. That was the beginning of a pragmatic relationship between Jeff and me that lasted until the end of his post.

Our paths would cross again in quite an unusual way. Less than a year later I received a phone call from a friend of Jeff's. The call was so out of the ordinary, especially since I wasn't considered an intelligence case officer at the time. I was an operator, and as such, not perceived as someone who could cultivate civilian contacts with foreign agents.

After two hours of questioning and a polygraph test, they were convinced I wasn't a double agent. I sat in an office full of KGB, GRU, and a handful of my colleagues in order to return the phone call to Jeff. The cigarette smoke flooding the low ceiling and the monotonous humming of the old VAT computers was the only evidence of movement in the room while I placed the call to Guatemala City.

"Hello?" I said into the receiver, rather unsure of how to start.

"Leo?" came the response at the other end.

"Yes," I said. "How are you doing, Jeff?" I asked, just to break the ice.

"We're doing okay. Are you busy right now?" he asked, sounding unsure of the circumstances of the call.

"Oh no, I'm resting. Are you in your . . . house?" came my query, with emphasis in the last word. I wanted to know if he was free to talk.

"No, I came to a friend's house to visit and I thought about calling you and asking you for help." This wasn't a sanctioned call. He was reaching over the fence. I was getting excited already.

"Certainly Jeff, how can I be of help?" I replied with all familiarity.

"We have a family problem, you know." He paused but didn't wait for my response. He was phrasing and choosing his words. "He is kind of a distant relative but family nonetheless."

Plausible deniability. It was just the ability to say, under oath if necessary, "I didn't know anything about _____." Because there was always someone listening, a benign conversation was always that—a simple conversation.

"Leo, this cousin has emotional problems. He has a substance abuse issue that has pushed him to the edge and he is becoming violent at times. I know that you're a counselor and have expertise in dealing with such situations." The description was explicit enough that I was able to determine the fact that I knew the relative in question. He was looking for a "fixer."

"We tried to convince him to come to treatment but he won't. At this point, involuntary commitment is the only option," he explained. His choice of words was precise and eloquent, but still veiled. "Because the rest of the family is kind of afraid of him, we're seeking outside counsel to deal with him. We can't reach him, but we have an idea of where he is right now." His speech was premeditated. Although his Spanish was perfect, the intonation gave him away. He was reading a script.

I smiled; I was enjoying this one. "These cases are complicated, Jeff, especially dealing with a violent individual under the influence. We have to make arrangements with the hospital and local medics for transport. Do we have time to make arrangements? Do you think he'll stay there long enough for us to reach him?" I was getting the hang of things.

"He is partying right now. He'll be there at his friend's for another week or so. After that, we're not sure. Use whatever you need in terms of medical staff, since money is no object. We want the best care in this case." The response was clear. Timing was critical and there was plenty of money available.

That sounded like my kind of operation, the kind the Soviets were into in Eastern Europe. No jungles, no bugs, no dirty water. Smash and grab and get paid. At least it might make getting shot at mildly rewarding.

"Okay Jeff, please pass the medical file to my assistant and let's make an appointment to gather some more history on the patient. You should also make arrangements for the retainer at that time." It was a very businesslike exchange.

"Thank you, Leo. You should have medical information first thing in the morning," he said in a more natural way. That came from him and not the script. "I thank you on behalf of the family," he said, and the line went dead.

Silence engulfed those of us in the room. My boss, a scar-faced general, of whom it was rumored that he ate human flesh in Africa in order not to starve, blinked at me and left the room. I waited a minute, distractedly scribbling stick men on a notepad. Now that was an unusual wrinkle, I thought, a quiet smile dancing on my face. I gathered my papers slowly and left the room.

In the Cuban military, you weren't supposed to grow a brain unless you were ordered to do so. It was frequently hazardous to your health. If you were suspected to be an independent thinker then you could be accused of sedition, of being "penetrated and brainwashed by the enemy," or some other absurd description.

Ideological or any other kind of dissent was seen as political opposition and punishable by the firing squad. Appeals were accepted and denied in the same day. No supreme or any other court was available. As a consequence, hyper-vigilance was a defense mechanism, not a mental disorder. In Cuba, only the paranoid survived. So, no one dared say anything until those at the top of the pyramid had made up their minds. The rest would fall in line in a collective hypnotic trance.

I walked into General Cabrera's office, if one can take such liberty as to call that termite nest an "office." He was smiling, enjoying his ten-inch long cigar. I went straight to open his windows and then sat across from him in the small metal chair. I speculated that a general would have better furniture in his office. Then I remembered he was a renegade and an embarrassment to the echelon.

In Africa, in order to feed his troops, he'd sold military equipment, dug for diamonds, and sold long distance telephone service in the villages using Soviet satellite links. They didn't kill him because they couldn't. Cabrera was a legend in the military in his own right, and venerated as a war hero by the men who served under his command. He'd been shot twelve times and burned half his face in a plane that was shot down. He was tortured by the French in Algiers. Some said the man couldn't be killed because God didn't want him in heaven and the devil was afraid of him.

"So, Lieutenant," he said, "when were you going to tell me about this 'friend' of yours?" he asked, sarcasm dripping from his chair as he spoke. He relished the fuss that the call had made in the corridors of power. It had come through an encrypted secure line from a foreign agent nobody knew anything about.

"I made a report about a chance encounter I had in a soccer game a year ago. I knew him through David." I let it hang. I'd said my piece.

He puffed leisurely on his cigar, staring at the ceiling with a smile like a swamp wild boar. I grabbed a piece of paper from the desk and scribbled.

"David was our asset, remember?"

"I don't know what the fuss is about," I said, trying to get comfortable in the hard metal chair. "The man has a family problem," I said stretching the syllables. "It's that nutcase of a captain, Urbide, you know? He has been doing cocaine for six months straight since they dismantled his base in Gualan."

Cabrera rested the cigar on a crowded ashtray. "What is it that he is doing these days?" he asked while mixing a tablespoon of baking soda and water and some other green liquid in a cup. So many bullet holes had left his liver and pancreas doing only a part-time job. He was known for expelling dangerously loud and putrid burps and intestinal gases.

"He is killing people left and right, civilians mostly. He's out of control and the gringos don't know what to do with him," I said, still a bit surprised and pleased that the Americans were looking to us to rid them of a nuisance they created.

"When do you leave?" Cabrera said with his face contorted in disgust after swallowing his bitter medical formulation.

"Do I have to go do this thing? I don't want to cross paths with that butcher again," I said.

I had narrowly escaped an assault on one of Urbide's safe houses where we found three detainees in a torture room, drowning in blood and feces. The place looked more like a slaughterhouse. I couldn't get rid of the stench for a month.

Cabrera just shrugged his shoulders and handed me the phone to the deployment center.

We went into Guatemala via Belize early the next day. We then made our way into Guatemala City and the embassy to get briefed. They had received the package via courier with pictures, phone call transcripts, maps, psychological profiles, recordings of radio intercepts, and other information. A stir was caused by the five hundred thousand dollars also in the package. We pored over the materials until nightfall.

Our own intelligence was even more disturbing. Fires are common in the jungle in the summer due to lightning strikes. By the same token, the torrential rains, which fall in the season almost every day, extinguish them with equal speed. But when fires burn for more than ten to twelve hours in the same location, with no observable variance in intensity, day and night, the fuel source isn't natural. Only napalm burns in such a fashion, and it had not been used since Vietnam; it's extremely dangerous to transport and can't be easily obtained. The other fuel possibility is human remains. The infrared satellite pictures showed a fairly stable and intense smoldering fire very close to a remote village. Daylight photographs didn't show signs of life or habitation in the same village.

We traveled south out of the city and then east. We reached the small enclave of Los Palacios at daybreak where we geared up. Last reports put Urbide and his two-dozen men fewer than twenty miles from our current location. If we kept moving, we could reach him by dusk.

By mid-afternoon we had reached the deserted village. A few dogs rummaged through the empty, smoldering huts. We searched the surroundings for survivors or victims but without success—just broken rustic furniture, empty pots and pans, and scattered clothing, but no bodies.

We left the village and regrouped on a small hill overlooking the valley below. The fire was about three miles downhill. We opted for a tangential approach in order to preserve the element of surprise. As we descended into the small valley, the rain came upon us fast and hard, cutting our speed and visibility in half. I was afraid we'd lose the trail if the enemy platoon moved, or that we might stumble onto them sooner than we expected. We stopped and waited for the rain to subside. Two hours later, we were on the move again and within two more hours we had reached the location of the fires.

I've seen death and dying. War is the ultimate reminder of how fragile human life is. But nothing could have prepared me for what my eyes saw that humid evening in an empty valley in the highlands of Guatemala.

At the bottom of a scorched ravine, between the charred stones and tree trunks, were the bodies. There were women and children, both young and old. Hundreds of bodies piled like waste, discarded and cast aside like chaff after the harvest.

As we got closer to the heap of bodies, it was evident the brutality and terror these people had endured. Some carried their children still cradled in their arms. I saw children clasping their toys in a deadly embrace. The smell of seared flesh permeated in every direction, the simmering vapors and the dripping of the bodies burned in my memory forever.

I climbed back up from the ravine and instructed the men to pick up the trail. I walked a little ways from the edge into the trees and sat facing away from that infernal orgy of destruction. That day my eyes were opened to the pit of the devil and his minions. With my senses saturated with the taste and smell Satan's relish, I sat under a tree and wept. I'd seen his handiwork. With blood he has paved his own way to that pit from which he'll never escape. With terror he has fed his own fury and anger; with rage he has justified himself before those who worship him and do his bidding.

I sat under an ancient ceiba tree, praying to God to help me do my work but not to seek revenge. I prayed that I could free myself of the anger roiling within me, so I could keep my peace. I needed a cool head and a steady hand. I rested that night but I couldn't eat. I slept in a stupor, no dreams, no noise, all the way through until 4 AM. There was no time to waste.

We received intel reports before midnight that Urbide and his host of bloodhounds were still camped five miles to the east across a small ridge. We broke camp before sunup and climbed the hills that separated us from our target. The morning was cloudy and fresh, which helped our neck-breaking pace. We reached the top of the hill at early dawn. The sun was held hostage by heavy cloud cover. We saw the enemy encampment from the height of our position, but there was no visible movement.

We gathered in a group for planning. The camp was on a ledge leading to a brook surrounded by mountains. The enemy soldiers could only go north, or try climbing south or east away from us. We planned to approach them from the north and south and take positions there, then launch our attack from the west on high ground. If they tried breaking away, they would be giving the ledge up as they pulled back from us.

C.T. was on the radio, arranging for the extraction. We didn't want to stick around too long after we "neutralized" the target, just in case there were other military units in the area.

I approached him as he was storing the satellite link. "Are we good to go?" I asked him, giving him a pat on the shoulder.

"They'll be here in thirty minutes, Lieutenant. So let's make this a snack," he said, smiling discreetly.

"Let's put this scavenger hyena out of his misery," I said, loading and locking my weapon. I slowly screwed the silencer at the tip of the barrel.

I looked away at the mist-covered mountains and murmured a prayer. I hadn't asked for this assignment, but it was mine to finish. I prayed I'd never have to witness such an atrocity again in my life. I prayed that the souls of those who had been killed by the hand of this monster had found peace in heaven.

I was determined to carry out this task. I hoped that this dirty, inhumane war might be over before I surrendered my own humanity in the process. I was determined to carry out my mission because I felt it was the right thing to do. I had never felt more justified in doing my job. In my heart, I was convinced that this animal had done enough damage; he had destroyed the lives of hundreds of people for no reason other than greed or pent-up frustration. There weren't any soldiers among the remains that were still burning on the other side of the hill. That wasn't war—it was a slaughter.

As we moved on the target, I couldn't help but reflect on the words of my grandmother. If I was always to be truthful with myself, I knew I must continually question my own motivations and feelings. I was descending on the enemy not in rage, not in vengeance, but on a mission. I could, in good conscience before the eyes of God, say so. Prior to that day, my work had been limited to intelligence gathering and planning quiet and surgical strikes. But this day we were on a hunt. The full intent of the mission was to find and exterminate a group of beasts that doubtfully passed for human beings. This was different altogether. I wanted to make sure my heart was in the right place.

An act of such cruelty had to be opposed. "Any honest and decent man would agree that a limit has to be set so that the innocent won't suffer," Grandma always said. "To stand and do nothing in the face of such atrocities would be an affront to God. He'll judge us for both our sins of commission and our sins of omission."

So that morning, without guilt, with no anger or thirst for revenge, I realized my role. It was no coincidence that God had put me there that day. If this were His measure of justice for the crime they had perpetrated, I'd oblige. I wielded the weapon, but it was His battle.

Our team cut through the perimeter without a sound. There were six tents and four men standing watch. The snipers took down the enemy lookouts before they could sound the alarm. We moved quickly downhill and hit the tents hard with grenades and automatic fire. The few men that managed to come out of their tents and slide down the ledge onto the brook were cut down swiftly. Urbide was among them. In two minutes it was done.

Within the camp we found cases of liquor, a substantial amount of narcotics, currency, and silver bars. We also recovered numerous reams of documents. We filmed and photographed the aftermath of the short battle and fingerprinted the dead. Then we piled the remains, including the dead, and burned it all. In the end, they suffered the same fate as their victims.

The roaring of the helicopters signaled that the ordeal was over. We flew east into Belize on a civilian aircraft. I was home for dinner that night, forever changed. I was now a witness to the kind of abasement and depravity I had never imagined existed.

The massacre made headlines the world over. The operation was classified and almost twenty years to the date not much true information has surfaced. I never shared the event with Grandma, but my work in the military was transformed from then on. That experience opened a window for me into the entrails of hell and the work of those who dwell there.

GOD'S WILL OR YOUR WILL?

War is exhausting, especially when there's no clear purpose or objective. Even in the face of "victory" and operational success, I felt hollow, drifting in a mist of intangible ideological premises and abstractions.

The social environment was highly sensitive to internal strife. It strived constantly for control, self-sustainability, and gyroscopic stability. There was no space for pragmatic, intelligent discourse, no room for commentary. It was all understood as vulnerability and lack of resolve, which in turn became a risk. And risk was never tolerated.

I kept all doubts to myself. I only engaged in reflective reasoning while pounding the pavement mile after mile during my morning runs. There was no confidant, no private discussion or friendly exchange. Survival depended on shielding my thoughts and feelings from those around me. Guerrilla warfare is quite different from "conventional" combat. The killing is up close, face-to-face. The nightmare splashes onto your face and stains your hands. I couldn't tell my friends, I couldn't bring this horror to their minds.

Spring brought rain to the island in abundance. It also brought the most impressive display of colors. Fireflies were always my favorite insects. They defied nature and simple logic and took it upon themselves to be distinct, in a significant way, from every other insect.

"I guess you're no longer going to be a bug doctor, are you?" Grandma once asked me with a chuckle.

I'd been quite a serious amateur entomologist a few years prior. I still kept my field book with drawings and notations of the specimens collected a few dozen yards away in the ravine behind my house. I had lost my enthusiasm for the insect world when puberty hit.

I smiled. Now I was more like the fireflies, I guessed. A night creature, different, mysterious, somewhat visible, but unrecognizable in the daylight.

"Abuela, why does God let good people, innocent people, suffer so much?" I asked in a reflective tone.

She contemplated the possible answers for a while with a frown on her face. This was the sort of question that lent itself to a prolific and explicit response. But she never wasted words; she took her time.

"Well son, there are many reasons, I suppose. I'm not sure where to start, but why don't you give me an example?" she answered. I thought she was baiting me.

"Well," I said, "imagine us here in this little quiet fishing town and a band of bad men comes and kills a bunch of us, for no reason, just to rob us or whatever. Why does God allow it to happen?"

She slid her right hand back and forth in a repetitive motion over the table. She was organizing her thoughts, measuring and pondering her response. Her old Bible was resting on a corner of the table. Her next move was to reach for it.

"I think that we don't know how God thinks or what He is planning or why. So these are Florence's thoughts and feelings based on what the Bible says, okay?" she said, and I smiled.

She rarely took such liberties but it was always fun to hear Grandma's take on some issue. There was no teacher, no scholar of any sort to confer with, so she was left to her own insight.

She didn't disappoint me. She stretched her hand and slapped open the Bible. In a few seconds she found what she was looking for. She read softly, tracing the verses with her finger.

> And all the inhabitants of the earth are reputed as nothing: and he doeth according to his will in the army of heaven, and among the inhabitants of the earth: and none can stay his hand, or say unto him, What doest thou? (Daniel 4:35)

"Son, this is what I think. This is His world and whatever He does, although we may not understand, it has a purpose. Sometimes the purpose is beyond our awareness or, sometimes, the purpose may be years away from today. Since time doesn't matter to Him but purpose does, we should just accept His will."

She rummaged through the pages for a few more seconds, reading softly to herself until she was sure she had found what she was looking for.

> For the wisdom of this world is foolishness with God. For it is written, He taketh the wise in their own craftiness.
> And again, The Lord knoweth the thoughts of the wise, that they are vain. (1 Corinthians 3:19–20)

She paused for a second to gauge my reaction. There was none, since the passage was a bit too intense for me.

"Son, we can't pretend to know all the things of God with our puny minds. It's simply impossible, but there are some like 'you-know-who.' And they indulge themselves thinking that they know," she mimicked Father Fumes, making a pompous sign of a cross in the air and folding her hands over her chest in faked piety. It was hilarious. "This I know: only the prophets knew what God was doing, what He was about to do, and why. Because He told them!" she exclaimed. "So, in a nutshell, in that regard we don't know why sometimes things happen that seem totally out of reason, as if God was asleep at the wheel. But rest assured, my God never sleeps." She continued reading:

> That upon you may come all the righteous blood shed upon the earth, from the blood of righteous Abel unto the blood of Zacharias son of Barachias, whom ye slew between the temple and the altar.
> Verily I say unto you, All these things shall come upon this generation. (Matthew 23:35–36)

After a brief pause, she continued. "I guess—how do you count yourself before God? You have to live a good life, obey His commandments, and have your conscience free of guilt because you haven't caused harm to the innocent. There must be darkness, so there is light also. There's always right and wrong, and right and left. The choice is always ours," she said, leaving the phrase somewhat incomplete. She seemed to be reflecting on her own words. She looked over my head at the tree branches sliding across the dusty glass window of the living room. She leaned back on her chair still deep in thought.

"Those who shed innocent blood will have to account for their wickedness before God one day, son. That's His justice and His will. The innocent will receive their reward in time and in due season. Meanwhile, God looks after them in heaven," she said, pointing her index finger up to the ceiling.

It made perfect sense, and Grandma's explanation was solid in logic. It also seemed to link with what the Bible said, but it was still hard to reconcile with the carnage I'd witnessed. *How can God just sit back and let the bad guys have a field day, and then later call them onto the carpet?* It was a very tough proposition. Such a hypothesis appeared, at least to me, to abandon all elements fundamental to equity, fairness, and humanity.

Then the thought just came to me fast, from some unexplored corner of my mind. *What if, indeed, we're really here to do just what we supposed to do and nothing else? What if, since God knows everything, as long as we stick to the script, it doesn't matter if we die as long as it's our time?*

Through the dining room window I saw a large pelican gliding in the blue afternoon sky. I hoped that all those who had died in the massacre had found peace with God. The hands of wicked and evil men had taken their lives from them, but God knew the victims and the predator. He would dispense justice in His own way.

As I said, I never told my grandmother anything. I couldn't bring such horror to her doorstep.

By 1987, the bulk of the Cold War operations had already taken place or were coming to an end. The Iron Curtain was coming down in a grand finale that would take place in a few months, when the Berlin Wall was chiseled to the ground in one evening.

It was becoming increasingly more difficult to get logistical support from the Soviets for Latin American operations. Suddenly, they had lost all interest in what was happening on this side of the world. Something simple that was usually accomplished in minutes, like re-tasking a satellite to take a peek at enemy positions or troop movement, now took days. Many of the officers I was used to dealing with were no longer available. They had transferred, retired, or were just not there anymore.

By far, the strong ideological undercurrent that toppled the Fulgencio Batista dictatorship in Cuba couldn't be duplicated on the continent. The experiment failed miserably everywhere it was tried. Both the government and the insurgents lacked the doctrinal fortitude and academic background of the engineers of socialism in the Soviet Union and later Cuba.

Without a clear political agenda, logistical or ideological support, and with no distinct leadership, those movements folded one by one. The fractured military units (formal and informal) turned to survival rather than politics. And often that meant taking a walk on the very dark side of multinational crime syndication.

Surplus weapons and supplies began flowing toward the open markets in the continent. It wasn't uncommon for Soviet-made MANPADS (surface-to-air missiles) to be found for sale in Colombia. Soviet-made trucks, weapons, high signature satellite communication gear, and other items made their way into the highlands of Sinaloa and Michoacan, Mexico.

There was great concern within the high echelon of the Soviet military intelligence for the satellite relay stations and other gear that they had installed all over the region. One by one these were dismantled and destroyed, sometimes at great cost. Many times such stations were far inside hostile territory. Without the logistical support of former years, many lives were lost in these "salvage operations."

Early in 1988 the death squads, at the service of Barrios Mederos, a wealthy landowner, targeted a Honduran farm cooperative leader for elimination. With the help of underground insurgents and indirect support from settled operatives (Cuban spies living in Honduras) Bernardo Rivas was able to make his way out of the danger zone. Cuban intelligence had operated in the region since the sixties and had hundreds of native and non-native sleepers in the isthmus.

Our assignment was to cross into Honduras from Nicaragua, connect with the runaway group—including this young leader—and escort it to safety back in Nicaragua.

March marks the end of the trade winds season. The night incursion through the Gulf of Fonseca on a small fishing vessel was death-defying, to say the least. Our six-man team went on the water one mile off the coast and battled the surf for three hours until we touched land near El Cacao. We sought the refuge of the mountains before daybreak and remained out of sight in a thicket until sundown.

We proceeded to our pickup point on a north by northeast direction to the outskirts of Soledad. There were no incidents that night and just a few horse-drawn carts on the deserted country roads. However, the incoming radio traffic every hour was a bad omen. Not only was it unusual, it signaled that an undisclosed agenda was being drafted. The Cuban Command Center needed updated position information to unload an unscheduled assignment at the last minute. At that very moment, they were estimating how far we were from the intended target. My blood started to boil. In my experience, the more I was ordered to deviate from the original mission, the more likely it was that somebody on my team was going to die.

The group was spread out on the trail across two hundred feet or so. C.T., my communications specialist, was in the middle of the team. I raised him on the radio and he joined me on point a few minutes later. "Lieutenant," he said as he came from behind on my right side.

"Can we claim tech difficulties on the next radio contact?" I asked, stretching the sentence to emphasize my intentions.

He scratched his head and smiled softly. He unfolded a map from one of his pockets and pulled me aside. We stopped on the edge of the trail and he turned the black light onto the piece of paper.

"There's a small canyon ahead," he said, pointing to the map in front of us. "We could be going through it when the call comes in," he said, making a snarl, both hands covering his head.

I smiled and nodded. "Double pace, people. I have a breakfast appointment," I said, pressing the radio microphone on my neck. The shadows moving on the trail quickened their pace in silence.

The radio call came less than an hour later and the charade was on. C.T. made quasi-human, animal, and ghostlike noises for a couple of minutes until Central command gave up. They tried an hour later. I pushed the team hard until we reached our point of contact.

We waited a mile from the small rural community. It was still dark, but daybreak wouldn't delay. After the signal came, we moved quickly into the abandoned hay barn and the underground hideout that had been carved years ago by insurgents.

The cellar was well built, well-ventilated, and dry, though a strong chemical smell dominated the confined space. It seemed like an insecticide of some sort had been sprayed not long before in preparation for our arrival.

There were candlesticks and oil lamps, old newspapers, and magazines. It all pointed to the dwelling having been occupied for at least ten years, on and off. There were cans of preserves and sardines, which I kept at a distance. No self-respecting Islander ate canned fish, We settled for the day. The southwest winds kept pushing against the forest, shaking the trees and dragging with it leaves, branches, and everything else not sturdy enough to hold onto the ground. We could hear the banging of a loose metal sheet on the corrugated tin roof.

We sprayed the outside of the trapdoor leading to the cellar with neutral animal scents. It kept the dogs and the hogs away so they wouldn't alert others to our presence. Children were the next hazard to take into account. The visual acuity of those mountain little ones is astonishing and not to be underestimated. They can, literally, find a needle in a haystack.

In the meantime, I slept, I read, and I pondered. Garcia Marquez, the famed Colombian writer, was rude, mundane, and even vulgar, but I found him entertaining then. He was the kind of writer that spoke without inhibition and allowed onto the page the unspeakable thoughts of the average, unrestrained man. He spoke of old times, ancient times distant from my current reality. I always kept a copy of one of his titles in my pack for moments like this one.

The current mission was a flat line operation. I've seen zombies carry out more complex tactical assignments. The global conflict sponsored by the two superpowers was in its final hours. The Soviets were spent, both ideologically and economically. Perestroika had blown strange winds into the old, dusty hallways of the Kremlin and ripped the curtains from the frosty windows of the secret corridors. The empire that had stood for seven decades face-to-face with the Americans was being dismantled piece by piece from the inside out. There was no nuclear explosion, no Red Square demonstrators, no tanks in the street. The change was silent, away from the headlines and almost imperceptible to the people inside the country or out.

As far as we were concerned, we, the poor orphans, the adopted children of convenience, had no future. At least, not one that seemed very appealing. We kept running these small cat and mouse, comatose operations in the region, but it made no real sense. The plate tectonics had moved a mile out into the ocean, and the generals were still pretending it was just a pothole in the middle of the street.

How long could we pretend? How much longer could we keep being the objects of misguided idolatry by our young and ignorant Latin American peasant brothers? They were in love with a dream, a fallacy, an ideology that attempted to make a new man by fear, force, and intimidation.

Grandma's theory on the issue was quite pessimistic but apparently also quite accurate: "Men have no reason to be good," she insisted.

"Everywhere you go there are before you multiple opportunities to enjoy yourself, indulge yourself, abase yourself, and people tell you that's the way it is now. Today, most everything we call good and sweet and attractive is bad, and some of it is really bad in the eyes of God," she said, pointing to her old brown Bible, its cracked cover showing much use. "Only God can make a man good when such a man decides he wants to please God more than he wants to please himself." That was her case in point.

Most people were bad but didn't know it, didn't believe it, or didn't care if you told them. We were all dirty and yet we believed we smelled like roses. That was certainly discouraging for some people, but according to Grandma it was in the Bible. If you didn't believe in God, follow His commandments, and do the things that He wanted you to do, you were, as far as He was concerned, wasting oxygen on the planet.

But through ideology, governments attempted to create a standard of goodness and value for man. Also, they attempted to regulate private and public behavior. They elevated loyalty and devotion to the government above faith and consecration to God, since they advocated that there was no God. In her opinion, government was just a delusion.

I sat on the floor of the cellar trying to shake those thoughts from my head. I was a soldier, uncomplicated, precise, efficient. There was no room for those kinds of mental gymnastics. I did as I was told: research, plan, and execute. The rest was beyond my immediate concern.

I called Francisco, my second-in-command, a short, muscular soldier. He was a mechanical engineer by training who grew claustrophobic inside the tanks. He came from a long line of military men. His father was a military surgeon and his grandfather served in Korea.

I began giving directions. "Frank, let's get ready to move our package as soon as the sun sets. You and Benny change attire and retrieve it from the house across town; we'll meet you by the roadside. I have a feeling we're taking a detour." I shrugged my shoulders.

"Why do you say that, Lieutenant?" he asked.

"This tagging-the-donkey game they're playing. These calls every hour are just so they know where we are, and then they'll pitch the curve ball. You watch." I got up and stretched.

I ate some of the canned beans and Spam available. It wasn't bad, just not my kind of food. I'd rather eat the gooey protein mix I carried. I was used to it, and it didn't give me gas.

Two hours later, it was dark as we sat waiting between the trees. Frank and another sailor were back with the package: a thinly-built, pale character wearing thick glasses and limping from a wounded knee. He was slightly older than me, and wore faded denim pants and a checkered shirt. He was able to walk on his own, but the pain was evident. He smiled nervously, glancing at the heavily armed men surrounding him.

I shook my head in disbelief. How was I supposed to take this man across twenty-nine miles of mountains if he only had the use of one leg? This was beyond ridiculous. I walked away to talk to C.T. privately.

"C.T., we have to bring the chopper closer to us. He isn't going to make the trip with one busted knee," I said, pointing discreetly to our passenger.

C.T. got on the radio and started to argue. After a few minutes of cursing and haggling, he passed the commander to me.

"Nest, this is leader. We have a wounded passenger. He can't make the trip," I almost screamed into the radio.

"Standby, leader," came the answer.

I didn't wait. "Let's get moving, double pace, people, I have a date tomorrow," I said. I signaled to two of the team members to help the wounded. They positioned themselves on each side of the wounded and pretty much carried him, his good leg tiptoeing now and again over the floor.

"Leader, this is Nest—we'll work out a solution for you. Contact when you reach location 11 Alfa and stand fast at that location," crackled the voice on the radio. Basically they would make us detour to do who knew what, thus changing our extraction point.

"I knew it, I knew it," I said, anger burning the soft tissue inside my nostrils. "Let's just push this trail, people. Dinner just got canceled," I said, spewing some of that anger onto the jungle floor. It was always the same. We were pawns, pieces in a game that bordered on the morbid at times—with so little regard for the safety and integrity of the men involved. The scenario repeated itself numerous times through the years at a very high cost in terms of human lives that weren't honored or remembered, lives that faded from public discourse but not from my memory.

The new coordinates sent us to an abandoned lumber mill on the edge of the Choluteca River in Honduras. The site wore the vestiges of violence. Bullet holes dotted the metal doors, the sides of the buildings, the low tin roofs, and just about every vertical surface. Ultraviolet light scans revealed that a fair amount of blood had been spilt on the site not long before. The workers or occupants of the mill had either been forcibly removed or had abandoned the location in a hurry.

After surveying the area, a perimeter and watch was set. C.T. got on the radio to report our location. We had arrived at the location four hours ahead of schedule. I wasn't really surprised, but I was afraid they'd had no time to plot our extraction.

We received instructions to retrieve a metal box buried nearby. It had a low-frequency radio emitter attached to it. The signal was so faint that even after we were given the exact frequency it took us another five minutes to locate it. The box had a rusty locking mechanism but I didn't open it up. I didn't care what it was, and it wasn't important to my mission. My primary concern was to deliver the limping package while he was still breathing and in one piece. All I cared about was reaching the extraction point without incident and then going home.

These little detours were often lethal. Training and planning were just tools of the trade to improve the odds of a safe return. They helped to anticipate, to explore possible scenarios, and to prepare for the worst. Although the expectation was that, all things considered most missions were routine, there was always space for the exception. Trouble along the operational continuum was always possible. Departing from the plan increased the chances of encountering variables for which we had no contingency or equipment.

The coastal mountains of Central America are fertile grounds for fables and bar room stories about treasures and buried bounties. There are also stories of wealthy landowners hiding their wealth from guerrillas and government troops alike. A group of armed men digging around in the middle of the night was bound to attract attention.

We transmitted and waited for extraction instructions. Daylight was just a few hours away. If we were forced to wait ten hours in the open, we were inviting trouble in a serious way.

C.T. came running to me with bad news. With his bushy eyebrows cropped together across his forehead and his right eye halfway closed, his grin was unmistakable to me. "Lieutenant, we have a group of men on our six. Infrared imaging puts them about two hours behind us," he said in a low voice.

"How many, C.T.?"

"Maybe twenty and they're moving fast."

"They knew what would happen but they wanted their darn box." I turned away and choked on a less than mild curse. My insignificance as a person and as a soldier, and the value of my entire company were clear. We were nothing to those in charge.

"C.T., get on the horn and tell them that I want an extraction solution in thirty minutes and that we'll make the original point by daybreak," I said, breathing heavily. I felt my ears burning. Somebody was going to eat my fist when I got back.

"Lieutenant, we won't make it. Not with the package limping."

"Tell them if I'm going to risk my men they need to put someone on the LZ in three hours. If the package slows us down, we'll leave him behind. We lost two hours and it's their fault."

I walked away and called the rest of the team. Two of the snipers went ahead to secure the high ground and keep an eye on our tail. It was going to be close—we needed them to hold back the enemy's platoon while we made the LZ.

I approached our guest and stood before him while he sat on the ground, massaging his bum leg.

"Comrade, I know you're injured, but we find ourselves in a bit of tight situation here. I'm going to need your cooperation," I said, doing my best to keep my animosity to myself.

He stood up with some trouble and tried a painful smile. "Whatever you say, Lieutenant," he said, breathing a bit heavily.

I called Joaquin, our unit medic. He was a tall, ebony-black soldier who moved with the grace and agility of a cat. He also had the bedside manners of a family doctor. He was actually a sports medicine resident on duty. How he managed to make it into Special Warfare Division was a mystery to all. Some speculated he was a mole on some secret mission. I had no complaints about him. He was a skilled, competent soldier who had always performed well.

I addressed our injured guest trying my UN-diplomat tailored speech. "In order to make our extraction point, we have to move fast. Your injury is holding you back. The medic is going to give you some pain medicine so you can move faster. You'll need surgery when we get to safety, but at least you'll be alive." I smiled and he got the joke, I thought.

"I'm ready," he answered.

"Pull your pants down," Joaquin instructed our guest, whose face got one shade lighter.

"I have to inject your leg above the knee and I can't do it by rolling up your pants," Joaquin explained. The patient breathed a little more normally and color came back to his pale cheeks.

As the patient looked away, Joaquin skillfully flooded the joint with cortisone and applied a patch secured with bandages. In a couple of minutes it was done and the patient was ready, already working his knee in a more functional way.

"Thank you, Doctor," he said, flexing his leg with a smile on his face. "The pain is gone, totally gone."

For a moment, I thought our package might start dancing in place. I patted him on the shoulder. "Are you ready?"

"Yes, I am," he said, starting to walk.

"Joaquin, keep close to him," I instructed the medic. He winked one eye playfully. He'd put enough cortisone into the man that if his legs disappeared, he wouldn't feel a thing. In two days, he wouldn't be able to stand the pain but by then he would be somebody else's problem.

The advanced team reported no movement but the satellite infrared feed showed the group of men moving toward us. I instructed Frank to leave some surprises behind to slow them down a bit. We had been located anyway—a bit more noise wasn't going to make a difference. We might as well cut into their numbers and slow their pace a little.

We jumped on the trail and had been pushing hard for an hour or so when the explosives we left behind went off. That was minus four or five enemy combatants to deal with; a few less guns pointed at us if it came to that.

We moved even faster to seize the advantage. We assumed they would leave the wounded behind with two or three men and try to catch up with us, but we were even now. We would be able to take them if they came at us while we held the higher ground.

I pressed the radio microphone on my neck to raise the sniper team ahead. "Firefly, this is leader. How's the night sky?"

"Beautiful, leader, it's all clear. Continue your stroll," he responded.

Ruben was barely eighteen but had ranked higher than shooters with twenty years of military training in the program. The kid had eyes like an eagle and the pulse of a dead man. During training at the range you had to look at his biometric registry to see that he was out there and that he was still alive. He could slow his pulse and breathing to the point that most people would think he'd passed out. A second later, he would nail a target at sixteen hundred yards. Months before, on a mission, he'd knocked down the power to a whole town with one shot. At more than a thousand yards, he hit a control panel inside the small electrical substation through a dirty window in a darkened room. We hit our target and left before anybody knew what happened. I knew that if there was something out there, he'd see it.

"C.T., let's get HQ on the horn," I said on the radio.

"Right away, Lieutenant," he said. Less than a minute later he was next to me with the handset ready.

"Nest, this is Leader. We'll be on the LZ in less than an hour but, as you know, we have company on our six—maybe one hour behind us."

"We're aware, leader. Continue on your course and we'll advise you," came the protocol answer. I bit my tongue until it stung.

"Nest, we don't need advice. We just need the bus to be there when we arrive," I said a bit more forcefully this time.

"We copy, leader. Standby for instructions."

Frustration was beginning to impact my reasoning, and that wasn't good. I took a deep breath and tried to regain my composure. Commander Montes was there at the Ops Control Center but since the mission had been taken over by others, he couldn't speak to me directly unless in extreme circumstances. I kept moving and tried to forget about the OCC chess game.

The leader of our sniper team broke the quiet on the team open frequency. "Leader, this is Firefly. We have incoming birds, at least two bearing on you from the northeast," he reported.

I more or less shouted back on the radio, "Okay people, we've been made. Let's find some cover and wait to see where these birds are going.

"Firefly, how far out?" I asked, hoping to gain a mental image of the situation.

"Leader, they're about five kilometers north by northeast of your position and closing at about forty knots. We're in the midpoint and there's still nothing on your six," he reported with surgical precision. The kid was tremendously insightful.

We sought cover in thick brush a few hundred yards off the trail. The wind had picked up and that helped a little. They would have to find a low spot to land. It would take them a bit longer since they had to fight the trade winds from the southeast.

We waited. It wouldn't be long and we had to do something about whatever was left of the patrol behind us—they might crawl out of the bushes on us.

"Leader, this is Firefly. The birds are looking for a place over the trees less than a kilometer east of us. Looks like they're just unloading rather than touching down," he reported.

So they were trying to cut us off from the ocean route on the west with another group closing from the southeast. While I was trying to organize my thoughts, a thunder-like tremor shook the ground and fiery lightning illuminated the dark sky.

"Leader, there's only one bird now. The other had an accident," the sniper reported in a flat voice. "It was so close, I couldn't let it pass," he concluded.

"Son of a—" I found myself exclaiming, a malevolent smile tickling my stomach.

He'd found the side of the craft at night at over a thousand yards and hit the hydraulics. That shot would place him in the legend category within the Cuban military for generations to come. "Firefly, your position is most likely compromised. I want you to move south and join us since that's where we're going. We have to forget about going skinny dipping for now," I said. The ocean route was blocked.

"Understood, leader."

"C.T., get me Command," I said to him. He extended the handset to me with a smile. He had them on ready for me.

"Nest, the outing just got complicated. A bird just brought more guests to dinner on a northwest position and we still have the small party on our six. We're going to make a run for the fence. Be ready to help when we call you. We're going to get as close as we can but you have to bridge the gap."

"Standby, leader," the response came.

"Nest, I can't wait. We're on the move so come back to us whenever you can. Out."

I'd made up my mind. We had to make a run for the Nicaraguan border twenty or so miles south of our current position. The downside was that we had to keep moving even during daylight, which was dangerous. But we had no choice.

"C.T., how far behind is that group?" I asked.

"Maybe an hour."

"Okay, let's wait for them here. The first group is probably still reeling from the explosion of the chopper. They're about four hours from us. Let's just finish this."

I directed the men to form a defensive perimeter and give the incoming unit a good welcome. They were coming fast and hard, expecting us to continue moving west toward the sea.

"Rolando," I uttered on the radio.

He came running, maps in hand.

"Roli, I need the shortest, fastest way to get to the border."

He flashed a small light on the crumpled, weatherproof field map. He slid his index finger across it, aiming finally at a point in the red line denoting the Nicaraguan northern border.

"Is that the best we can do?" I asked, already dreading the answer.

I'd been through that canyon before. It was bare, with little foliage coverage and the foothill was made of loose gravel that came down from the mountain during the rainy season. The ground moved with every step, traction required an extraordinary effort. But it was indeed the shortest route to the border.

"Okay," I said. "Let's put out the red carpet and handle these scarecrows. Then we head up the canyon."

We had no choice but to face the group of soldiers almost scratching our backs. We'd lost time and without the cover of darkness, it was difficult to keep moving unencumbered.

The group came on the double, making as much noise as a stampede on the prairie. Our team was split in half with a fifty-yard gap between the first group and the second along both sides of the road. The first group let them pass and waited until the enemy hit a wall of lead that fell on them without warning or mercy. We opened fire and cut their numbers by one-third within five or six seconds. The enemy pulled back and our second group finished the job—also in a few seconds. One more time, it was over before they knew with any certainty what had transpired.

I could hear the cries of the wounded. We didn't have time to videotape and photograph the wounded and the dead, fingerprint the officers, or gather any documents. We had to keep moving.

Two of our men suffered moderate wounds. The unit medic stabilized them and we got underway. We broke away from the trail across the high grass in an attempt to gain time and shorten our route. Radio contact an hour later confirmed our worst fears. The enemy was still on our tail.

We were almost at the top of the ridge when the pursuing troops came out into the open and fired at us. A rain of RPGs and heavy machine gun hellfire rained on us and chopped the rocks nearby. The side of my face and forehead burned from the debris, but I kept climbing. The sooner we cleared the top, the sooner we could return fire and hold the enemy back.

I was almost at the top when I heard a scream behind me. I turned to see one of my teammates lying on his back, clasping his shattered leg in his hands. He was bleeding out quickly. I fired down at the enemy to gain a few seconds and slid back down to where the injured soldier was. I grabbed his arm and he looked at me—fear and pain mixed in a contorted mask.

I dragged him behind a small bush. Not much cover, but at least we were away from the direct line of fire. I ripped his pants to expose the gruesome injury. Part of the muscle in the lower calf was gone but the bone was intact. I applied a tourniquet to stop the bleeding and gave him some morphine. That was just about all I could do under the relentless gunfire.

I looked at him and smiled a bit trying to ease his tension. "What is your name, soldier? I asked.

"Rene, Sir," he answered, his voice trembling.

"Rene, are you ready to go?" I asked, grabbing his belt with one hand, my other hand around his waist.

"I can't," he said, almost crying. He was a young specialist out on his third mission.

"Rene, is this your first time being shot?" I asked.

"Yes, Lieutenant. I don't think I can make it. I think I'm done." His face was now pale and his pupils were beginning to dilate. He needed critical care immediately.

"Look soldier, do you want to die?" I asked, almost screaming at him. It seemed to shake him a bit. He bit his lips in pain and shook his head.

"Because if you do—I'll let you die right here. No sense in trying anything else if that's what you want."

"No, Lieutenant. I don't, but—maybe if God wants . . . maybe it's my time."

I took a second before I grabbed his shirt and shook him. He was going into shock and both his strength and will were leaving him.

"I've seen men die many times. Not because they couldn't be saved, not because it was their time, but because they gave up. Are you giving up on me now, soldier?" I was shouting in his face now.

"No," he answered faintly.

"Then don't die. Help me out and let's get off this cliff," I said, yanking him by the belt to his knees.

I looked up the hill and measured the distance to the boulders on the edge. "I need some cover, people. I need two minutes to clear the hilltop with a wounded man. Two minutes," I shouted on the radio.

"Roger, Lieutenant. Will do," came the reply.

"Now," I said.

Eight or ten muzzles flashed, spitting fire downward right over my head. I pulled, dragged, and tugged Rene up through the sand and gravel to the top. Just when I thought my strength was exhausted, half a dozen hands materialized from amongst the rocks to pull my broken comrade and me up to safety.

"Are you okay, Lieutenant?" a voice asked behind me.

"In one piece. Just take care of him," I answered, pointing to Rene bleeding behind me.

I walked away from the edge of the hill, my weapon still smoldering in my hand. And so was my head. How dare this soldier say that maybe God wanted—I turned around and pushed the medic tending to him aside.

"Soldier, don't you ever guess about what God wants or not!" I screamed at him. "If He wanted you dead, that bullet would have blown your head off right there on the cliff. Don't second guess me ever again, especially when I'm getting shot at while trying to drag you up that hill to save your skin," I yelled. I took a deep breath. "If you want to die, do it on your own time."

I was done, at least in terms of the public display. I was furious about how people found excuses for everything, even dying. Implicating God in such situations, especially when I was trying to do something to change the outcome, was simply repugnant. Grandma's words ricocheted in my mind then: "Sometimes people die not because they have to, but because they lack the faith to survive." I made a mental note to make sure that Rene was never again under my command.

We tended to the wounded for the next half an hour or so. The enemy platoon retreated down in the ravine to the tree line for cover. We planted antipersonnel mines and other explosives at the top of the hill. It would be impossible for them to climb behind us and circling would take them five to six hours.

We reached the border in three.

The debriefing and after-action review was anything but amicable. It was a miracle I didn't end up in a court martial. The use of profanity and expletives were standard operating procedure in such situations. Even though it wasn't necessarily my style, I made use of them anyhow.

I made it clear then that if I lost another man in one of those shenanigans, someone was going to walk with a limp as long as he lived. It wasn't a threat, but a warning—and they knew it.

The longer I remained in the military, the more cynical and cunning I became. I also became more astute in terms of protecting my men from the whims and secret schemes of the political weasels with influence in intelligence operations.

Back home, I tried to explain to Grandma how I'd lost it with the soldier who wanted to die. Later, I wondered if I might have been too harsh with him. By then I had realized that at the time I had just been feeling hurt and frustrated. I had, after all, been risking my skin to save his—and he'd been talking about dying?

The thought occurred to me that I should have been more understanding. Perhaps I should have allowed for some room on the battlefield. What if it had happened to me? Would I have been afraid? I certainly had been before, a long time ago.

When did I learn to subdue my fear? Maybe the need to remain in control (or at least maintain the appearance of it) had forced me to assume a completely mechanical response to the situation. After all these years the subjects and the people had no names that were of any concern to me. They were targets, some soft, some hard, and they were to be handled accordingly. They were almost less than human, or at least of no real importance other than their level of military interest.

I was getting good at this—and I hated it. Trading in human lives, making split-second decisions about who lives and who doesn't—it robs you of your connection with others. As your friends leave the realm of the living, it becomes more and more difficult to make new connections with those around you. *They'll be gone tomorrow, or next month. Why bother?*

"Son, war finds us even when we want no part of it," Grandma said. "But it isn't you; don't become the war. Pray that God may sustain your heart so that it isn't lost in the carnage," she advised me. But at the time her meaning eluded me.

I memorized my grandmother's prayers—her strange song for me. I kept it in a crumpled piece of paper in my breast pocket.

> O Lord, rebuke me not in thine anger, neither chasten me in thy hot displeasure.
> Have mercy upon me, O Lord; for I am weak: O Lord, heal me; for my bones are vexed.
> My soul is also sore vexed: but thou, O Lord, how long?
> Return, O Lord, deliver my soul: oh save me for thy mercies' sake.
> For in death there is no remembrance of thee: in the grave who shall give thee thanks?
> I am weary with my groaning; all the night make I my bed to swim; I water my couch with my tears.
> Mine eye is consumed because of grief; it waxeth old because of all mine enemies.
> Depart from me, all ye workers of iniquity; for the Lord hath heard the voice of my weeping.
> The Lord hath heard my supplication; the Lord will receive my prayer.
> Let all mine enemies be ashamed and sore vexed: let them return and be ashamed suddenly. (Psalm 6)

I had very little left. Humanity was one of the concepts that could keep me sane in the madness I inhabited, or that perhaps resided in me.

Grandma was hand-washing a light-blue dress, one of her Sunday dresses. I wasn't sure if the color was light or if the dress was so faded that only a faint sky blue tint was visible—most likely both. Her gnarled hands gently scrubbed the garment while she listened.

"Why do people do stuff like that, Abuela? I mean, after all, I'm right there trying to keep him alive and he's talking about God's intention," I said, my tone steaming with frustration still.

She listened for a few seconds and answered without looking at me. "It gets them off the hook. You can always blame somebody you think isn't going to jump out of a bush and confront you right then and there," she explained. "Besides, people like that have other problems. Giving up when things get tough and pointing to God for an explanation gives them a way out and permission to drop to the floor and die," she said, handing the dress to me and pointing to the bucket with clean rinsing water.

I rinsed the paper-thin dress mechanically, reviewing details about the soldier in my mind. Yeah, he had problems, I concluded. In hindsight, he shouldn't have shipped out with us on that mission. I had ignored the signs and mistaken his odd demeanor for apprehension, which is normal before any operation.

"Abuela, do you know when you're going to die? Would God let you know?" I wondered.

She thought for a few seconds again. "Well, I guess He could tell you or prepare you if your work was done. I'm not sure, but I must suppose it's possible. He knows all the times, after all," she said smiling. "I really don't care. I'm ninety years old and my time is well past. After eighty, we're all on vacation. He can call me any time now." She had said that before and I knew she meant every word of it.

The fact that I saved the soldier's life proved that it wasn't his time to die. "You're here, aren't you? And so is He," she concluded.

BROTHER AGAINST BROTHER

The Cuban military has been involved in every major conflict on the planet since the Vietnam War. Soldiers, specialists, medical, or technical personnel have been sent to every corner of the globe where a rifle has been fired or a flag waved in agitated revolutionary fervor.

Africa is no exception. Hundreds of thousands of Cuban soldiers fought and died in diverse conflicts in Africa from the sixties until the collapse of the Soviet Union. From Congo to Ethiopia, the blood of these unnamed soldiers was spilled.

These conflicts were abstract, void of conventional reasons, and politically too distant from my own reality to make any sense. Yet, my own experience was characterized by similar feelings of detachment and "de-real-ization." It often seemed like an out-of-body experience.

The fighting in Africa was brutal and constant. The bloodletting had no restraint. The factions attacked each other with a hatred I hadn't seen before. The enemy was anybody and everybody who wasn't from a particular tribe. Children, women, old men, and even infants were considered fair game in the conflict. The rationale to kill children was that they would, at some point in time in the distant future, become enemy soldiers. So, dispensing of them now made sense. I thought it totally barbaric

These so-called countries were nothing but tribal societies: nomads, shepherds, hunters, and gatherers clustered by geopolitical boundaries imposed by the United Nations. The drama of ancestral fighting for wells, hunting grounds, a bride, or a similar Bronze Age skirmish continued. The

introduction of gunpowder had simply made killing more efficient. That
was the only visible difference.

The high altitude drop from the AN-225 Soviet transport plane went
according to plan. I landed on target after gliding almost ten kilometers.
The hot air updrafts helped, and the entire team touched ground within
one mile of the target a few minutes past midnight.

Lights from the enemy camp were visible. The wind brought intermittent laughter and the sound of celebrating gunfire. The rowdiness of
the camp evidenced, not just their lack of training and preparation, but
also the fact that they weren't expecting combat. That changed quickly.

Our unit was composed of twenty-four men. Except the four replacements due to last minute illnesses and an unexpected leave of absence, I
knew them all. We encircled the enemy camp and turned on the radio
signal-jamming device. There was no call for help and no one was coming.

Our task was simple: "Reduce the target," more or less a coined phrase
for "plow through anything that moves," and secure the airstrip nearby
for a massive landing and buildup. The plan from the Cuban command
was to build up a contingency force large enough to stop the cross border
incursions of the CIA and South African troops from the south.

The enemy camp was a collection of old United States Army surplus
tents placed around several fires. There was music playing from an old
radio interspersed with sporadic gunfire. The storage units were identified, and our instructions were to avoid destroying them. It was possible
there were documents and equipment of interest in them.

Our unit closed in and the occupants of the tents in the perimeter
died without resistance. As the soldiers moved into the center of the camp,
the alarm sounded and the battle intensified. Without cover and being
surrounded, they had no place to go. Within minutes, three-dozen men
lay dead, scattered across the camp. Among them were children who had
been kidnapped from their homes and forced to fight—children no more
than twelve or thirteen with weapons in their hands, thrust into a fight
they couldn't understand, robbed of their right to play and be children
for another season. They were taken from their villages and compelled to
fight against their fathers, their brothers, and their families—pushed at
gunpoint into a conflict as ancient as the sycamore trees on the savanna.

I felt my stomach convulse violently and a second later a gush of bitter fluid filled my mouth. I held it there and walked away. I went around the storage shed, spat on the ground, and turned into the wind. I took a few steps away from my second-in-command. He understood.

"Damn you," I said quietly. Those in control had to have known about the child soldiers. That's what military intelligence is for. It's their business to know who is there and who isn't—who dies and who should live. We all knew about the soldier boys, but the encounter with them was unexpected. They weren't supposed to be here, not this far south. They were always kept close to their villages where they could provide intelligence to their captors about their communities, food sources, people, and other useful information.

"What kind of screwed up war is this, Lieutenant?" asked one of the mission specialists. His face a mask of disgust and confusion. I had no answer. None that would satisfy him anyway.

"It felt like killing my own brother," he said, almost in a whisper. The words escaped, just as tears dripped from his eyes. "I didn't come up here to kill children, Lieutenant," he said and then walked away.

We all walked into the night to hide our tears, to hide our despair.

"None of us did . . . none of us did," I replied to myself.

"Is it a sin, God?" I whispered. "Is it? To lay waste against him who points a weapon also against me? How can I distinguish? How?"

I labored to keep my breathing slow and even. I walked a dozen yards and kept my back to the troop that waited for me. I turned off the small light and squeezed the stained, crumpled paper with the handwritten Psalms that Grandma had given me.

> Unto thee, O Lord, do I lift up my soul.
> O my God, I trust in thee: let me not be ashamed, let not mine enemies triumph over me.
> Yea, let none that wait on thee be ashamed: let them be ashamed which transgress without cause.
> Shew me thy ways, O Lord; teach me thy paths.
> Lead me in thy truth, and teach me: for thou art the God of my salvation; on thee do I wait all the day.
> Remember, O Lord, thy tender mercies and thy loving kindnesses; for they have been ever of old.
> Remember not the sins of my youth, nor my transgressions: according to thy mercy remember thou me for thy goodness' sake, O Lord.
> Good and upright is the Lord: therefore will he teach sinners in the way.

The meek will he guide in judgment: and the meek will he teach his way.

All the paths of the Lord are mercy and truth unto such as keep his covenant and his testimonies.

For thy name's sake, O Lord, pardon mine iniquity; for it is great.

What man is he that feareth the Lord? him shall he teach in the way that he shall choose.

His soul shall dwell at ease; and his seed shall inherit the earth.

The secret of the Lord is with them that fear him; and he will shew them his covenant.

Mine eyes are ever toward the Lord; for he shall pluck my feet out of the net.

Turn thee unto me, and have mercy upon me; for I am desolate and afflicted.

The troubles of my heart are enlarged: O bring thou me out of my distresses.

Look upon mine affliction and my pain; and forgive all my sins.

Consider mine enemies; for they are many; and they hate me with cruel hatred.

O keep my soul, and deliver me: let me not be ashamed; for I put my trust in thee. (Psalm 25:1–20)

The images of that particular operation lingered in my mind longer than any other. My sleep was disturbed for months with transient, horrifying images of the desecration. I couldn't help them, neither could I stop them. Sleeping pills weren't particularly effective since I couldn't wake up from my nightmares under their influence.

I couldn't bear to share the event with my grandmother. But as always, she felt my pain and watched me suffer in silence. "Only God has the balm to heal certain pains in a man's soul," she said.

She watched me while she hosed the chicken cages early one morning. I had spent most of the night before reading. I could hear her tossing and turning in her bed. She didn't sleep much either.

"Abuela, why is Africa today as violent as it was five hundred years ago?" I asked, reflecting on my own question, unsure about whether I really wanted an answer. "I mean, these are all black people who look the same; they grew up just a few kilometers from each other and have lived for an eon next to each other. In fact, they don't remember when it all started." I piled up the questions. I was sure she wouldn't mind.

She passed me a long handled brush and stepped back a bit. She pointed here and there to a particular spot in the chicken pen like an orchestra conductor. I knew she was thinking so I scrubbed while I waited.

"They have no God. They have forgotten. Now they fabricate these stories to soothe themselves and find some comfort, but they're cut off from the real God," she said with sadness but conviction. "Because of it," she continued, "the devil has set himself in their midst. And war, my son, is his favorite weapon. To tear and to destroy, to cut down and to burn, that's his pastime," she said. Her voice filled with bitterness and sorrow, she spoke the words with pain.

She turned off the water and gestured to me to follow her inside the house. She poured some hot chocolate in a mug and brought it to me on the table. I hesitated. Food wasn't very attractive to me these days, but not eating would raise her concern. I took some timid bites at a slice of bread and sipped the beverage slowly.

"But they have lots of saints and gods that they sacrifice to and offer to, every day in some instances," I pointed out. "Surely some of it has to contain some truth."

"It's all garbage," she said rather harshly. "We're their descendants and here we are, slaves to the same garbage that our ancestors left five centuries ago in the old continent," she said, making a circular motion with her hand. "We may have changed the names a bit, the dialect has certainly changed, but we keep calling those 'saints' by the same names and killing animals and sacrifices and offerings the same way," she explained, as she tapped her finger on the table.

It was true. And what was worse, in order to appease the slave masters, the Criollos (island-born slaves) had brought the Catholic saints into the mix. They dressed the statue of each saint with African colors. Beneath the statue rested the stones, shells, irons, and colored beads of the African deity. Quite an innovation, but it was still the same.

Her voice went up a decibel. "Of course, these are gods you can bribe and cajole with food offerings, animals, or whatever else is available. And they, in turn, give you a green light to hate, malign, interfere, and even kill somebody else with their approval and support. Son," she said, holding one of my hands, "without God, the true God, men are free to pursue the vilest and basest desires of their hearts. Never mind that they have to kill a million or two in the process . . ." Her speech trailed off for a second. "It has happened before," she stated, opening her clear blue eyes a bit in emphasis.

She was right. I'd seen it, and there was nothing I could do. All I could hope for was that I wouldn't find myself in the middle of it any more than was absolutely necessary.

"The world is a continuous round of war and bloodshed," I said, almost in a murmur. "Do you think, Abuela, that Jesus Christ will come any time soon? I mean, some people say He may be already here." I said, my last statement quite tentative.

She smiled and pulled her battered Bible from the corner of the table where it lay.

> Behold, the Lord maketh the earth empty, and maketh it waste, and turneth it upside down, and scattereth abroad the inhabitants thereof.
>
> And it shall be, as with the people, so with the priest; as with the servant, so with his master; as with the maid, so with her mistress; as with the buyer, so with the seller; as with the lender, so with the borrower; as with the taker of usury, so with the giver of usury to him.
>
> The land shall be utterly emptied, and utterly spoiled: for the Lord hath spoken this word. (Isaiah 24:1–3)

I leaned over to read with her. It was Isaiah, again, where she seemed to be able to find most every answer.

"I think," she said, "that if the Lord had come we'd know." She laughed a bit, tapping the Bible's page. "Everybody would know. And He would come and heal all His people, comfort them, destroy all His enemies, subdue the whole earth, and conquer the devil and chain him for a thousand years, as the scripture says," exclaimed Grandma with excitement.

Her eyes glowed, but her voice was serious, almost a whisper. "But before that, son, the whole earth will know about Him. All people will come to know that He is the Son of God, that they nailed Him to a wooden cross for our sins, so that no more blood would be shed but His. And," she continued, "that we may find salvation and freedom from the spiritual captivity of the devil if we believe in Him . . ." Her speech trailed off.

She looked out the window, speaking softly now as if muttering to herself. She shook her head and looked down on the table while tapping softly. "But," she paused again. "We're left with faith in Him alone since there's no baptism. He took with Himself all his apostles and prophets."

I found myself treading swamp water now. I knew that Grandma didn't believe that the priests, at least the ones we knew, were actually priests and that the church in Cuba was actually a church sanctioned by God. *But some good must come from it*, I reasoned.

"Imagine I've done some horrible sin, Abuela," I offered. "If we must be baptized to get forgiveness of all our sins, but you say the baptism offered by Father Fumes is no good, what then? Isn't something better than nothing?" I asked.

I was avoiding being explicit but I wanted a straight answer. I needed it, especially in lieu of the pain and difficult events of the previous months in South Africa. That much I understood. You can't be forgiven just by asking. There must be a physical, public act of humility and repentance.

"Sin has consequences," Grandma always said. Thus a simple apology couldn't suffice. "The things of God may be sacred; they may appear secret, but just for the eyes of the wicked. He doesn't do anything in secret, but in plain sight His wonders are revealed," Grandma taught me

"Son, if you're found wanting according to the things of God, but not because of your lack of diligence, God will judge you according to what you knew and did. Just because somebody claims to do something in the name of God doesn't mean a whole lot," she said while flipping through the pages of her Bible.

> Not every one that saith unto me, Lord, Lord, shall enter into the kingdom of heaven; but he that doeth the will of my Father which is in heaven.
> Many will say to me in that day, Lord, Lord, have we not prophesied in thy name? and in thy name have cast out devils? and in thy name done many wonderful works?
> And then will I profess unto them, I never knew you: depart from me, ye that work iniquity. (Matthew 7:21–23)

"Son, these folks walk around with their big robes and their wooden crucifixes, and they love to be seen and revered. They stop on the street, so people may bow before them and kiss their rings," she said, her voice boiling with contempt now. This was a sensitive subject for her. "They ask for money to baptize children—innocent creatures of God who have no sin. The 'holy men' speak in Greek and Latin, move with pomp at the rotten pulpit, and before the altar they worship their own sin."

Her eyes were watering, her forehead was swollen with a bulging vein coming from the left side of her temple. Her voice was becoming deeper, and her words dropped out of her mouth as if they nauseated her. "They stay in their pestilent and dark buildings to hide their daily sins. But they can't hide from the Lord. He will discover their secrets for all mankind to see. He has reserved a place in the pit for those who won't repent."

Her face had transformed into a mask of disgust. Her eyes took on a fiery look that made my blood freeze. She took a deep breath, and then became aware of my bewilderment. Smiling timidly, she got up to get some water. She returned after a few minutes.

She sat down and smiled again, smoothing her old apron, and then she touched her frosty white hair. She looked at me again, and I recognized her usual soft and gentle stare. "In a nutshell, son," she said, both hands flat on the table, "you must seek repentance on your own. Now, be truthful, for the Lord knows absolutely everything in your heart and every thought that will come to your mind even before it does," she said. I nearly gasped at the thought, but she continued, "confess to Him and ask Him to heal your heart, to take away your pain and your sorrow. Plead for His merciful hand to lift the weight you carry, for it's more than you can bear. Then wait. You'll know when that's done. You will feel when the good Lord has granted you forgiveness."

I was shocked, and it probably showed in my face, for she came around the table and hugged me for a long time. I felt needles behind my eyes and my breathing got heavier for a minute, but I held the tears in check and felt better.

She could see inside my soul, could sense my pain and sorrow. She could hear my restless sleep, and she always came to soothe me out of my nightmares. Details weren't needed. All she required was to be near me.

"We're missing one step, and it will remain missing until further notice: baptism," she announced factually and without hesitation.

I was going to offer my argument, but she lifted a finger. "As far as I'm concerned, there are two things required for baptism, son." She took a sip of her drink. "One, the man has to be commanded by God Himself to baptize people, and this can't be substituted by seminary, schools, robes, rosaries, trinkets, or any other kind of gadget or assumed mandate," she pointed out quite seriously. "Second, there has to be an order, a registry—in other words—a legitimate church of some kind put together by God Himself," she said. "Do you remember in the Bible when Saul, who later calls himself Paul, is going to Damascus? There he was on his high horse coming and going, killing people and putting them in prison for being Christians? Do you remember that part?" she asked.

I nodded in agreement. I'd read the passage in Acts chapter 9 before.

"Well, to make a long story short, Jesus appears to him, knocks him off the horse, scares the living daylights out of him, and leaves him half-deaf and blind for three days. After that, the Lord tells him to go into the city and look for one person that will heal him. This person is a servant of God, a Christian, and he heals Paul. Soon after, he also baptizes him."

"Right," I said, not quite following the line of reasoning.

"Son, the Lord already had a church going with prophets and apostles and all kinds of people. They were already commanded by Him to go and teach the gospel to everybody—to baptize and do miracles. Paul was a latecomer so he had to join the band, not make a new one," she said, accentuating her words.

"So, Abuela, isn't this baptism that we have now in our country a continuation of the same thing that was done a couple of thousand years ago?" I asked.

She shook her head. "No, son. All the apostles were dead and God didn't leave any instructions, as far as I know, to carry on." She drew an imaginary line on the table. "And these folks, the so-called priests," she slurred her words a bit for effect, "claim to have some kind of inheritance from the apostles, but I just don't buy it. For two thousand years they have killed millions, robbed, incarcerated, punished, and condemned the innocent, all in the name of Christ? I don't buy it—not a chance." She was serious now.

This was her reasoning hat she was wearing now. Not much emotion—but pure intuition and years of reading the Bible. She was convinced that, although some portions of the Bible remained sort of a puzzle to her, she could read others very well. She was able to glean enough to develop a strong judgment about this and a host of other issues.

"When I'm convinced that there are men on the earth commanded by God Himself to baptize, then I'll consent to do so gladly. I've waited a lifetime for that day and I can wait until I die," she said, a twinkling of a smile now dancing on her lips. "And I can always tell the Lord if I was wrong that I'm stubborn as a mule and that I didn't see the writing on the wall—if it was there," she said, half laughing. I could tell she was serious about this, though. Her laugh had the ring of truth to it.

"I keep a prayer in my heart day and night, son. I let the past be, and worry about how God wants me to live today. In time, after much suffering, God lets me know that I must go on living and that a change of heart and a new way is sufficient for now, since I can't have baptism," she said. She was speaking more thoughtfully now—her pace slowing as if she were weighing each of word.

I believed her. I thought of the Psalms. I started a silent prayer in my mind or my heart—I wasn't really sure which. I got up from the table, kissed my grandma's forehead, and walked briskly out into the cloudy afternoon, the pinching of tears stirring behind my eyes again. Finally, by age twenty, some of the teachings of my grandma were beginning to take root. At last, I was gaining some clarity. The harsh realities of my life required the solace and comfort that only God could afford me. Suddenly, I felt true faith rooting deep in my heart.

"Oh God of my grandmother, my God—be merciful and forgiving. Please, restore my peace—let my heart rest. . . ."

I found solace and rest in those prayers. I found refuge for years to come. And I found the realization that indeed the God of my grandmother could ease the pain of my heavy heart.

GOD OF MY GRANDMOTHER, ARE YOU THERE?

The world was in shock. Mikhail Gorbachev had publicly announced "Perestroika." It represented a quantum shift in the political and ideological heading of the great Soviet Union. It was a radical swing in priorities and the intent of the super power sent shockwaves across the globe.

The world was changing. Years of theories, constructs, and assessments became worthless and obsolete within weeks. The true effects of this announcement didn't come to fruition until almost five years later when, in one night, the Berlin wall came crashing down before the astonished eyes of the whole world.

On our side of the world, the Iran-Contras affair turned up the heat in the United States' political arena. After years of tacit agreement with the official political agenda for the region, dissenting voices in Congress awoke to a situation that public opinion couldn't digest. The immediate impact was a 90 percent decrease in financial and logistical support to insurgents in Latin America.

So, the Soviets drew inward as their social and political universe imploded, and the Americans launched a witch-hunt that scared all the soldiers of fortune and unofficial operators from the region. With them went the purse that fed the civil war for thirty long years.

As expected, with the decrease in funding came a scarcity of goods, spare parts, food, and supplies on both sides. The conflict was never settled; the ideologies remain divorced from each other to this day, but the bloodshed was coming to an end. The cause of the forced settlement— simple economics, it seemed.

The Soviets had been involved in a bloody and impossible war in Afghanistan for close to a decade. They were demoralized, exhausted, broken, and bankrupt. They wanted to go home but were waiting for a dignified retreat. The Afghan mountains had become the Soviet's Vietnam.

The resources squeeze led to recurrent breakdowns in infrastructure, especially electronics and surveillance equipment. The sophisticated satellite-guided anti-aircraft batteries began to fail. The ground radar stations on the northern Nicaraguan border, which were critical for tracking southbound US air support to the insurgents inside Nicaragua, started to go down one by one.

A mission was put together in order to bring a group of Soviet specialists and some much needed supplies to repair the stations and to install less expensive, more flexible ground level radar to track movement of troops and vehicles inside Honduras and El Salvador going south into Nicaragua.

My unit was tasked with accompanying two Soviet "technicians" on a forty-mile, two-week maintenance expedition. Not a glamorous assignment, but still one of high priority since our side was becoming blind and deaf to the movement of the enemy in the northern Nicaraguan border.

The last portion of the mission included a quick insertion into Honduras. It was "a 36-hour round-trip gig" as the mission commander described it. It didn't sit well with me, since we were already low on supplies and ammunition. We also had a skirmish with a small paramilitary group a week earlier. The small group of enemy soldiers had been looking for a way around a flooded lagoon and walked into our advanced patrol. Neither they nor we had been poised for a long engagement, so we had allowed them a breach for them to continue. They weren't looking for a fight but stumbled into one. I guess we were all relieved when it was over. Still, four of our team members were now injured.

For the sake of speed and expediency, I divided the unit into two groups of about ten men each before our incursion into Honduras. The rear group served as a lookout, cared for the wounded, and acted as a relay for radio and satellite traffic from mission control. We needed to hold radio silence for more than two days while across the border.

A strong rainy season had changed the landscape. Existing trails had become impassable due to flooding and vegetation growth. Mud slides had destroyed small bridges and man-made passages in the jungle.

Our unit, and previously the ground listening station, had recorded telemetry from cameras, radio scanners, and ground-level radars installed in "enemy territory." Rain and nature had rendered most of them inoperable or lost. We were tasked with replacing, repairing, and recovering some of them.

We reached the objectives on schedule and conducted field repairs when possible. The "technicians" were miserable because of the overwhelming heat and humidity but did their best not to complain too much. In two days we were done, which was record time for the mission. We climbed a hill facing south and broke radio silence. I felt uneasy about it, since others might hear us. But those were the instructions.

At the appointed time, the communication specialist signaled that he had a link. I approached him with apprehension, though I didn't know why. A soft rain had started to fall earlier and clouds had moved in. The day had turned gray as far as the line in the horizon to the west. Maybe it was a bad omen, who knew?

"Control, this is Vector, we're looking good and en route to the rest point," I said, using my best non-descript Central American accent. It was a way to keep curious ears guessing about the source of the exchange.

"That has to be a record, Lieutenant. Standby for instructions," came the response.

A different voice came through the radio this time. "Excellent, Lieutenant."

My blood stream changed directions a second later. Whatever came next through the comm unit wasn't going to be good. My hand tensed around the handset.

"We have one more recovery point, Lieutenant," the voice said.

I dropped the handset, blood rushing to my temples. I could feel the air in my nostrils becoming hotter by the second and burning the back of my throat. I despised the voice and the man behind it. This was his mode of operation, and countless men had paid with their lives for his games through the years. If I'd ever been close to taking another life in cold blood it was when that man had stood before me a year or so prior, to "congratulate me for a successful operation." Never mind that three of my men had died in the process. That night when I received a medal for my "extraordinary valor," I imagined the subtle and creative ways in which he could die "accidentally." I thought I had enough internal support and political leverage to avoid a court martial. It would be a scandal I could survive, I believed.

The Major Veraz was a political appointee that cheated his way through the military academy, went through post after post a thousand miles away from any military action, and climbed the military echelon tree like a snake. He had no friends and only convenience allies because of his political connections. He had no regard for the men that had the misfortune of coming under his command, and his trophy wife was a disposable fun bag, as the joke went.

His wife was an old flirt. That was a vulnerable spot. I imagined I could pretend to have an affair with her so he could barge into my office in a jealous rage and "struggle for his gun." The press release, if there were going to be one, would read like this: "The aftermath—a regrettable accident—in which Major J. Veraz, a "distinguished" military officer lost his life." In Cuba, leaders die in combat, accidentally, or of a long illness. The scenario was predictable.

Three seconds later, I discarded the whole idea. He wasn't worth the bullet, much less the months of silly protocol inquiry about "the accident." Not even his father could stomach Veraz Jr., but the poor old man couldn't bring himself to put him out of his misery.

I listened motionlessly as the instructions came. My second officer took notes diligently. I was, on the other hand, mentally reviewing the details of my encounter with him upon my return. I was going to make sure that he never, ever had anything to do with me or any of the operations I was involved in.

After the transmission ended, I briefly discussed the details of the "detour" with one of the mission's specialists. The change of plans included moving back north-by-northeast, across into enemy territory. Since the enemy knew of our incursion, the chance that we'd encounter some enemy units was extremely high.

We doubled our pace but nature had her own schedule and plan. Torrential rain, and even more troublesome—long, intense lightning kept us from moving for two to three hours at a time. In the tropics, rain can be as pernicious as a virus. There's no respite—everything is wet for weeks at a time, including the body. It's not uncommon for fungus to grow in the most unimaginable places in and on one's body. Wounds won't heal, weapons and equipment will fail, all on account of the rain.

After three days of a painful and treacherous march in the jungle, we reached the recovery point. I decided we should split one more time in order to secure our extraction. Aerial intel showed no potential threat in the area. There was no evidence of large cohorts of men moving in the jungle or aircrafts, but just in case we proceeded with caution.

Two men accompanied me to the recovery point to retrieve the equipment. The rest proceeded to the extraction point about ten miles south to secure the LZ. My expectation was to join them by the end of the day. We took our leave from the larger group at daybreak with the rain pounding our heads. The sky was still dark with a faint gray in the east. I felt the same way after so many days without sunlight.

By midday we rested a little. After so many days of insipid field rations, my taste buds were numb and unable to register anything short of battery fluid. The difference between food and nourishment becomes ever so great after weeks of foil-packed Soviet military recipes. Yeah, it sustained me, but was it food? There's no data on long-term exposure to Soviet field rations, as far as I know. I derisively wondered why.

As we were getting ready to move on, one of the soldiers lost his footing on the soapy soil of the trail and slid almost sixty feet down a ravine. The fall was brutal, and the rescue effort took almost an hour. After close examination, it was evident that this soldier wouldn't walk again without assistance for quite some time. One of the ligaments in his right knee was severely torn and in need of surgical repair. The situation precipitated another slight change of plans.

I would continue on my own to retrieve the equipment while the other two soldiers waited in a secure location. My failure to return in six hours would signal that something went wrong and they'd radio for help. Breaking radio silence before that would compromise our ability to extract without attracting significant attention. It was settled.

Anger is, for most people, quite a difficult reaction to master. Grandma's views on the matter were radically different from just about everyone else I've asked, even to this day.

"Anger isn't an emotion, it's a reaction," she reminded me, to exhaustion. Her reasoning was that, regardless of the situation, we have choices in terms of how we react to it. So, in fact, an angry outburst was more or less either deliberate or a programmed response.

"More often than not, pain is what we feel," she said. "Sometimes even sadness. But of course, rage is more like: 'I'm about to take care of this' kind of a reaction. It brings action and energy to the front, which we feel is what we need to deal with the situation. But it doesn't have to be that way," she concluded.

She thought that letting our "real" feelings out was always more productive and healthier.

"Maybe not what people expect, but—" she'd comment.

I was never the angry type. But a flashing flame of red-hot anger was expected in certain circles within the Cuban military. It was a sort of evidence of strength and courage, and even a desired leadership trait. I had mixed emotions about this tradition but I delivered, occasionally, since it was expected of me.

That day I felt angry. It wasn't a runway display, nor was it macho bravado. It was a 'you stepped on my toes once more and you pushed me around for the last time' kind of anger. It was frustration, which couldn't find a target, at least not for another two days.

I made my way, spitting profanity and deadly curses at everyone I could remember or suspected at the Central Command who might be behind this sideshow. The rain in every physical cavity of my body, the heat, the insects attracted by the CO_2 transfer of my skin, and the ground that refused to hold my weight pushed me over the edge. I'd seen happier days.

What was so important about this piece of fixed monitoring equipment? Nothing, I screamed, abandoning caution and feeling overwhelmed by the deadly force of my anger. What do they know that I don't? It actually stopped working a few days ago, so it has become "a non-performing asset." It happened all the time; it was unavoidable.

I tried to subdue my wrath by reviewing the reasons why I was there. I looked at scraps and pieces of my beliefs, my conviction and ideals, my loyalties. I stopped and leaned on a tree, water sliding down through the cracked bark like a creek. I wasn't sure anymore about what to believe or how to feel. The longer I remained in the middle of this senseless war, in the midst of the carnage and destruction, the more distant and obscure my mission became.

I pressed on again, wiping the rain off my face with my forearm. The wind shifted, bringing the rain almost horizontally, completely blinding me. I froze in the middle of the trail. What was that smell? I felt it, just for a second, but I knew it was there. I sought the cover of the trees on the edge of the almost invisible trail and waited there. I wasn't sure for what, but I waited.

Was I wrong? Was I so distracted and deep in my present misery that I could no longer discern fear and apprehension from potential danger? Did a simple and accidental chemical reaction in the environment trigger my alert? It was certainly possible. I scanned the area—a futile exercise. Too much rain, not enough light, and my eyes were irritated and tired of battling both.

I slid down a small ravine to a thicket of pino ocotes, large pine trees that clustered at the bottom of the cliff on the edge of the gorge. It was a small valley, maybe two hundred yards across to the edge of a large grove of oak trees pushing against the hillside.

The smell of the resin from the pine trees flooded the ravine, softening my mood for a few minutes. It reminded me of home, the pines and meadows right behind the house. I wiped my face from the rain and refocused on the task. The wind battled furiously against the pine needles that fell to the ground around me. My eyes were fixed across the small clearing. The gear was set on a rock outcrop twenty yards away. To retrieve it, I had to cover the distance to the boulders, circle them, climb four feet off the ground, and pull it from the crevice where it lay. The only problem was that I'd be completely exposed and facing away from the tree line across the gorge. The thought made my stomach tighten a notch.

I waited. There was nothing, at least I could see nothing across the clearing into the tree line opposite my position. Still, there was "something there." I hesitated, being pounded by the rain and with no appealing choice.

I quietly cursed a few more times as I released my shoulder pack. Ninety pounds of assorted lifesaving or, death-causing tools fell softly to the soggy leaf bed. I clasped my weapon and broke into a soft jog to the massive rock formation in front of me. My eyes remained nailed to the trees across the valley.

I swung my weapon to my back to free both hands and rubbed them against each other. They were wet and wrinkled after so many hours of constant rain. I squeezed against the rocks in a soft but quick motion, circled the obstacle, stepped up, and reached inside the crevice. My fingers made contact with the slippery, cold surface of the camera. I pulled, and the array slid out without effort.

The next moment, as if in a dream, my head exploded, jerking my cervical spine upwards in a counter clockwise motion. And then there was silence. Nothing but the dark, bottomless, and insipid silence that accompanied the fall of my body to the muddy ground two feet below. It seemed like two miles.

The report of the weapon fired across the gorge registered in my traumatized brain a full two seconds later. It sounded far, like a distant echo of thunder. I laid face down, my mouth quickly filling with the unsavory mix of my own blood and the clay and grass of the flooded valley floor. I lay there, my brain in shock and unable to process any of the higher motor functions.

I could hear my own breathing, fast, labored, insufficient, with blood gurgling in my throat. After a few seconds, or minutes, the realization of my impending death sparked through my consciousness like lightning. I was dying. I lay there broken, unable to move for what seemed like a lifetime. I sobbed quietly, helplessly.

I lost all sense of time as I waited for the sniper to return. Occasionally they do. They come close to "confirm the kill"; they come for a souvenir. After all, he'd been hunting me for a few days. He never came, fearful perhaps of being caught in the open and alone by a larger enemy group. If he felt safe, he'd have watched the fallen prey for half an hour or so, observing for signs of life. He was convinced I was dead and I believed it myself. Most people have never truly and intentionally considered what happens to human beings when they know that their lives are certainly about to be over—especially if there's no prolonged illness or chronic condition. Popular media has attempted some romanticized interpretation of the pre-death experience. I haven't seen a convincing one.

Fear. Overwhelming and undiluted terror seizes you. The realization that, conclusively, in just seconds you'll stand face-to-face, eye-to-eye with the God of the universe is a frightening experience without equal. For me, the thought of being under the all-searching eye of God wasn't appealing—not with the life I'd led.

The fear and apprehension that gripped my entrails, the physical pain that accompanied that moment of despair had no parallel in my life's existence. I had no words, no explanations, and no excuses. I wasn't ready to die but I couldn't escape what seemed the unavoidable outcome of my injuries.

I sobbed, quietly at first, the pain and fear intensifying every minute with the decrease of my physical strength due to the loss of blood. I cried bitterly like never before or since.

I thought of my grandmother. What would she have me say? What could I say to her God? Life, mine at least, seemed distant, disconnected, and almost like a dream. It occurred to me then that I'd wasted my life. For all my accomplishments, scholastic and military, the painful fact remained that nothing, absolutely nothing I'd done at that point was of any real relevance. There was nothing in my life that had been noteworthy. There was nothing that could transcend time and impact others. In fact, away from a few trinkets stored at home and a few black and white photographs in serious peril of extinction, there was no evidence of my existence.

I'd spent my life and time on the earth in a useless and futile struggle. I'd exhausted every opportunity and hour "in the endless game of nothingness," like Grandma used to say.

I'd seen it before. A "political officer" went to the home of the fallen soldier early in the morning, then read or rehearsed a script about "patriotic duty, heroism, and invaluable service to the country" and so on. It was some meaningless rhetoric designed by someone who had no children, at least none that were in harm's way, none that had died in a dark and lonely jungle.

"What do I do, Abuela?" I asked myself, my voice barely audible.

I knew what I needed to do. The "how" was the dilemma. Speaking to God has always been a serious, very involved process. First, there was the issue of, what do you say to God that He doesn't already know? For me, there was always a certain amount of trepidation in approaching the God of the whole creation.

"Son, we don't deserve to be heard, but He does hear us," Grandma used to say. "Humility is the key. Be aware that we're unworthy of His attention and His care but He offers it to us nonetheless." I remembered. Amidst my tears, my fear and sorrow, I remembered.

I spat the blood and mud from my mouth and twisted my body painfully, slowly to face heaven. I cried some more. "God of my grandmother. I know You can hear, for my grandma says You can hear even the creatures that creep in the grass. I'm about to die and maybe I deserve to die; only You know that. I won't tell You of the things I've done wrong for You know them all, God. I pray to You today so that You may be merciful to me. I pray that You may forgive me of all my sins, that You may not look at them anymore, God."

The wind and rain abated for a few minutes. The treetops danced softly in the warm breeze as if unwilling to interrupt my prayer. Now and again I could see the stars in the sky in between the dark clouds rushing across.

"God of my grandmother, I know about You, and I believe in You because I've seen the things that You have done for my grandma. Even if You won't do anything for me, I believe in You and everything Grandma has taught me about You. She says You're a God of miracles and I believe. I know that You sent Your Son, Jesus Christ, to be killed for our sins. I pray today, God, that You will forgive me because of Your Son, for then He also died for my sins. Yours is my spirit and You will be my God. I pray to You today that though I have nothing left and am about to die, the sound of my voice remains here on the earth even though my spirit leaves. But I say this before I die so that You know that I believed in You before I saw You in Heaven, God.

"Take me then, God, and don't let me suffer any longer. Comfort my grandmother, God, for she is old and she loves me. Help her, God, that she may be able to bear my death and live until You take her to heaven that I may see her again. Forgive me, God. Forgive me, God."

I wept again, now however, with a tingling in the pit of my stomach. I felt almost happy. I'd made my peace and acknowledged before God the insignificance of my existence. I felt complete. I was now willing to surrender to His will and die.

The rain returned but not the wind. It fell thin and soft, warm and quiet over the already saturated valley floor. I listened and lost myself in memories of distant laughter and children's play. I remembered Grandma's warm and aromatic kitchen, the rumor of the seashore, and the wind chime made out of seashells hanging in the patio window.

Inconsequential memories, perhaps, but those were the only meaningful things in my life, I realized. The long talks over the dinner table, the silent moments of quiet reflection while digging about in the small vegetable garden, those were my treasures. Absorbed in those and many other scattered memories, I slipped into unconsciousness.

"Not yet." I heard it inside my rattled brain with astonishing clarity. No cymbal, no trump, no earth-shattering tremor, yet the quiet and simple phrase startled and surprised me at the same time.

I was in shock due to the loss of blood and my rattled brain had but a spark or electrical impulse barely enough to keep my body alive. The magnitude of the event, the realization that I had been a witness and a recipient of a true miracle and how this event would transform my life would come days later.

I wiggled my soggy toes inside my boots and wiped the blood from my face. The pain on the side of my face was gone, replaced now by a strong pressure over my right eye. I touched my head and the tactile experience was horrific. I could feel the mangled mass of bone and tissue loose on the side of my face.

I rolled over and sat on the swamp underneath me. I could see the outline of my surroundings although there was no moon. I stood and stumbled to the location where I'd left my pack. I searched mechanically for the emergency supplies in order to dress my head wound. After some primitive triage and a shot of wide spectrum antibiotic in my arm, I rummaged through my pack for something to eat. The usual protein mush tasted slightly better that night.

As I quenched my thirst with chemically treated jungle sludge, I meditated about my options. Four hours had elapsed since my close encounter with the "pale rider." Soon, members of my team could assume that I was wounded or worse. Their mission was to extract and then look for me. That could take another two days. I had to get moving.

The pack was heavier than I could carry under my current conditions. I dropped most of its contents and got ready. I opened a small field map under the dim light of a multipurpose magnifying glass. I couldn't wait for daybreak. That could bring more people to the zone, and I was alone. I had to risk making my way to the coast.

Moving in the jungle at nighttime is no easy feat. Sustained rain, mud slides, fallen trees, and unstable ground just about make it impossible, but I had to try. I walked almost by inertia. No rush, no concern, just the primal, pre-programmed drive to reach the geographical point recorded in my brain—what was left of it.

I walked for six hours with a coppery mix of rain and blood in my mouth and an unbearable pressure of my cephalic mass pushing through the bandages. I had to get out of the jungle. Perhaps the injury wasn't fatal, but infection could make it so. I reached the coastline before daylight. I opened my communication equipment and punched in the codes.

The female voice that came through the comm link was coarse, cold, disengaged. "Initial transmission incomplete, please authenticate again," she said: all protocol, no love. I needed love that night, at least a little.

My brain's shot, I lost half my weight in blood, I don't even remember my name, and they want me to repeat the codes? Wait until I get back, you heartless witch.

I repeated the codes.

"Welcome from the dead, traveler," a familiar voice replied this time. I felt a bit better. It was the voice of Commander Montes.

"Commander, I'm broken, repeat, I'm broken," I said trying to sound casual and just informative rather than alarming.

"How bad, Lieutenant?" he asked.

"Very bad, Commander. But I can wait—a few minutes until I stop breathing," I said. Only I thought it was actually humorous.

"Copy, Lieutenant. There's a grasshopper in the neighborhood and it's being detoured to find you. Standby."

I was too exhausted to reply. The next thing I remember was the noise of the chopper shaking me out of my stupor. The navigation light flashed over the dark, still ocean water. I switched on my dark light and the chopper pitched its nose high and hovered. The medic jumped out of the craft. As he approached, his eyes grew bigger by the second, as if they were ready to pop out of the sockets.

"Don't worry," I said. "It looks worse than it actually is."

He ripped my sleeve and filled my veins with morphine. Now, that stuff was demonically good. I made a mental note not to try that juice again, even if I was dying. I woke up a week later at a hospital back on the Island, hoses coming out of every orifice in my body and a symphony of monitors, bells, and whistles serenading me in the hospital room.

The neurosurgeon approached me slowly. He was a short, dark-skinned man, too young to know so much about people's heads. He opened his eyes a little as he came closer, medical chart in hand.

"Lieutenant," he said. "I've seen plenty of dead people. You were plenty dead," he concluded, trying to stress the point. "Somebody sure likes you up there."

I winked with my left eye, my only usable eye for the moment. The plastic feeding tube was burning my throat. I tried signaling with my hands to disconnect me from the machinery attached to my body and he got my message. He turned off the monitor orchestra and put on some surgical gloves. He pulled out the IV lines from one of my arms and my leg.

"Now, this is going to feel weird a little, but it won't kill you," the doctor announced just a second before he pulled the feeding tube from the deepest recesses of my digestive system. It was weird, all right. A spastic reflex overwhelmed me but no vomit came. They had been feeding me liquids for a week. My stomach was completely empty.

A few hours later, the nurses helped me up from the bed. Nothing could have prepared me for the shock of the first glance at myself after the injury. My head, what was visible, was obviously swollen and misshapen. I had a scar from ear to ear, and stitches like a baseball. My right eye and orbital socket were enlarged to an unnatural size, my eye bulging behind the blackened eyelid. Most of my head was covered in white bandages. My romantic life was over, I thought. Images of the hunchback of Notre Dame flashed before my eyes.

I spent three long months reading, writing, and sleeping in the twentieth floor of my "hosp-tel", as I came to describe my living arrangement during recovery. It had a view to kill for, overlooking the waterfront and the Habana Bay. I had a steady stream of visitors most afternoons: friends, neighbors, colleagues, passersby. In summary, I was a local celebrity. The wound was indeed gruesome.

After a month, the shock and pain of the injury were gone. I started to feel restless, physically and emotionally. I'd run out of books to read and the nurses bored me to death with their complaints. "Too much work, not enough money, too little rest, not enough time to find somebody to marry," one of them said rather frequently.

I started walking up and down the stairs as a way to exercise. A month later, the physician caught me running in the dark in the stairwell. He prescribed some sleep aid and forbade me to jog. I just about checked myself out of the hospital the day after.

Recovery at home was a bit more pleasant. I had, once more, access to all my familiar things. Physically, "normal" seemed to be an attainable goal. The "alien-shaped" head resized to quasi-human, including my right eye. More importantly, my friends didn't seem disturbed by the sight of the injury, especially my female friends. That was certainly a relief.

Going back home also meant that I had to talk to my grandmother about what happened. Some kind of long, drawn out, non-specific explanation was necessary. Not that she demanded one, but it was an inescapable fact: I had to offer something. Otherwise, how could I stand before her, half my scalp gone and an acrylic cap propping up my cranial box. Top that with stitches from ear to ear and a goldfish inspired right eye.

Grandma cared for me in her customary selfless fashion. It was confident care, not overindulgent, not an ounce of concern, no overbearing attention. Yes, I was injured, I was still wearing my head bandages around my skull and I was in no condition for a photo opportunity with GQ magazine. But there was no other visible change deserving extra attention. She acted accordingly.

I walked around the house behind her, talking while she did chores. I leaned against the fence in the back garden while she dug about. I followed her for days, unsure about how to approach the subject. The story, as far as I was concerned, had all kinds of implications. Beyond that, it was the most vulnerable moment of my life and an experience as personal as none other I'd lived until then.

The late afternoon light permeated the faded curtain high on the doorway skylight. A short but intense rain shower had swept across the hillside, bringing us the smell of the fruit trees beyond. You could always tell when the mameyes were ready. The blood-red colored fruit was everyone's favorite. The aroma was soft, almost sensual.

I could hear Grandma talking to somebody in the kitchen about some non-descript illness somebody was suffering from. I saw Leonor, our next-door neighbor, exit through one of the patio doors as I walked slowly to the archway that separated the kitchen from the dining room. I leaned against the wall and looked at Grandma tapping the counter and grabbing a small bottle. She was almost blind but she was able to find every single spice bottle, pot, pan, and whatever else she had in that ancient kitchen. Moving anything and leaving it out of place was punishable by starvation and banishment from the kitchen. No snacks for a week. Memory and precision were her allies and disrupting that system was frustrating to her.

"Abuela . . . I've been meaning to talk to you . . . about what happened," I said, trampling over my own words. I felt my breathing get a bit heavier. "Do you want to know what happened to me out there?" I asked, not completely sure if I wanted her response.

"I figured you'd tell me when you felt it was right," she said without turning, sprinkling some of her secret herbs into a boiling pot. Both my tactile and olfactory senses had been impaired due to the injury. I couldn't smell, nor could I feel very well with my left hand.

She pulled a jar with fruit preserves out of the refrigerator and put it on top of the dinner table. She brought a paper bag with toasted bread and a knife. I joined her at the table, almost on autopilot. My response to sweets was almost ritualistic, wired into my brain.

"There's no easy way to say this, Abuela," I said avoiding her gaze. She waited.

Skipping the most gruesome details, I proceeded to describe the incident. "Abuela, I was dying. I knew I was dying. And there was nothing I could to help myself," I said softly, trying to hold back my tears. Until then, I'd spoken about it only to one other person, Commander Montes. The experience was cathartic, almost therapeutic. She listened without interruption and almost with no visible reaction but attentive to every word. She waited until I was finished.

"So, what do you think, Abuela?" I asked.

"What do you think happened, Son?" she asked in response, her blue eyes scrutinizing me.

I thought for a second, biting distractedly on my toast/fruit preserve combination. I'd asked myself the same question hundreds of times. What happened to me out there in the jungle? What was that all about? What was I to make of it? Is there a meaning hidden in the pain and the blood and the agony that I endured for so many hours? I failed to grasp it, miserably.

"I don't know, Abuela," I said, looking for a vague way out of the conversation. "I mean, I know that God does everything He does for a reason, but—" I let the sentence trail off. She waited. "I haven't been a bad, bad person. But I haven't been good either, I mean not as good as I should have been, at least in the eyes of God," I reasoned aloud. "Truth be told, I didn't deserve to live, Abuela. I was dying out there and I knew it," I said, feeling my throat tighten a little.

"So—," she said finally, after what seemed a cosmic wait. "What was different, beyond your fear of dying?" she asked.

I thought for a long while, trying to summon the event, trying to recall the emotions I experienced.

"I asked God to forgive me," I said almost in a whisper, tears threatening to burst free from my eyes.

It dawned on me that, during my ordeal, I was convinced of my impending death. I'd lost all hope of surviving and at the critical moment I'd chosen to ask God for forgiveness rather than for Him to save my life.

"I thought that's what you do when you're about to die," I said.

"But did you ask Him because you're supposed to? Or because you wanted to, you needed to, and you knew it was the only thing you could do?" she asked in a flurry of words, as if she wanted me to explore every angle.

I paused again. Grandma was speaking now as if the scene was familiar to her. I'd felt this way before but she'd never shared her very personal experiences.

"I had nothing else, Abuela," I said, my voice now trembling and tears in the corners of my eyes. "I was dying. I was there alone, in the dark. I knew that within a few minutes I'd have to stand before God," I said, a wave of emotion sweeping over and overwhelming me for a few minutes.

I sat quietly, tears falling on my chest. I made no effort to hide them. Grandma didn't move; her eyes squinted a little quizzically. She kept waiting.

"What is it about this God of yours, Abuela, that makes Him appear when you're broken down in a thousand pieces and about to die?" I asked. "I mean, if all He wanted was to shame me and bring me to my knees, He can do that any time He wants, right?" I said, my voice inching up a decibel or two.

Her mouth arched a fraction of an inch in what seemed a poorly timed attempt to a smile. She spread more orange-hued preserve on a piece of toast and offered it to me. She was lining up her thoughts.

"Well, son, the issue here is that beyond what actually happened to you, the rest was a heart-to-heart with God Himself. It was you who called on Him. This is the way it always happens," she said, her smile almost visible. The angle of the conversation pleased her. I thought about her words for a second until she spoke again.

"This is basic, son. We all have the thumbprint of God inside. It's almost by instinct to seek Him when we know we've run out of options. He is the beginning and end of all roads," she said, gesturing with both hands. "I'll spare you the sermon, son," she said, placing her hand over my arm. "This experience will change you forever. Now you know of the awesome power of our great God. Now you know that He is there, on the edge of the universe and right here with us. Now you know that He hears yours and everybody else's prayers—and that He answers them. Now you know, Son, that life is His to give and to take away; that He spared you for a reason known only to Him, for now. Now you know that faith is about what you know to be true, even when it seems impossible, because for Him there's no such thing as impossible. People call them miracles, I call them His handiwork. The earth is filled with them from east to west. And now that you have heard His voice in your mind and felt His Spirit in your heart, don't you forget it. Don't you dare forget it," she said, her voice gaining momentum and intensity. "Son, His is the forgiveness, mercy, and the peace that you felt, and that's the foundation of faith. Don't let it die, don't forget that day. Let it be the day that the seed of knowledge and your acquaintance with Him began. The day will come when you'll learn and realize that by trusting in Him you can do all things, you can overcome all things. You'll see how in His name rests all the power to face whatever this life will bring before you."

Her words came in a barrage with such intensity as I've never seen or heard before. Her eyes were lit with a strange fire that had taken a life of its own. This wasn't just good advice, nor was it a suggestion for good living. This was a statement of fact, a clear and explicit declaration of her faith and undeviating belief in her God.

We spoke about many things that day—about how the apostles walked the earth with great power in words and deeds. We spoke about the future, the end of days, the Resurrection, about worshiping God, and about the possibility of other people scattered around the earth who felt the same way she did. Sometime after that afternoon, she spoke words that I later described as almost prophetic.

"I know, son, that God listens to all people of faith wherever they assemble themselves or wherever they seek Him. We find ourselves in a dark and dreary country. People that offend and profane the name of God daily surround us. But I've worshiped Him according to my faith and with the knowledge He has given me from the pages of the Bible. I have peace in my heart and I know that He will bless me in the life after this as He has blessed me in this one," she said. A long pause followed as she gathered the bread crumbs distractedly.

"You," she said. "Things will be different for you, son," she added, smiling softly. "One day you'll find the church that will fill your heart. You'll come to know God in a more perfect way than I could. And come to understand and discover much of His mysteries upon the earth," she said, still smiling.

With one soft gesture she placed her fingers over my mouth to muffle the question rising from every corner of my badly bruised brain. "One day . . ." she concluded with a broad smile.

PART THREE
MY NEWFOUND FAITH

A Change of Scenery

Recovery was a long process. I progressed well physically and felt stronger with every passing day. The emotional aftermath of the episode lingered months after the scars were no longer visible.

I could hold a grudge for a long time. I actually prided myself on that fact. I could recall the most insignificant details about an otherwise not-so-significant argument, insensitive comment, or, according to my definition, an unpleasant event.

The circumstances that led to my life-threatening experience were of the sort that demanded a payment in kind, to say the least. I had chips to cash in and stowed them in a safe place until I could collect on them. Secondhand information circulated on a bet about how long a certain person—that would be Major Veraz, aka The Snake—could live before he had a so-called accident. Of course, his accident would be on account of what had happened to me.

I decided to wait. I reported for duty reassignment a full three months after getting home. The meeting with my commanding officer was cordial, but the tension under the surface was as thick as the wall of a bank vault.

It was a known fact that politics kill people. In my case in particular, a lot of people got hurt. It shouldn't have happened. But because of the nature of the military organization, the operating ideological dogmas, and the unspoken rules, nothing happened—no court martial or military review tribunal, as they called the mockery of the brass gathering to examine the circumstances. They were often convened when the son of a high-ranking political and military crony landed in hot water. It was all a charade. In my case, it was all swept under the rug—or more like pushed discreetly out the window, as the saying goes.

I arrived at the gray-bluish building before 7 AM. A slender, tall female receptionist smiled at me from behind the old mahogany desk at the entrance. I tried to smile back, but I'm not sure it worked. She curbed back into a pleasant hello.

"You're early, Lieutenant," she said, handing my identification back after scanning it. Her light brown eyes sparkled, and her manner was pleasant and completely atypical of the anal-retentive type of person they usually hired for sentries and gatekeepers.

"I need to get to the archives before my meeting," I said, motioning toward the stairwell as I kept walking. She pointed at the open door, inviting me to proceed. I smiled back. I think I did better this time around, judging by her response.

The declassified archives, meaning those available to high-ranking intelligence officers and military analysts, were located on the third level below ground in the Interior Ministry building. Several doors and sentinels later, I entered the dark, musty room.

The floor was adorned with row after row of metal cabinets, with ladders and drawers fifteen feet high. A dozen or so information officers, all of them women, moved around with stacks of papers and files in their arms. Access to the actual cabinets wasn't permitted. A thick red line clearly demarked the so-called danger zone. The archives were the domains of these women, many of them close to retirement age, and all dressed in ill-fitting olive green uniforms, uncomfortable boots, and haircuts too short for my taste. One of them approached me, trying to appear diligent. It was barely 7 AM, and she looked exhausted, apathetic, and even sad. Some of their faces were known to me.

"Good morning, Lieutenant," she said, looking at my name on the ID hanging on my uniform jacket. "What are you looking for today?"

I opened my notebook and glanced at my notes for a few seconds. I made my request, trying to sound uninterested, burdened by the task. She stopped writing on her notepad as her eyes narrowed a fraction. She interlocked her fingers and rested her hands on her slightly bulging stomach.

"Lieutenant, I know who you are. Those files are flagged—but again, you know that. Would you like to see the files by yourself without the fuss?" she asked, slowing the sentence down to a word at a time. She was giving me a window of opportunity.

"Martha, don't worry" I answered, smiling a little. "It doesn't matter if somebody upstairs finds out I'm down here smelling around." She hesitated a few seconds and shrugged her shoulders. With that she turned and disappeared behind the metal cabinets.

I walked slowly to the dusty wall to my right. Old handwritten notes, stamped documents, and other relics from the early revolutionary period adorned the walls of the archives. Black and white pictures of Fidel, Camilo, Che, and a host of almost-forgotten former heroes of the revolution hung there, frozen in time.

"Lieutenant—." Her voice startled me, breaking my wandering. "Your documents are on table nine," she said, pointing to the far corner of the floor.

She walked in front of me until we reached the table. She winked and then was gone again. I sat down, opened my notebook, and opened the first file. I worked there for over an hour until one of the assistants passed me a handwritten note. They were ready for me upstairs. I got up and made my way across the tables to the exit. I waved good-bye to Martha. Her reply was almost imperceptible. She lifted two fingers, but her hand remained on the desk. My acquaintance, or better yet, my curiosity, had become a liability.

The tenth floor of the ministry was almost entirely populated by the Foreign Operations Bureau. Nothing was there but the well-connected, multilingual, multi-national staffers. It was the refuge of the foreign-born sons and daughters of military personnel and political officers—those who never saw the blood of those they sent to bleed.

It was also the brain of the foreign operations division. All the intelligence reports from all over the relevant world were analyzed and collated there. An impact briefing was put together daily and spoon fed to the principals at the top of the food chain before breakfast every day. Action initiatives were drafted from those reports in order to influence operational environments wherever in the world the government or the block of allied nations (for example, the Warsaw Pact) had interests.

I sat in a spacious conference room for five or six minutes until the door opened. An attractive female officer, wearing a uniform skirt that probably violated every dress and conduct statute in the military code, stood at the door.

"Can I bring you some orange juice, Lieutenant?" Her honey-thick voice dripped from her lips.

I swallowed air before words came out of my mouth. "I'm fine," I choked. She disappeared again as I exhaled.

The three senior officers, one of them my friend Montes, trailed each other, gathering around me at the corner of the table. After the trivial pleasantries, Lt. Colonel Montes spoke.

"How do you feel, son?" he asked. His tone was, as usual, transparent and without pretence.

"I'm as good as new, Sir," I responded. "Actually, Sir, now I'm a hero. Girls love wounded, half-dead heroes." I smiled. It was, after all, true.

He flipped through the pages of a thick dossier for several minutes, the paper's shuffling being the only sound in the room. The meeting was, in fact, a formality. Whatever he said next had been planned, discussed, and previously agreed upon some time before.

"It has been suggested, Lieutenant, that you come to work here with us at the Central American Group," he said without lifting his eyes from the file in front of him. I didn't answer. "You have lots of field experience in the region. In fact, Lieutenant, you have the skill and exposure that takes years to acquire. Some believe you'll be ready to head the section in two to three years." He paused this time, put the file down, placed both hands onto the table, and looked at me.

These weren't his words. This was a script, and he was doing rather well, but not well enough to convince me. There was a better chance of having snow in Habana than me taking a desk job, never mind the title.

"I think somebody is trying to force me into early retirement, Colonel," I said.

His laughter almost blew the glass windows out into the street below. The other two officers either didn't have a sense of humor, or missed the joke altogether. They looked baffled.

The people upstairs wanted to assess my level of political skill. Since I made it a point to stay away from the verbal fencing and social intrigue that permeated the walls of the building, very few people really knew anything about me.

"I understand if you don't want to take a job here at the CAG," he said softly. "I want to bring you into an ad hoc team we've assembled for a special operation. It will take six to eight weeks from start to finish, and then we'll find you a job. How about that?" he asked with a playful smile on his weathered, cracked face.

"Are you heading the team?" I asked, not sure I understood the offer.

"Yep, this is my baby," came his reply while he tapped on the table with a pen.

It seemed genuine and uncomplicated. "Sure, Colonel. What time tomorrow?"

"I'll send for you at 0600. We'll meet at the ranch," he said, gathering the folders from the table.

The other two officers briefly came to life and followed him into the hall.

That was the end of the meeting, and that was the last time I entered the inner sanctum of the Special Warfare Operations Command Center. The reasons were many. The facts: a geopolitical shift had altered the dynamics of the region.

In 1990 the last of the indictments for the Iran-Contra Affair were handed down after a four-year, quasi-political court procedure. Although all the convictions were later vacated on appeal or rescinded, the affair had a chilling impact in the Central American conflict. The resolve of the CIA to support insurgency in Nicaragua melted away.

As the Soviet empire collapsed amidst a never-before-seen political and economic meltdown, the political weather map in the region changed radically. No more Cuban–Soviet support for Nicaragua. The Contras in Nicaragua and every other group of ragtag insurgents suffered the same fate.

After eight weeks of training and planning for an operation in El Salvador that never materialized, I found myself in the house of Colonel Montes once more. Early on in my career I'd spent a lot of time with him. He was my mentor and friend. Operations and ongoing duty had prevented me from spending much time with him in the last few years, and I missed his company.

His house was located one hour west of the city in the quiet backwaters of the former yacht clubs and vacation homes of the elite in the pre-Castro era. The large but unassuming home was surrounded by fruit trees on all four sides, which not only provided shade most of the day, but also discretion. No evidence of "excess or access," as the items bought outside the country in foreign currency were referred to. Such items were the pinups and the trinkets that exemplified success in Cuban society. Of course, I'm referring to color TVs, VCRs, washers and dryers, large stereos and, without exception, Johnny Walker bottles refilled with colored water.

His standard government-issued personal car rested at the side of the house. The box-shaped, Soviet-made LADA was tucked away behind a nylon curtain. A variety of garments on a flax cord flapped loosely in the wind. The sweet aroma of fruit preserves ran through the house. The nearest home, which wasn't visible from the perimeter fence, was half a block away. Another high-ranking government official called the domicile home. Such were the perks of loyalty and obedience.

We slowly walked among the low branches of the mango trees. "I'm getting old, son," Montes said, his eyes lost on some distant point along the hills in the background. It was disconcerting for me to hear his faltering tone.

"The world is changing, and we have to change as well. But change into what?" he asked. He took a sip of his iced fruit juice and crossed his arms at chest level, still holding the glass.

"I mean, all I know is how to make war. We've prided ourselves in being able to bring war to the enemy's doorstep. And now there's no enemy!" he exclaimed, opening his arms wide, juice sloshing a little onto the ground.

He was still coping with the frustration of his clandestine operation being cancelled. Beyond that, at some level he was sensing that his career was in its final chapters. The world had changed in an unforeseeable way, casting a whole generation of people and a world view into irrelevance.

Not that the hostilities in Central America had ceased. The conflict became unsustainable for both sides. On the one hand, the Soviets were exhausted, financially and politically, after a ten-year incursion into Afghanistan. The threat of nuclear war now seemed more like a childish ghost story.

The billions of dollars spent building up a "mutual annihilation" war machine had corroded the already faulty foundation of the Soviet Union. Soldiers were going hungry and cold in four continents, on land and at sea. In the jungles of Central America, a civil war closer to a tribal feud than to an ideological struggle was, at the time, the least of their concerns. Aid to the Nicaraguan government via Cuban intelligence had all but stopped that year.

"They're afraid you're going to hurt the son of the swamp meister," he said, patting me on my shoulder while he snorted his traditionally loud, colorful laughter.

He was referring to The Snake of Major Veraz at the command post the day of my fateful encounter with the sniper's unfriendly bullet in the jungle. I smiled just a little in quiet satisfaction. So, they were afraid of my "measured response," as Montes had described the lingo of the unit's psychologist. This was better than actual injury; the uncertainty of when and what I was going to do with him for playing god with other people's lives.

"Good," I said emphatically. "Let them hold their breath for a while. I heard the miniature captain—as Major Veraz was also nicknamed—had diarrhea the other day when I went into the office." I was trying not to laugh.

"Well, son, the problem is that they want you out of circulation. They're trying to bury you somewhere out of sight for a while," Montes said in a more serious tone.

This was a high stakes game of survival, and political influence peddling of the worst kind. In a country where the ruling class came to power under the banner of equality, fairness, brotherhood, and justice, such situations turned my stomach inside out. The Snake got people hurt and killed in his incompetence, and now he was not only trying to cover it up, but he was also trying to dispose of the living evidence of his negligent disregard for the lives of others.

"Montes, if they try to tuck me away in some training farm in the mountains to kill my career or break my resolve . . ." I let the sentence drift. The certainty of my thoughts scared me.

Injuries can turn an otherwise normal and balanced human being into an unrestrained beast. The urge to assign blame and fault, the drive to make somebody pay for the pain is almost irresistible. The anger crawls from the bellows of hell to consume your soul day and night. The fantasies about what and how long the offending party will suffer can be quite elaborate.

"I swear, Montes, I'll put him a wheelchair for the rest of his life." I could feel my heart doubling its pace. My fists clenched instinctively as I tried to push the thought away. I had to find a way to let go of these dark thoughts. "Vengeance is God's domain, son," Grandma said often.

Montes said, "We're soldiers and puppets to an insane master and the politicians next to him are the corrupt casting agents of the play. Let it go. Let's find a way to do what we do and stay off their radar." He squeezed my shoulders as he steered me into the house for dinner.

His wife, Miriam, was a slender, polite, highly intelligent woman. She seemed much younger than she was, especially since they had children my age. Her hazel brown eyes were restless, scrutinizing every frame of the scene before her. There was a precision about her, an economy of movement and gesture that seemed calculated. She wore no make up. Her shoulder-length black hair was tied at her neck, and she wore a simple blue dress. The quality of her movement reminded me of felines, the hunters.

She was always polite, courteous, and accommodating, but never intrusive. It seemed she knew instinctively when to come, when to leave, and when to reappear again. Montes and Miriam looked at each other with confidence. There was definitely a subtle exchange between them, but it seemed fluid—no threat, no imposition—just a natural understanding of what they each needed. This kind of synergy was simply unimaginable to me.

The table was set for just the two of us. We spoke little during the meal. Some casual conversation about fishing and repairing an old boat diverted our attention. He seemed preoccupied and I was the source of it.

We walked outside again into the gentle, late-afternoon sun. The wind swept through the trees softly.

Montes thought for a few more minutes and broke the silence again. "I've arranged for you to go to Europe for a while, son," he said without looking at me. He sipped from his lemonade glass slowly.

I was expecting something of the sort. Now, Europe was way out of the neighborhood and certainly light years away from my former field of operations. I calculated my response for a minute or so.

"Is it that bad?" I asked in a rhetorical fashion. Of course it was. They were terrified of me, of the fuss I could make, and the careers I could ruin.

"You have friends in high places, son," Montes replied, smiling coyly now. "Not only God likes you, but some earthly people also seem to be fond of you—me included," he remarked.

"Montes, I hope the price of appeasing their fears wasn't too steep," I said as sadness swept over me.

I could only imagine him going to battle for me in the snake pit to preserve my future in the service. He may have jeopardized his own future in the process. He had great survival instincts but even greater integrity. There were things that I knew he wasn't willing to do. I hoped it didn't get to that point.

"Don't worry about me, son. I've gone as far as I can, and now that the war is over, I'm gonna find me a shady tree and rest a little. Maybe

I'll take Miriam to visit her folks up in the mountains next year," he said, almost with contentment.

"You know, I found her out there in the mountains in Canasi. She was fourteen and the most beautiful girl I'd ever seen." His eyes flashed in remembrance. "It's been twenty years since the last time we went that way. Her folks are about to die. We have to get there soon, and next year seems to me as good as any other."

His eyes held onto the skyline in the distance. There he was, a warrior if I've ever seen one. He was a man with no fear of mortal men, proven under some of the most grueling and heart-wrenching circumstances, and he was now worried about me and my future. That was more than I had a right to expect. He'd chosen his last battle, and it was for me.

My eyes burned. "So what happens next?" I asked with hesitation.

"Let's go in the back. Let me show you my experiments," he said, smiling.

He took a long sip of his lemonade and left the glass on a concrete block bench as we made our way to the far left corner of the patio, forty or fifty yards from the house. Once there, he pointed to a patch of carefully tended grounds where extraordinarily large tomatoes rested on the soft, red soil.

"Now, this is something, Montes. Where did you get these?" I asked, bewildered.

"My daughter, Sara. She is working at the Biotech Institute, and she got me some stems. I grafted them to my house tomatoes and—ta-da," he exclaimed in theatrical fashion.

I laughed as well. Gardening was his secret passion, his balancing act, and his stress-relief therapy. After returning from operations, I found him on his knees digging in the dirt, day after day.

"Son, listen very carefully and don't interrupt. I want you take this assignment in Europe. There will be an eleven-month tour and a scheduled rotation back to the home base. Come back with the last group. On the layover in the third country, get off the plane and don't look back. We'll never talk about this again. And tonight is the last time we will see each other."

He took a step across the rows of tomatoes in an attempt to inspect some of them. My tears flowed unrestrained. I walked slowly to the edge of the vine-covered fence and rested against it for a few minutes, my face turned away from my friend. It was a bitter good-bye, quiet and unceremonious.

We walked back to the house in silence, not for lack of words but to avoid the pain of pronouncing them. A million memories raced through my mind in those few precious minutes. The weight of the future was unbearable. I pushed it out of my mind, for at least a while, so that I might stay in the here and now. I searched in vain for something meaningful to say, but silence descended upon us instead.

He stopped at the threshold of the kitchen door and turned. There, in the dark, he embraced me and I saw his tears. I was, after all, the son that he found along the way. I always sensed I was in the presence of the father I never had and that I once needed. The shadows of the spring evening were the only witnesses to this quiet but personally significant departure.

He patted me on the back what seemed to be a thousand times, and then he went into the house, the sound of the hinges betraying the solemnity of the moment. I stood listening to the wind rattle the branches of the fruit trees. I circled around the house quietly and slipped through the wood stakes of the fence. I resisted looking back.

The weeks following this surprising and, to a certain extent, unexpected farewell were fraught with internal and emotional turmoil. Montes had placed before me a choice that I hadn't contemplated before, not even in my wildest dreams. The idea of leaving my country and my family behind had simply never occurred to me. Besides, as far as I was concerned, the places I'd seen when it came to foreign countries didn't appeal to me in the least. Central America wasn't a place to which you plan on traveling, but rather a place from which you try to escape.

Intellectually, at least, Montes was right. The world had changed on us while we were busy trying to keep the one we had from being annihilated. Former enemies were now friends, and the age-old animosity and enmity between East and West were now fading into history at a neck-breaking speed. Ideals like country and revolution were becoming increasingly irrelevant and less frequently invoked, especially in the sphere of influence of our Soviet comrades.

The collapse of the central government in Moscow created a political vacuum that wasn't lost to the enterprising breed. Military bases in the fringe north of the former Soviet Union found themselves cut off from the central command. Without food, salaries, or direction, they turned to the West for sustenance. After all, they were sitting on a weapons stockpile worth billions, which of course, found its way into the world bazaar at an alarming speed.

Highly trained operatives made their way into Western Europe and melted into the influx of new immigrants. With substantial expertise and contacts, it wasn't difficult to access the employment market in activities that were marginally legal. Industrial espionage, blackmail, offshore financial services, and private security were only a few of the activities appealing to the newly displaced former intelligence and military specialists from the dismembered Soviet Union.

I struggled day and night in silence about my future plans. Not being able to tell my grandmother generated significant anxiety and a profound sense of despair. The thought that I may never see her again was heartwrenching. I couldn't rationalize that fact.

I shared with her the news of my future assignment. She seemed content that I was going to experience a change of scenery. The idea of me having a smart job instead of one where I was being shot at from nine to five was attractive to her.

I walked behind her, holding a basket of wet clothing in my arms. The sun, bright and high in the sky, forced my eyes into an unnatural facial gesture that reminded me of my Chinese ancestors. Saturday was laundry day. With the passage of time it became more difficult for her to navigate the large patio with several pounds of wet clothing in tow. I waited around to help her with this small task.

I tried to conceal my internal struggles regarding the future. I avoided lengthy conversations about it, but some casual exchange was unavoidable on a daily basis.

"I hear it's very cold in those parts, son," she said while stretching herself to pin the freshly washed linen sheets on the line.

"Yes, Abuela, I have to go get winter clothing on Tuesday. The winter lasts four months there. I'm worried about not being able to see the sun for so many weeks," I said, trying to sound distracted.

"It may be a year or longer before you come back," she said, still flipping the laundry over the flax cord stretched across the backyard.

"Yes," I answered quietly. I was dying inside.

She stopped for a second, and after hanging a green and yellow tablecloth, she turned to me.

"So, you're not going to the jungle anymore?" she asked.

"No, Abuela, I don't think they want to send me out that way anymore," I responded, the weight of her eyes on me. It seemed as if gravity had just doubled its pull.

"It has nothing to do with you getting hurt. You're as strong as you've ever been," she reasoned out loud, dangerously approaching a subject I was determined to avoid. I didn't answer.

She took another large cloth and spread it over the line. She handled the fabric with dexterity and without effort. She was thinking.

"What did Montes say about . . . the change?" she said slowly.

"I think it was his idea, Abuela. He is trying to get me a break. You know—help me relax a little after so many years." It sounded unconvincing, even to me.

"It doesn't sound right, but what do I know?" she asked.

I thought about what to say for a few minutes. I couldn't be more explicit. I couldn't put her in danger that way, if by any chance my plan was exposed about not coming back after my tour of duty. It hurt, but I had little choice if I wanted to protect her.

"I think, Abuela, that some people feel I shouldn't go back to the jungle anymore," I said. It sounded more like an apology—unsteady and flaccid. With her back to me, she continued to stretch clothing over the line. I'd run out of excuses.

We walked slowly back to the steaming bucket of boiling suds. With a long wooden stick, one by one I hoisted some of the white linens into a porcelain bin. She silently stood across from me, her face hidden behind the rising steam.

"I think a career change will be good for me, Abuela. New environment, new people, and also new skills to learn," I said, shifting gears in tone and subject. I still didn't get any response.

She pointed to a bottle of chlorine on the shelf underneath the wash sink. I poured some in the plastic cap resting on top of the bottle and then poured it into the laundry. I stirred the contents of the bin again and let it rest. Grandma turned and started walking toward the house. I stood there a few more minutes with a clutter of thoughts loitering my mind.

The conversation was certainly not over, but I had very little to add that was safe. The smell of sudsy clothes was drifting through the air, and I could feel the breeze behind me push aside the steam. I slowly followed her into the house. She was sitting at the table, a mound of beans in front of her. She sifted through it quietly and unhurried, her gnarled fingers picking up bean after bean and transferring the edible ones into a small pile. I sat across from her and joined in almost mechanically.

"Are they trying to punish you for something you did or said?" she asked a few minutes later. She was still absorbed in her task. I couldn't see her eyes.

"Maybe," I said. "It's possible. I said some unkind things about the man that was at the command post the night I got hurt." I paused for a minute to gauge her reaction, but none was visible.

"Most people suspect it was spoken in anger but—" I said. I let it linger and waited.

"So they're afraid of you, then?" she asked.

I nodded softly. This old woman understood more than I gave her credit. Time went by, revolutions arrived, and people were born and died. Man was, as far as she was concerned, elemental.

She had said it before in so many words: "Men covet and they fear. Most realize they have wasted their lives when it's already too late to change anything." Basic but true. "And to get what they covet or to cover their fear, they'll do just about anything, even shedding some blood," she said, pointing to the Bible before her.

"Well, son, I hope this will serve as a lesson for you. People take threats seriously, even more so than those who issued them," she said, breathing finality. "Tell Montes thank you, from the bottom of my heart, for looking after you. I hope you will never forget what he has done. God will protect him and reward him when men won't. Do you understand?" she said, her eyes penetrating my silence.

It was done. She understood as if she'd been in the same room when my impending assignment had been discussed—different circumstances, but the same dynamics of fear and greed.

"Only time will tell, son, but beware. I don't know what you said, neither do I know if you should stand or take it back. But this I know, they'll do anything if they believe you're a danger to them. They'll try to destroy you or your future. Maybe both," she said, pointing at me emphatically. "Don't let them—don't. Do whatever you have to, but don't let them. Go with God, my son. Let Him guide everything you do from now on. Now you know Him, you have heard His voice, and you felt the strength of His hand. Don't be afraid of the future and where it takes you. After all, He has brought you this far. All will be well with you, son. Don't worry." And with that she was done. She swept the beans into an empty pot and went into the kitchen. We never spoke about it again.

I agonized for weeks afterward as I prepared for my trip that summer. I stayed home as much as I could. I sat quietly for hours searching, digging in the darkest bend of my memory for bits and pieces of forgotten events, forgotten stories, or memorable incidents. I wanted to remember. I wanted to hold onto her and a lifetime of experiences near her so that she was never forgotten.

For years to come, phrases, expressions, and her wisdom permeated every facet of my life and every corner of my experience. It seemed as if her presence remained connected to my consciousness. I sought to see through her eyes when I felt uncertain. In a thousand ways and even when I didn't intend to, I remembered her—always.

THOSE WE CALLED FRIENDS

The fourteen-hour flight to Moscow could easily be described as cruel and unusual punishment. The massive turbo prop plane was crammed with military attachés (a euphemism for political appointees), Soviet poli-bureau protégés, disgraced senior officers on the verge of retirement, and the like. There were also technical and political envoys from every corner of the Soviet empire on some kind of quasi-legitimate errand. The air inside the aircraft was a nauseating mixture of cigarette smoke, explosive alcoholic beverages, cheap flowery perfume, and rancid sweat.

A well-traveled stewardess with a ruddy, peeling nose offered me an object that looked like a sandwich. I was used to taking carefully calculated risks, but eating it would have been suicidal—plain and simple. I smiled and politely declined. She smiled back, uncovering teeth that had seen better years.

A group of young cadets clustered together in the back of the plane. It was their first trip abroad and they were brimming with excitement and anticipation. Their ultimate destination was the Institute of Science and Technology in Baku, a barren peninsula exposed to the fury of the Caspian Sea. The gale force winds in winter are legendary. They had no idea what was waiting for them. I didn't spoil their enthusiasm.

My schedule took me to Kiev for a month of tundra infantry training. Later, I traveled south to Odessa on the Black Sea for another month-long training stint with the *reydoviki* or special forces, an exhaustively trained group of country boys from the backwaters of the Soviet expanse, emotionally in comas and hormone-driven. It made for a very dangerous pack of wolves.

The training was completed after a three-week course in Arctic training and underwater salvage operations. That experience proved to be the most difficult in my entire—albeit brief—military career. Hours of exposure to subzero water temperature pushed the limits of my physical and mental endurance beyond unthinkable thresholds. I'd never imagined that one could be so cold for so long and live to tell the story.

One of the exercises involved a simulation in which a submarine suffered a catastrophic mechanical failure at two hundred feet under the ice cap. We were tasked with reaching the submarine, assessing the integrity of the haul and the strategic weapons systems, ascending to the surface again, and preparing a salvage trench to bring the sub up to the surface.

After hours of grueling underwater work, and regardless of the protective gear, the freezing temperatures begin to take a toll on a body's ability to cope with the environment. Hypothermia is often called the silent killer. Respiration, pulse, and one's ability to think slows down until one is barely aware of their surroundings. The body is so absorbed in preserving vital functions that even memory and recall are compromised. It's not uncommon for a diver not to be able to say his name when asked if he is suffering from hypothermia.

Some twelve weeks later it was clear to me why my ancestors chose to settle down in Africa. The Nordic countries became, in time, a distant memory for me, but I made a mental note to avoid the neighborhood altogether whenever possible. My genetic makeup was ill-equipped to handle that landscape.

After a few more weeks of typical bureaucratic limbo, I found myself making my way into East Germany. Summer in Eastern Europe is quite short. Transitions from one season to another can be violent, sudden, and with little warning. Beyond the beautiful foliage changes and the deceiving Indian summer days in the middle of the season, the brittle cold fronts rushing into the land from the north and Baltic Seas change the landscape overnight.

For the most part, East Germany prior to November 1989 was a somber and somewhat dreadful place. The gray and dirty terra cotta buildings spread a shadow and a sense of gloom over the citizens. Indeed, gloom seemed like the most explicit adjective to describe my overall impression of the city.

I had never felt so foreign and lost, not even in the jungle highlands of Central America. Fall is the concert season in Germany, at least in the west. In the east they tried, mostly unsuccessfully, to bring some high art and entertainment to the masses, but it left much to be desired. The few shows and venues in working condition were, to say the least, a heartbreaking tale of human existence. Even sadder was the fact that Eastern Germans weren't aware of it. The old, dilapidated theaters, the faded winter coats sporting exhausted, fused colors, and the tired faces filled the landscape with disturbing ease. The contrast with still-fresh images of my own land created the kind of cognitive dissonance that reinforced my notion of displacement.

Time brought some consolation, and the nostalgia dissipated as the workload increased and haste replaced placid reflection. One of the perks of genetic diversity is novelty. For a while, I felt truly a celebrity of sorts in Eastern Europe. People of African ancestry enjoyed, at least at that time, a level of notoriety that helped diffuse my loneliness. Most common people assumed that I could run, jump, lift, and who knows what else, better than the average man. At the time, my physical condition also helped stimulate such speculation, and I did absolutely nothing to dispel the myths.

The work was everything but stimulating, however. It was just that—a job. I avoided thinking about what lay ahead of me. I wanted to keep my mind free of loose associations in case I had to face a polygraph. Indulging in fantasies could complicate things. What would I do if I had to look straight-faced at some glory-hungry, middle-aged, going-nowhere spook eager for promotion, while I sat strapped to a maze of electrodes? I didn't allow myself to speculate about my future.

My time passed between training young operatives in how to assess psychological vulnerabilities on potential targets, and performing after-action reviews for those coming back from West or North Africa. It was nothing glorious nor notorious, but it seemed initially ideal. I had no immediate supervisor at the station. My reports went somewhere, though I never knew exactly where. And in the ten months I did this job, whoever received them never contacted me. I often wondered if somebody really knew where I was. For some people, the assignment was a step up from paradise. On the other side, I was burning with boredom.

Berlin was a strange city broken in half with a grotesque wall and barbwire fence twisting and turning capriciously through the urban maze. There was no logic to the divide. It seemed like a school child had irreverently drawn across houses, buildings, parks, schools, creeks, and every other human and geographical element without regard. It seemed, at least to me, a sadist display.

Nighttime was the sad reminder that I was in the east. Darkness descended and remained. There were few displays, and little, if any, life about the streets after dark. The west, in contrast, was a cauldron of activity. The city lights blinded the horizon with a multicolor display that rivaled sunrise. They were once one united people, but not any longer. It seemed that those in the east had died long ago, and only their souls wandered the gray streets in search of meaning.

Berlin was also unique in many other respects. Long-standing conflict, animosity, and enmity gave way to a more subtle, dangerously addictive game of sorts. Violent encounters were unheard of here among the intelligence services of the world, and they were all there. Berlin was an agitated bazaar of information, but a quiet garden as far as operations. It was, I came to know later, a previously agreed upon and universally accepted neutral ground. The city was a place of respite for the tired warriors and those who had ascertained the level of sophistication that deemed the shedding of blood as unnecessary. Berlin was the city of the power brokers, deal-makers, and information merchants of the world. Some had residence in the east, some across the wall in the west.

Since the issue of nuclear war was a misnomer, a more sophisticated game had emerged in the years of the Cold War: the very expensive and entertaining game of pretense. The United States and their allies placed intelligence officers in their embassies under various titles. The Soviets pretended they didn't know who the intelligence officers were, but they did, and the Americans knew the Soviets knew but pretended they didn't know they knew. It was sick and silly to oblivion, but it worked. Plotting how to outsmart the other side rather than how to kill them kept everybody busy.

The killing was done through proxies. It was those not smart enough to understand the intricacies of the game, those for whom the shedding of blood was still "normal." In Africa, Asia, Latin America, and the Middle East, natives stained the streets with their blood in civil war. The superpowers just provided the weapons after a heavy dose of ideology.

I had time on my hands in Germany. That was a first for me after years of hyper-vigilance and stress in the jungle. I could read, take long lunch breaks, schedule appointments out of the office, wander endlessly through the wet, cobblestone-covered streets of Berlin without care.

Access to historical information was somewhat limited. The archives at the station only contained information in the European theater of operation. I wasn't particularly interested in the subject, but it helped pass the time. Much of what came to shape my conception of the world and current operating reality came from these readings.

The principle archival administrator was a moderately overweight, German-born Cuban woman in her thirties. Beyond the stony face and cold, detached mannerisms lay a lonely, hungry, desperate woman. In private she was pleasant, smart, and even friendly. She was a security risk and she knew it. My guess is that she was the illegitimate child of someone in a high place back on the Island; someone who left a souvenir while on tour in Germany in the early years of the revolution. Things such as this were well-kept secrets, and as in this case, a smart way to keep past mistakes close at hand. Viera Marin surely fit that category.

Viera seemed baffled by my lack of an even passing interest in her. I was told she'd made a habit of helping single male personnel adjust to the new environment in the station. The cold weather, loneliness, and nostalgia can be difficult to deal with initially. She was there to help in the process. However, she made me uneasy. She was too wanting, readily available, and too desperate for my taste. And the once-a-week shower, hairy-legged style for the winter was just too much for me.

She took my subtle rejection fairly well. She seemed to believe it was something to do with my taste in gender. She'd seen it before, and she knew that in that kind of circle it had to be a quiet affair. We could still be friends. I said absolutely nothing to contradict her assumptions. She always smiled at me, even when her day had given her no reason to.

I gained access to information for which I had no legitimate use, which caused flags to be raised and questions to be asked. She gave me unlimited access to the classified files. The girl was a bomb waiting for a fuse. As it happened, it wouldn't matter in the long run.

As my reading progressed about what had taken place in the previous decades, the jigsaw puzzle of the geopolitical map of the world began to take shape. As months went by and spring approached, my level of disappointment overcame my initial bewilderment. Nothing had prepared me for the information I'd been reading. As I began to weave and connect the past with current information, equipped now with a new situational awareness, the events that were beginning to unfold made absolute sense.

The fall and early winter air had been heavy with anxiety. The Hungarians lifting their border guard with Austria earlier in the year, the resignation of Eric Honecker in October, and the withdrawal of the mid-range artillery battalion from the Polish border signaled that change was to be the norm rather that the exception for years to come.

The Stasi had been evasive and unresponsive on some routine information requests. That was certainly uncharacteristic of the East German secret services. They were the epitome of precision and efficiency. I tried to triangulate with the Soviets, but my contact had no response for me either. The agitation and constant movement of trucks in and out of their headquarters finally offered a reason on November 9 of that year.

Without further warning, without gunfire or upheaval, and following an interview on the nightly news with a mid-level East German official, thousands of East Germans went to the wall-crossing points. The sentries weren't there for the first time in almost fifty years. That night alone, twenty thousand East Germans crossed into the West for the very first time.

During the next three days, people from France, Switzerland, Belgium, and as far as Spain drove to Germany to see the wall torn down at dozens of places along its former divide. The world witnessed in astonishment how the ultimate symbol of oppression, at least for the western world, had shattered in one night and without one drop of blood being shed between sunset and sunrise.

The scene in my building was eerily calm. All the staff was accounted for, and four additional secret service personnel had been summoned from Poland. The brass on the Island feared that some of the staff might find the recent events too tempting and decide to take a walk west. Nothing happened, and all the staff remained in virtual lockdown for one week. After that, all covert operations in Germany stopped, six tons of documents were shipped to Poland and later to Cuba, and the station staff was reduced by one-third.

I spent the next three months developing situational assessment reports about people I knew nothing about and trying to speculate about future developments. It was a completely useless exercise, but there was no one else to do it. The European specialists were grounded and recalled to the Island, because they failed to see and anticipate the collapse of East Germany. Silly. Actually, no one saw it coming. At the US embassy, some were growing bald scratching their heads over the subject.

In East Germany where it had lived for four decades in a less visible, less public way, Communism had evaporated in one brittle winter night. The strident, convoluted system that had incarcerated, starved, and killed more of its own countrymen than both world wars combined, vanished without so much as a cry or a whisper.

After that, time seemed to linger in suspended animation. My many and often insipid tasks felt even more disjointed and incongruent. We continued to receive orders and planned, researched, and explored for a universe that had disappeared weeks earlier. Those on the Island seemed unable or unwilling to comprehend that the world as it existed was gone. There was no threat, no enemy, no conspiracy—not even those who were formerly identified as friends. The boundaries, ideologies, and people fused, morphed, and disappeared. I stood with shield and spear in hand, ready to fight while my former enemy had abandoned the battlefield.

The useless exercise continued for a few more weeks until I stopped responding to the wire requests. I left early in the mornings and walked without purpose or destination along the busy, agitated streets of Berlin. I missed every communication brief every morning for three consecutive weeks.

I felt a void, as if something fundamental had shifted inside of me, but I was unable to identify the cause. Suddenly, by some sick and sinister design, my life stopped being relevant. I discovered, in a nauseating wave of awareness, that all the assumptions, beliefs, constructs, and references that supported my life and gave sense to my existence were gone. Nothing I had done, dedicated my life to, or risked my life for was worth anything. In the new reality being shoved down my throat by forces distant, foreign, and disconnected from my past and current level of comprehension, I was a mute item. In one night, I'd lost my existential axis.

The station secretary was more pale and tense than usual, which was probably due to her near-death situation. She always seemed on the verge of cardiac arrest.

"They're waiting for you," she said, pointing to the conference room that was up a flight of marble stairs. Her finger was again trembling more than usual. I figured it was from too much caffeine.

The three men in the conference room were absorbed in their reading. I slid out of my long coat and hung it on a rack by the door. Armand, the station chief, was visibly distressed by the unannounced visit of the two other characters. He was, after all, biding his time until retirement. This was trouble he didn't want and was not ready to deal with.

I sat at the far end of the table, away from the trio, both hands resting on the large mahogany surface. As if lit by thunder, the political officer stood and pointed a menacing finger at me. He was a short, flabby-looking man in his forties. His military uniform was crisp regalia in full display. His face was pale and dry, demonstrating that his skin didn't agree with the German weather. He wasn't there by choice or on a routine mission.

"Who do you think you work for?" he shouted. The station chief got up and closed the door. The issue was embarrassing enough for him.

I didn't answer. It was a rhetorical question. I could see the aorta pulsating on the plump man's neck, his eyes pushing the confines of their orbits. The man was enraged.

He was a politician turned spook. He had no formal training, operational experience, nor aptitude for the job. He was a political appointee and protégé of somebody higher up. Only the devil knew how he got where he was. Most intelligence officers I knew believed the man to be a scavenger.

"Do you believe I'm stupid? Don't you think I know what you're doing?" he asked angrily as he held a file in his trembling right hand. He slammed the file on the table and pushed the chairs before him as he made his way to me.

When he reached me, he stretched his hand and grabbed the neck of my sport coat. I felt a wave of anger wash over me slowly, my face becoming warm.

I said softly, "If you don't let go of my coat, I promise you won't be able to use that hand for weeks." I pronounced the words with my best casual, non-threatening tone. He got the message and let go. He stood there, breathing fire through his nose, hyperventilating two feet away from my face. He had no options with me. There was little he could do, and he knew it.

"Chief, I'll draft a reprimand for his permanent file," he said, referring now to the station chief. "And I'll recommend that the disciplinary council convene once he returns." Putting on his best bureaucratic air, he gestured toward me and said, "And I'll decide what to do with you later." I didn't answer, and that made his blood boil. "In the meantime, you'll report every morning to the communication room at 0700 and provide the requested information for the area briefing. Do you have anything to add in your defense?" he asked with ridiculous pomp.

I barely held my laughter. "I didn't know I was on trial," I said, leaning back in my seat.

He swallowed air and almost gasped. "You're pushing your luck. It'll cost you," he said, once more the tone and gesturing of a frustrated, impotent human being.

"Are you done?" I asked, softer still, trying to avoid laughter while gesturing my intent to leave.

"Where is the report on the target of interest that I told you had priority?" he asked, holding his hand up, gesturing for me to wait.

"The man is gone, retired, disconnected, out of circulation in a villa in the south of France," I shot back. "I told you people—the game is over. You keep playing wars on a sand pit back on the Island instead of just walking around for an hour or two. You must have seen the rats bailing out of the sinking ship. It's over, can't you tell?" My voice now raised a decibel or two. "There are no more Stasi, no more bridge wires," I said, referring to inter-services' daily briefings and communications between allied intelligence agencies. "Go across town and realize they're gone, the building was looted and halfway burned. On the east, the Soviets have their own problems. They can't, nor do they care any longer about what we need. It's all over!" I said, almost screaming.

He looked at the station chief in disbelief, who in turn looked out the window as if the windswept street could offer some cover from the storm boiling inside the conference room.

There it was. So many weeks of tangential and poorly explainable excuses came crashing to a stop. I don't recall a more satisfying moment in my life up until then. His facial expression was a mixture of shock, disbelief, confusion, and even fear. That picture was worth a thousand words—and a million dollars.

The political officer fixed his bewildered eyes on me for a few seconds. As he drummed on the table for a minute, trying to gather his thoughts, I pictured the top of his head just blowing into hundreds of tiny gray pieces all over the room. I almost smiled at the visualization. Yep, I had just, in fact, blew his mind. I was savoring the moment.

He slowly got up, gathering his papers as he rose. The quiet, quasi-invisible man sitting next to him imitated his gesture and rose almost simultaneously. He stood there for a second, also looking out the window. I followed his exhausted movements and troubled face as he left the room. I could hear the metal doors of the elevator opening and closing as the political officer descended into the communication room in the basement.

The political officer spent three or four hours that day reading my reports of the last four months and then left. I never saw the visitors again.

The exchange had huge implications. On one hand, I managed to alienate one of the most influential officers in the military foreign core. I disobeyed a direct order and, to add insult to injury, voiced a political opinion as a statement of fact in public. That amounted to professional suicide, to say the least, if it didn't land me in front of the firing squad.

I was done. My life as an intelligence officer in the Cuban military was conclusively over. The encounter precipitated the inevitable. I couldn't go back to the Island if I cared for my life. My plan to jump the fence, as defection is known in those circles, began to hatch as soon as I left the meeting. In my short years inside the paranoid and ruthless intelligence world, I had seen men lose their lives for a lot less. I knew my fate was sealed.

Europe wasn't safe. It had permeable borders by land and sea. Besides, men of African descent don't blend in very well there. North America offered the only true refuge for me and those who dared defy the regime. They dared not make an incursion in US territory and give the trigger-happy Yanks an excuse to blur the Island sky with airplanes. "Yeah, California it is," I said to myself.

"Did you have to lay it out in front of him so hard?" Armand asked. The question seemed flaccid, uncalled for, and inconsequential. In fact, I thought I'd done rather well and spoken in a way that had protected Armand, the station chief. Whatever it was, the trouble was well above his pay grade.

"Don't worry, Armand. I've covered your backside since I got here," I said, a sliver of condescension trickling through. I shouldn't have said it quite that way. "All this is well over our heads. And you had no decision-making authority to affect change," I said, trying to offer comfort to the embattled station chief.

This was a "global climactic shift of monumental proportions. Not even the total brainiacs at Neustädtische Kirchstrasse 4–5 (formerly the US Embassy/CIA building) had the foresight to predict the events of November 1989 in Germany.

I was, to my surprise, pretty much left alone and completely disjointed from the larger unit. I couldn't be happier, however. I took long, heart-stopping drives along the world famous autobahn, the granddaddy of the United States' freeways. Speed there wasn't the end but the means by which thousands of people traveled two hundred miles in a little over an hour.

I mingled with the people and ventured as far south as Austria and Switzerland. The French were less inclined to believe my diplomatic credentials. Plus, they insisted on associating me with North Africa and speaking to me in French. I found the whole event taxing. I told the border-crossing officer at Strasbourg that as far as I knew, my ancestors had left Africa about five hundred years before. Sorry, no contact with them in recent history.

The year 1990 didn't fare better for the former Soviet republics. Perestroika, Mikhail Gorbachev's brainchild, swept over the Soviet hinterland like a tidal wave.

The former empire began to collapse and implode like nothing ever seen before or since. Suddenly, high-ranking military officers in the Red Army began to hold swapmeet-style fire sales of war supplies of every kind at bargain prices. The far-flung military bases of the north became the bazaar of the world. The former apparatchiks chiefs began to surface in Switzerland, Belgium, Italy, and Greece as the new venture capitalists. They later found their way to New York and California, and settled quietly amidst the ethnic communities of the United States.

Snow in Spring

Spring in the Caribbean is no doubt one more testimony of the mercies of God to the inhabitants of the earth. The breeze, the tempered weather, the early bloom of flowers of every kind, and the millions of birds that fly in both directions over the islands soothe the soul. In summary, the beauty of the land is beyond compare.

Not so in other latitudes. In fact, there was snow in Berlin that year in early March, which didn't melt until the end of April. After seven solid months of snow, I was ready for a break in the weather, the landscape, and life itself.

Almost without notice, anxieties found a niche in some dark corner of my stomach and settled themselves there. Increased running time at the athletic club didn't help. I tried herbal remedies of every kind, less food, and monitoring certain kinds of food, but nothing seemed to work. I felt as if I'd swallowed a small watermelon, whole and heavy, and it remained in the pit of my stomach.

The staff scheduled for rotation was eager to return to the Island. The three-month-long layover was a welcome reprieve from the cold social and psychological isolation of the embassy. People spent significant amounts of time gift hunting—or rather going on scavenger hunts, to be honest. The meager stipends that the Foreign Service gave to its employees didn't go far. The staff members had saved (more like deprived themselves) during the year in order to bring something home to their families.

These were dangerous times. The secret services were on the prowl during rotation times. These were the times when people jumped fences, drove across bridges, and walked into embassies other than their own. These were the times when escape plans were hatched, cracked, and frustrated every year. It was the only time when movement was allowed in one way or another, and thus came the opportunity to make a run for it.

I kept my usual cool. It was no secret that I wasn't really interested in much other than my reading. At age twenty-one, I had no family of my own as of yet. I'd managed to buy a few things now and again throughout the year. I kept my outings to a minimum and the watchful eye of the secret police off my back. They were everywhere around the clock, like hounds on a blood trail. I followed my routines to the letter.

The first group left in early April on a nonstop flight from Berlin to Martinique and from there to the Island on a merchant vessel. There were reasons for the unorthodox travel arrangement. Primarily, it provided a safer haven for agent infiltration, controlled surroundings to avoid desertions, and restricted the smuggling of materials, which savvy and sophisticated customs agents can detect in more developed western nations.

The replacement group arrived three days later, and our group left the same day. There were six diplomats and a group of four military attachés. The secret police staff traveled in the same flight but pretended to mix with the passengers. Their cartoon-like demeanor was laughable, except for the fact that that some of them were little more than government-sanctioned, bona fide killers. Their sole purpose was to summarily prevent people from the diplomatic core from escaping to a receptive country and seeking political asylum. Given the chance, spilling their own blood was for them the ultimate evidence of their zeal and duty.

Our schedule took us over the Atlantic to Canadian soil for a one-hour layover, and then on to the Island from there. A day before, I sought medical treatment for flu-like symptoms. I received a prescription for antihistamines and the like. I'd be asleep all the way through, I was told.

I stood before the mirror in my room fitting my tie. I slid into my formal coat with the regalia and other insignia hanging on my left breast. It was, no doubt, the last day I'd wear the uniform. I wasn't going to miss it. However, the fact that I didn't know how long it would be before I could put together a decent wardrobe concerned me somewhat.

I grabbed my zurka, the small, folding leather document case that rested on a chair next to my bed. I pulled my long coat off a hanger behind the door. There was no nostalgia, no longing, no good-byes to the room I had called home for a year. *They could be looking*, I thought.

I had sent my luggage ahead the night before. I was certain they had gone over the bags meticulously before placing them in the diplomatic containers. I had no concerns. There was nothing in them that could reveal what I was about to do.

The long black chaika pulled up on the side of the building. The Russian version of the limousine was more of a remodeled hearse than anything else. I walked down the long flight of stairs, coat in hand. I had little time to get acquainted with the new staff, nor did I care to. Keeping my distance and an air of mystery was part of the allure of the intelligence service. I didn't go that far. I just stayed out of the way in my last few days at the station.

I sat in the front seat next to the driver, a thin old man in his fifties. *Too old for this job*, I thought. The job was often held by young, not very bright "son of somebody." It was a prelude to similar jobs at home for influential members of the party and the like. These were coveted, dead-end jobs for those with little brains or opportunity to do anything else. Another alternative was what I called "pasture before retirement," usually the fate of mid-level bureaucrats that had committed pardonable sins but were deemed in disgrace. They were sent on out of the way assignments for a few years until retirement. It was the fate of the damned in the eyes of government officials.

The car was spotless. No adornments, no little flags hanging on the rearview mirror, no pictures or stickers. A sterile and efficient official vehicle. A copy of Poe's *The Purloined Letter* on the dashboard gave a glimpse of the breadth of the driver's interests. This was no ordinary man, but few knew him.

"Ready?" he asked, shaking my hand as I slid into the seat next to him.

"You bet," I said. "I can't wait to get out of the snow," I said, pointing to the small piles of snowfall swept onto the edge of the driveway.

"Yeah, we have another month or so until it gets warm enough to melt all of it," he added, his eyes scanning the corners of the garden. "Had a chance to brief your replacement?" he asked.

I hesitated in answering. I wasn't sure if drowning the man in files was considered a briefing. There was little else to do beyond that. In fact, going forward, there was even less work to do since the very existence of the unit, its purpose, and future plans were still empty canvases. The geopolitical shift of the previous months had cast our lives into a new light. I hadn't managed to make sense of it all yet.

I shrugged my shoulders. Who knew what he'd be asked to do? Maybe he'd have enough time to go to the ballet and the theater and date some pretty German girls in the fan club.

"I'm going home now, Amiel. That's all I care about right now," I said, looking through the window at the gray sky and the leafless trees in the courtyard.

"I hear you, brother. I hear you," he uttered, pulling on his leather gloves.

A large group congregated on the side of the building for a few minutes. The cold, damp weather didn't allow for lengthy farewells. A few hugs and handshakes later, six shivering people climbed into the car. The driver turned on the engine and the heater. Little did I know our paths would cross again years later in another place, thousands of miles away.

The airport was nearly empty. Groups of people, mostly German and Russian bureaucrats, dotted the scene. We were ushered into a separate, all-purpose room to await our flight. There was nothing in particular about the room; in fact, it seemed more like a waiting room in a hospital. Perhaps the only purpose of the room was to keep us from wandering away from the eyes of the secret police.

I unwrapped a package of over-the-counter medication and swallowed a couple of pills. My quiet but persistent cough broke the silence of the room now and again. I reclined on the vinyl-covered seats and rested my head on the plastic wall behind me, my eyes closed.

I could hear the soft, whispered conversation of the few around me. A few minutes later, two others joined our group. I could hear the sound of a muffled introduction and handshakes. I didn't open my eyes. I knew who they were, our overseers for the trip—people whose sad purpose in life is to keep other human beings from following the mandates of their hearts. They were the prison keepers, for we were all prisoners of the state.

Some time later, we were shown to our flight and we boarded the red and white Interflug plane. We took our seats all the way in the back of the plane. The overseers positioned themselves, one ahead of the group and another at the very end of the plane. No words or pleasantries were exchanged. They were there to unequivocally inspire fear.

The plane filled up quickly with the usual crowd. As soon as it took off I requested water and ingested more cold medication. I reclined the orthopedic device that was called a passenger seat and closed my eyes. I remained apparently deep in my antihistamine-induced stupor for nine long hours. I didn't move or acknowledge my surroundings at all. I could hear the almost constant chatter of my colleagues next to me, their senseless daydreaming and unrealistic expectations about romance, conquest, and appeal—all of it.

I rehearsed in my head the pictures, the sketches, the notes, and every other piece of information that I needed in order to achieve my goal. The satellite pictures had come at a very high price. What happened to friendship? How about camaraderie and brotherhood in arms? Well, I guess it died. Perestroika killed them, and now everything was for rent, sale, or test drive—for a fee, of course. What I would have gotten for nothing a few months earlier had cost me nearly a thousand dollars. All for a three-year-old picture of four corners in the city of Montreal.

Timing. That was the key to the success of my little operation. I'd rely on time-honored human responses and errors in judgment. All but the sharpest operators react in very predictable ways, and that was the trump card of the deck. A soft tap on my shoulder from the steward alerted me to the imminent landing in Montreal. I repositioned my seat upright but still reclined against the glass window.

We enjoyed a flawless landing in spite of a fairly good crosswind. The clicking of the seat belts filled the aircraft before we arrived at the gate. The air filled with noise and anticipation, the brushing of bags and coats, the nervous energy typical of the end of a long voyage.

I remained seated. A few minutes before the landing I ingested a small amount of quinine. Long ago it was found to be a natural remedy against malaria. It also produced a sweaty, swollen face and hands. In a few minutes it can give one the appearance of being quite sick.

As the passengers disembarked, the overseers sprung to life. One exited the plane well ahead of our group and took a position near the only exit out of the waiting area. We were to leave the plane and wait at this location for another two hours to connect with a chartered flight to the Island. His job was to prevent any member of the group from leaving the waiting area. The second agent remained behind in the plane until the group had disembarked. Our instructions were clear: stay together and stay close, just like cattle in a feedlot.

I left the plane handkerchief in hand, my quiet cough now more persistent. I sat calmly, lethargic, and obviously under a significant viral influence. I noticed everyone tried to keep some distance from me. The small group sat in two adjacent rows and chatted amicably. The two youngest members of the group walked restlessly about, glancing at the concession stand thirty or forty yards away. I motioned to one of them and he approached.

David was thin and short, a transcriber and translator at the station. This was his first foreign tour of duty and they kept him on a very short leash. I had heard him complain several times about his limited stipend, his curfew, and his bad luck with the German girls. He wasn't considered a security risk but rather a malcontent. They'd surely pull his ears and scare him straight back on the Island.

"See the vending kiosk almost around the corner?" I asked him, half-way through a coughing fit.

"Yes," he said eagerly, his eyes lighting up like a Christmas tree.

"Get some sodas for the group but hot chocolate for me, please, and hurry," I said, gasping for air and handing him some money.

David darted across the spacious waiting room. As he made his way to the concession stand, one of the overseers caught a glimpse of him and also began to move in that direction. The stand occupied a corner in the T-shaped room. There were no exits at the extremes except boarding gates, but it was possible that the young translator was out of the visual field of the security agent.

My cough returned. This time with fury, fluids, and the kind of noise that forces people to remove themselves from view. I got up, stumbling over bags and people. I pointed to the bathroom behind me and went inside. Once inside the stall, I continued to cough for a few more seconds until I felt the bitter, hot gush of fluid burning up my esophagus. I spat and thrashed inside the stall for a minute and no one came.

I took off my coat and hung it over the stall door. I climbed over the toilet, onto the divider wall, and removed the false sheetrock ceiling plank. I pulled myself over the aluminum frame and rested both knees on the main wall behind the bathroom fixtures. I replaced the sheetrock plank and darkness engulfed me.

The crawl space was dusty and damp. I had ten inches of surface to crawl, fifty feet to cover in order to move away from the bathroom, and two minutes maximum before the alarm sounded. I moved quietly over the narrow wall, my head and shoulders brushing against wiring and metal brackets holding more wires and unseen fixtures. I could hear noises, voices, but nothing that indicated alarm or urgency.

I reached the end of the crawling space. I hesitated for a second when a flash of light filled the space. It had to be them. In one motion, I swung my legs to one side of the wall, my feet pushing down the ceiling plank underneath. It gave way easily under my weight. I landed in a small, enclosed space full of wood sticks, rods, and plastic buckets. A strong chemical odor permeated the small room. Closer tactile inspection revealed that it was a utility closet of some kind.

"What the—" came from the other side of the narrow door.

I searched frantically for a doorknob, a latch, something to get out of that suffocating space. Suddenly the door opened and a small balding, red-headed man in yellow coveralls appeared framed against the blinding light of the office behind.

"Hey, fellow, what are you—" was the last I heard as I passed him. I reached the outer office door, ran down a flight of stairs, and to the main lobby in less than ten seconds. I heard shouting and what seemed like a rush, people running, cars braking. The symphony of unfamiliar noise flooded my senses—too loud and too incoherent to distinguish any details. The tension and situational stress was too high to discern what was taking place behind me.

I ran faster than I'd ever run and longer than I thought possible. I twisted and turned across numberless streets and the snow-covered sidewalks. The cool spring evening's early shadows covered my haste and my dark blue military uniform the anachronism of my presence. The French lettering meant little to me in general. I was following a geodesic mental map that had to do with city blocks, kilometers, and prominent landmarks. Trying to read names in a foreign language while on the run isn't a recommended practice.

The last thirty miles to the United States border remained a blur. Intermittent patches of colorful trees alternated with snow-covered mounds of earth dotting the landscape. At some point, I waved and a black-dotted yellow cab swiveled out of traffic to the side of the road. The Caribbean native taxi driver could sense that something was unequivocally wrong, but he couldn't point to anything specifically. He made small talk and at least attempted to engage me a dozen times with little success. I was dehydrated, hungry, and on the verge of collapsing after the adrenaline overdose of the chase. He kept nervously glancing at the rearview mirror but didn't inquire directly.

Highway 15 was littered with green banners and paper flags. Traffic was heavy onto the bridge, and my sense of orientation had begun to falter as nightfall spread over the terrain. I had only the negatives of the satellite overlays to guide me on the final leg of my task. I could see the lights of the border crossing a quarter of a mile ahead. The pedestrian tunnel shouldn't have been too far away, but my excellent navigational skills in the jungle proved totally useless in the urban environment.

The landscape was wrong. There were no trees, at least not enough of them with a leaf on them to over impose on the mental map I carried. I left the taxi and jogged slowly to the border checkpoint. A hundred feet or so to go, I slowed to a fast walk. I looked back for the first time in hours. The long line of vehicles stretched back for almost a mile. People with green shirts, hats, and even green faces stared back with euphoric eyes. The carnival-like atmosphere seemed to me out of season. If you asked me, it was way too cold to be celebrating anything.

I approached the border patrol checkpoint slowly now. I was, after all, dressed in a military uniform of a foreign country, I was sweaty and agitated. I was sure I looked like a demented war veteran of some kind. I didn't want to give the impression that I represented danger. I'd come too far to get shot right before I could sink my teeth into a Big Mac.

I stopped a few yards from the young border inspection officer. I took off my cap and wiped the sweat off my face and neck. I tried to compose myself the best I could.

I resumed my walk again toward the checkpoint, more slowly this time. The officer was young, in his twenties maybe. He sat inside his heated cubicle, coming out once every minute or so to inspect the trunk of a vehicle. The searches seemed random. He was dressed all in blue with a heavy jacket and a green neck scarf. He had his side arm high up on his right hip and under his jacket. He must not use it very often, I thought.

I continued to walk at a leisurely pace toward the officer. I held my cap under my left arm and my passport in my right hand. I slowed to a crawl and smiled. More than a hypocritical smile, it was an attempt to offer psychological control to the officer. Smiles are universal tokens of friendliness; certainly they demonstrate a lack of intent or hostility.

What happened next belongs in a comic strip. By the time he saw me, I was less than twenty feet from him. His eyes bulged almost out of their sockets. In a trembling and clearly confused fashion, he grabbed his radio upside down and yelled: "This is zero-nine, I need some help over here, stat!"

He was frantic. I stopped fifteen feet from him, both hands extended, my silly smile frozen on my face. He dropped the radio, attempted to pull out his weapon, and then tried to pick up his radio. Just like in the Marx Brothers' movies, he dropped his gun, picked up the radio, and pointed it at me.

"Freeze! Stop!" he yelled, the antenna of the radio pointing at me while he desperately tapped on the floor for his gun, his eyes glued on me the entire time. His agitated fingers recovered the gun and he clasped it in his left hand and put it close to his mouth as if it were the radio unit.

"I need help now!" he yelled at the top of his lungs.

Guns in hand, a handful of officers rushed to help their fellow agent. They surrounded me, their weapons pointing at the ground but in my general direction. They were ready but didn't appear in any distress. The situation was under control. They perceived no threat, and I took a deep breath. I had a good chance of eating that burger soon, and I'd be in one piece.

They handcuffed me and rushed me into the building. I was searched, x-rayed, and placed in a small room for a number of minutes. The room was almost bare, with a small table and two chairs inside its four walls. There were no pictures or windows, and the light was flush against the high ceiling. I'd seen rooms like this before.

A uniformed immigration officer came into the room with my passport and a file in hand. He asked me a hundred questions, took me to an electronic fingerprinting scanner, and brought me back to the room. His Spanish was fair, but it was obviously his second language. The rest was standard refugee processing procedures, at least until the rest of the feds showed up.

Three hours later, I was at the Federal Bureau of Investigation (FBI) office in Buffalo, New York, answering more questions until almost midnight. It was then that someone figured out that it had been perhaps ten hours since I'd had any food. That day I met Mr. Hoagie. After I was finished with the sandwich, a most delicious fare, I gave them permission to shoot me in the leg if they had to. I'd gobbled an American original and it was the most delectable food I'd ever tasted. They could keep me there a whole month if they wanted to, as long the food was that good.

And keep me they would, for six long weeks on a Virginia farm. There I received three hot meals a day and all the fruits, snacks, and Twinkies I could eat. There was a real junk food buffet in the pantry. My wardrobe consisted of nondescript blue jogging suits and running shoes.

The National Security Agency (NSA) just wanted to ensure that I was who I said I was. The debriefing sessions lasted two to three hours each day. Two agents were at the small country house at all times. It must have been some kind of assignment or fixed detail, because the same agents worked the day shift six days per week, with another pair working almost twenty-four hours on the Sunday schedule.

They all seemed moody, distant, and aloof. I was just an assignment to them. I understood the need to avoid attachments or complications, but I thought they went out of their way to keep themselves removed from me. I played chess almost two hours per day with one of them without saying a word. I went running in the woods with the other agent for thirty or forty minutes without a sound other than the heavy breathing and the crackling of the dry twigs on the trail under our running shoes.

The questioning revolved around verifying my incursions on foreign soils. The NSA captures video and photographic evidence from travel traffic in every country in which there's an American embassy. If a person visited Fiji, for example, at any given time since 1979, his or her picture is stored in some archive in Virginia somewhere. A quick search for the date in question will show him or her inside the airport, presenting documents to customs, boarding the plane. It's all there for eternity, some say.

Most of the questions were related to my former involvement in Latin America and the Cuban military presence in the region. I offered dates and times, and they verified them. After they were satisfied, they turned to me and administered a battery of psychological tests. Ensuring my mental stability and fitness for citizenship was as important as making certain I wasn't a mole.

Another agent came late one night. It had been raining heavily all day long, and my mood had suffered as a consequence. The isolation, the lack of alternative social contact, and the uncertainty of the future occupied my mind almost continually. He rehearsed some of the notes in the file before him. He asked me a few more of the same questions I'd answered before. When, where, with whom, and why I was in a certain location on a particular date.

After dinner he came again into the TV room. I was enthralled in an episode of *Knight Rider* and the wonders of KITT, the customized black Firebird. He signaled for me to follow him into the study next door.

"Do you have any close friends in the United States?" he asked in mild terms. He seemed sincerely concerned.

"No, sir. I have some acquaintances scattered across the country, but nobody I consider my friend," I replied.

I felt sad. I'd left my friends, my family, and my whole life behind. It was a painful realization, and until then, I'd given it very little thought. I was silent for several minutes. He didn't interrupt me, sensing some internal turmoil. "No, I don't have anyone," I said, matter-of-factly.

"Where do you want to go and settle?" he asked, looking me in the eyes.

I hadn't thought much about that. My country spanned from ocean to ocean, and I could go anywhere. I hadn't pondered this small issue in a long time. Of course, no snow, please. I'd had enough to last me a lifetime.

"Los Angeles sounds like my kind of town," I said, trying not to smile.

"Any particular area? I mean, the City is five hundred square miles," he said, smiling back.

"Do you have a map?" I asked nervously.

He disappeared for a few minutes and returned with a wall-size map of the United States. He pointed to Los Angeles and looked at me once more.

"I guess, maybe around here," I said, pointing to an area on the map. "Is it close enough to drive to the ocean?"

"Yes," he said. "It's about one hour north of Los Angeles, but you can drive down to Hollywood any time you like." He broke into quiet laughter, and I joined him.

"Have you been there, in California?" I asked, my eyes still glued to the map.

"I went to school at Stanford. It is—right here," he said, pointing to a location bearing that name.

"Did you like it?" I asked.

"Very much," he said, folding the map. "Okay then, it's decided. California it is, and Los Angeles for sure. Get some sleep because you're leaving tomorrow. Hold on," he said, stepping out of the room again.

So that was it. No more silent chess games or forest runs. I was finally free to roam and do as I pleased. I was also looking forward to a little warmer, dryer place. I'd had more than a fair share of snow, rain, and hibernation. I was definitely ready for some outdoor activity in the sunshine.

The sliding and whistling sound of nylon interrupted my thought process. The agent walked into the room holding a suit cover and a small bag. He placed them on the table and pointed to them. I unzipped the larger bag to uncover a navy blue suit. The paper bag contained a light blue shirt, folded and packed in a way I'd never seen. A tie, socks, and a shoebox were also in the bag. I smiled timidly. Something inside of me softened a little.

"Courtesy of the United States government?" I asked, with irony.

"No, this is from Agent Benson. He sends his regards and best wishes," he said, extending his hand with a business card bearing Agent Benson's contact information. "He thinks highly of you," he added.

"I don't know what to say." I hesitated. "Thank you very much, truly," I offered.

He came around the table and extended his hand. "It has been a pleasure. If you remember anything that you think has actionable value, give me a call. The number is on the card," he said, shaking my hand good-bye.

"I will, certainly."

He grabbed his briefcase and raincoat and left the room. I didn't follow him to the door—house rules. I saw the light inside his car flicker for two seconds as he got in, and soon his engine broke the sound of the rain in the quiet night. I went back to my bag of goodies and stared at them. *Now that's a real suit*, I thought.

I didn't sleep that night. I wondered about Grandma and how she had taken the news that I'd deserted, and that, in all likelihood, I would never set foot on the island again. I wondered about my mother, my brother, and my friends. I tried to anticipate what my life was going to be like in the next few months and years. I tried reading in the hope that distant landscapes, strange lives, and inexplicable plots could keep the anxiety and anticipation of my trip at bay. Somehow, Pamplona before a bullfight, the drinking, dancing, and general debauchery of the scene in Hemingway's novel didn't do the trick. I lay awake until dawn. A chapter of my life had just ended and a new one was about to unfold. The transition had been smooth, subtle, and free of upheaval.

However, the months ahead were anything but gentle.

VIVA MEXICO!

By 5 AM I was ready. I had to admit I looked rather handsome in my dark blue suit. It was a distant cousin to the tight, polyester drapes I'd had to wear in Germany. The two agents escorted me to the car outside under the porch. It was still cold and humid, but the rain had ceased during the night. The blue mist engulfed the woods like a veil. Visibility was restricted to about fifty or sixty yards.

I stopped for a few seconds, contemplating the quiet beauty of the place. I'd spent more than a month running every morning amongst those trees, and the microphones, the cameras, the ground level radar, and the motion sensors. Sometimes I wondered if there was a tree on that fifty acres that hadn't been drilled or mutilated in some fashion to accommodate a device of some sort. I failed to see the point.

I stepped into the car and we drove for almost an hour until we arrived at a small airport—very small. In fact, the only evidence that the place functioned as an airport was the plane idling on the edge of the tarmac. It could have been an old abandoned roadway. There were no towers, no buildings, just the landing strip.

We drove to the side of the aircraft and the side door opened, extending the ladder down to the ground. We exited the car and walked toward the deafening roar of the engines. A tall, young man in a dark brown suit appeared at the small door and waved me in. I turned and realized the agents had remained halfway between the aircraft and the car. I was going alone on this trip.

I climbed the narrow ladder and stepped into the plane. The door closed behind me, and the tall young man pointed to a seat two rows back. There were four other passengers in the plane but there was no time for introductions.

"Buckle up," he said as he took the seat across the aisle from me. A second later, the engine revved up and the aircraft made a 180-degree turn almost in the same place. In forty seconds, the nose of the plane was pointing skyward, pushed by the powerful jet engines at each side. The craft pierced the clouds and leveled above them in a manner of minutes. The flight lasted less than one hour, takeoff to landing. I barely had time to skim over a few magazines in the seat pocket in front of me. I never learned who the other passengers were.

The plane landed and was guided to a hangar where I was shown to a small golf cart and transported quietly to another side of the Dallas airport. The driver, a middle-aged man in a blue jumpsuit, didn't utter a word. I was beginning to worry about the long, drawn silences. It had to be an American thing. The small utility vehicle traveled for a minute or so across the airport and then through a mechanical door. A heavyset man with glasses greeted me. He shuffled some papers until he found the one he'd been looking for.

"Yes, that's you," he said, pointing to a file with my picture attached to it. "Nice to meet you."

We walked amongst the people at the airport terminal. The scene was intoxicating. I'd been secluded in the forest for over a month. To see so many colors, faces, and all the new environment had to offer to my senses was exhilarating.

We kept looking for a quiet place to sit, which was almost impossible. We settled next to a small perfume shop, and he pulled out a folder with several blank forms. He began what turned out to be a long, tedious, bureaucratic ordeal. He was a worker for Catholic Charities and was flying with me to Los Angeles in order to get me settled there. There were the typical forms and documentation to complete, and we spent two and a half hours in the process. We finished with just enough time to board our plane.

I slept for most of the flight. I awoke briefly to eat—I can't remember what it was to this day—and fused into my seat again for the rest of the trip. My travel escort awakened me just a few minutes before we landed at Los Angeles International Airport. I looked out the window, and it was cloudy there as well.

"I thought California was supposed to be sunny and bright all year around," I complained quietly to my travel guide.

"Well, I guess it sometimes rains here too," he answered, also peering out the window as the craft landed heavily on the runway.

After a few minutes of walking in the hallways and dodging people who were dangerously loaded with luggage, we breathed the L.A. air. It was different from what I expected. The faces were different from New York and Virginia. There were many more different faces, many shapes and colors. I smiled and thought, *This is my kind of town, the right kind of salad.*

"Yeah, I can live here," I said, smiling broadly.

We landed in L.A. on Cinco de Mayo, and Mexico seemed to have spilled a hundred miles north. I couldn't believe I was in the United States. For a brief second I thought the NSA smarties had shipped me down south to Mexico instead. We walked what seemed to be at least twenty miles from the airport inland. There were thousands of people on the streets, playing, eating, and laughing—and they were all talking in Spanish! From the street names to the business signs, everything was in Spanish. The few gringos around could have been tourists mingling in some Mexican city's holiday.

They found me accommodations in an apartment with another political refugee from El Salvador. A former union leader, Roman had been detained by the police during a rally and brutally tortured. Both his kneecaps were broken, making the simple act of walking an ordeal for him. He had cigarette burns all over his body, lacerations of all kinds, and more tragically, psychological scars that would last a lifetime.

Roman had found his only refuge in alcohol. He was physically and emotionally disabled. Bringing him to the United States was a humanitarian gesture of the American government. I seriously doubted he could be rehabilitated. He drank intermittently during the day and more heavily as night fell. He had recurring nightmares and agitated dreams almost every night. He woke up screaming and crying. My stay in the apartment was short but difficult. It was almost impossible to have a conversation with him without revisiting his ordeal. Roman was ten thousand miles away from the torture room where his body had been broken, but he remained in the grip of his captors. I moved to my own apartment six weeks later and never saw him again.

Adjusting to life in the United States took some time and some creative reasoning. I felt trapped inside my own brain. So much to say and no one to talk to. And, of course, no practical way of doing so because of the language barrier. Emotional isolation can be painful and persistent.

People who could speak my language were always around me, but their command of it and the depths of the discourse left me unsatisfied. For months I wondered if I'd made a mistake. Other countrymen I encountered had either been here too long or were first generation born stateside. Either way, I couldn't connect with them.

The first few years went by in a more or less inconsequential fashion. Learning a new language is quite a challenge, but one I could always undertake with confidence. Between American history classes, *Knight Rider*, *Magnum P.I.*, and *The A-Team*, I immersed myself in the culture at large. Within two years I'd mastered the language with enough fluency and ease to fool anyone. I worked odd jobs while going to school—bank teller, night auditor for a motel, night inventory crew at a retail store chain, and quality control at an electronics component manufacturer are some of the early entries on my resume.

One of my most ardent desires was to get rid of the little indistinguishable accent that I still carried. I visited one of the speech pathologists at University of Southern California where I was taking some graduate course work. The tall, cute blonde who attended me listened quietly and intently to my observations. I spoke of my desire to rid myself of any vestige of my former self, linguistically, that is. She took some notes and nodded now and again.

"But why?" she asked with a malicious smile that gave me goose bumps.

"Well," I said, "I think that's what I need to completely immerse myself in the culture."

Her response came after a few seconds. It was frank, disarming, and horribly insightful. "You're bright beyond belief. Yes, I can help you lose your accent. But then you'll be just another black man in a suit on the street." I was speechless. She continued, "I think it's extremely cute and appealing to sound just like you do. Your speech is soft, melodic, clear, and impossible to place. Talk more, open up, and you'll have girls dying to find out where you're from." She was trying to keep from laughing. I smiled timidly. I felt my face getting warm.

"Just say, 'Hello, how are you, can I sit here?' And you have the first thirty minutes to break the ice just having her guess from which part of the world the wind blew you onto these coasts." We were both laughing now with gusto.

"Come on, boy, I know half a dozen guys who would pay to sound like you," she said.

After a few more pleasantries I left her office, flattered, and with confidence to spare. I never again concerned myself with the sound of my voice.

Time proved her right in many ways. I made friends, worked, and continued my education. Between the benevolence of Uncle Sam and his student loan programs, and the most unusual and timely grants, I made my way through school. Although my social experience had improved and my circle of influence had enlarged to include many people and activities, I continued to feel incomplete.

I searched, sought to acquire knowledge, and developed a tremendous thirst for inquiry and research. I became convinced that researching and understanding the past were the keys to make sense of what the future had in store for me. I took on the study of history as a serious endeavor, as an academic task and a personal activity. But after a few years, it didn't bring the fruits I expected, although it was by no means a useless exercise.

Sundays were especially difficult for me in those early years. I missed my grandmother terribly. I initially hadn't been able to send letters to her directly, and there was no way to circumvent the governmental scrutiny inside the Island. I'd been declared a non-person, which in plain terms meant that I no longer existed. All evidence of my life had been removed from public view. Contact with me by anyone, or attempts thereof, could be extremely hazardous. I managed to send some notes with relatives of friends I had made in the United States. Sometimes they managed to bring back a note from home. That was all.

Sundays were sort of lazy days for us while we were growing up. Grandma sat and read, took naps, chatted with me, or listened to her old radio, but not much else. It was a day to rest and to prepare for another week.

It was the carefree spirit, the closeness of Sundays, the sense of reprieve and nourishment, the availability and the safety of my home that I missed. It wasn't until years later that I experienced something similar.

On one of those almost depressing L.A. Sundays, a neighbor invited me to what he called a confirmation at a nearby church. I had often thought about God, pretty much every time I looked at the mirror and saw the scar across my forehead. But for whatever reason, I hadn't mustered the courage to walk into a church. I hadn't been a church-going person ever, and the notion of venturing inside one wasn't appealing to me.

I was trying to be polite, and, of course, I was more motivated by the promise of the party right after—the most important portion of the event. The affair marked an important point of reference for me in terms of religion. It opened my eyes to the world of religious affairs in the United States and how many people interpreted, believed, and saw religion in a broad sense.

The experience in general awoke my desire to reconnect with God. I realized what I'd been missing for so many years. It also pointed to something that Grandma had discussed with me before—tradition versus conviction. There was, in most of those attending that religious ceremony, very little understanding or conviction about what they were doing. There was no sacredness or anything special, but rather it was casual and routine. It seemed to me that it was a mechanical, pre-scripted play with no clear message.

I attended a few more of those events. I came to understand that in general, they didn't mean much to my friends. It was more of a public act that reaffirmed their membership in a particular familiar and social group, and nothing more in my estimation. I needed more than that.

They Call His Name But He Is Not Here

I resolved to inquire on my own about local churches and other religions. It had come to my attention that in the United States there were a number of different churches. So many, in fact, that it was difficult to discern which one was worthy of my attention.

Throughout the week I began to visit the church buildings near my apartment and make notes of their meeting times on Sunday. Suffice it to say that other than listening to sermons of varying lengths, with their emotive intensity and messages, I wasn't impressed with any of them.

I spent most of the year, at least on Sundays, driving to church services around Los Angeles. Sometimes the prospect was my own. Other times, friends and neighbors recommended a church service of their acquaintance. The exercise proved futile, for the most part.

After months of unsuccessful searching, in my disenchantment I relented to other activities. It took almost a year and a very interesting conversation to motivate my search once more for the church I so desired.

The doorbell rattled me a bit. I wasn't used to receiving visitors so early on Wednesday, especially unannounced. I walked to the door, tie in hand, my feet sparking electricity over the new carpet. The doorbell rang again before I could reach the doorknob. A familiar smiley face greeted me with some unusual camouflage on it.

"What is that?" I asked in surprise pointing to the black cross painted across my friend and carpool partner's forehead.

"I went to church early. Today is Ash Wednesday, don't you know?"

he asked, genuinely surprised.

I shrugged my shoulders. I had no real clue of the date or its significance. This is the first time in a year that I heard him talk about church. I glanced once more at the black markings on his forehead and turned back to my room to finish dressing.

"There's oatmeal in the microwave," I said, pointing to the kitchen as I stepped into my room. I could hear him thrashing in the kitchen ten seconds later.

"Ash Wednesday?" I said. "What is it? Walk me through it." I got no answer for a minute or so.

"Well," he said, the words competing with pieces of fruit and oatmeal. "It's sort of a reminder that we are dust and that when we die we'll become dust again."

"And for that you have to paint your face that way?" I asked. It sounded sarcastic, but I really wanted to know his position on the issue.

Another prolonged silence ensued. I wasn't sure if it was because he was looking for an answer or he was munching on the food.

"Well, it's a tradition in the church," he replied. "I know where you're going with this, so leave it alone. It's something people have done for almost two thousand years," he argued.

I didn't reply. I'd find out and get back to him. "OK, let's go." I tapped my wristwatch.

He returned from the kitchen and grabbed his briefcase. I noted the black cross was still on his forehead. I raised my finger to call attention to that fact.

"I have to keep it till sundown," he said casually.

"You've got to be kidding!" I exclaimed in disbelief. He wasn't.

A few days later I enrolled in a class on comparative religions. I was determined to separate fact from fiction and tradition. From that point on, religion for me became a serious undertaking and a pursuit that led me to find what I'd been searching for.

HE SUFFERED FOR YOU, SON

Spring is a welcomed season in most climates. It seemed the only thing my friends were interested in was the next watering hole to visit on spring break. I couldn't afford the travel nor was I interested in the schizophrenic excess of those two weeks. The intensity of the event was like nothing I'd ever seen before.

Spring also meant Easter. The Passover celebration brought a spirit of solemnity and soberness that, even when I was thousands of miles away from home, I still remembered. For us at home it signified a time for reflection. Grandma externalized a sense of sadness, a dark mood, to a certain extent.

The emotions were complex. We often pondered on the fact that God had sent his Son to pay for the sins of all mankind. According to Grandma, most of the world ignored the true meaning of His great sacrifice. Tradition dictated, at least in our land, that people must eat certain foods, or that they abstain from eating others. There were processions with old peeled statues of saints, people with weights and chains walking on their knees for four blocks to the local church or four miles to sanctuary. All the same, the traditions were incomprehensible to me.

"God doesn't need that charade," Grandma said quietly. "It's all for public consumption." It sounded harsh, but it seemed to bother her greatly. I didn't understand, but I did see a possible act of contrition.

"You got blisters on your knees? Great, that will teach you not to crawl when you should walk! Your blood is useless and insignificant. It makes a mockery of the blood of the Son of God!" she shouted to a woman in the neighborhood once. She'd tried to impress Grandma with her devotion. I don't think that woman walked on the same side of the street as Grandma after that.

Traditions are like family recipes, I believed. They existed in certain homes and families but not in others. My neighbor Leonor loved sautéed liver and onions. In our home, we couldn't even mention liver, much less cook it—at least not while Grandma was alive. I saw our Cuban religious traditions the same way. They were there, part of the trunk of relics handed down through generations. They were foreign to our family but part of the social environment. Obviously Grandma had a different frame of reference.

Grandma lamented that we no longer knew how to worship God in His way. In other words, it was her belief that unless God sent messengers of some kind to bring back true worship like in the beginning, then we'd be left in the dark in terms of the things of God. At Easter, she lamented such a loss and the twisted observance of a cult that had been changed and corrupted over time.

Now, clear across the ocean, in a strange land, I contemplated the same things, and I longed for something that suited me better. Every year around Easter I initiated my search for "the church that would fill my heart," like she promised.

That week, I entered a small church not far from my apartment. I'd seen it before, but the sign outside had lost some of its letters, and it wasn't clear at what time the services were to take place. I reasoned that Sunday at nine o'clock in the morning seemed as good a bet as any other. I stood there a few minutes and was greeted by a member of the board, whatever that was. The elderly Hispanic man didn't elaborate.

Part of the sermon was in English, and part was in Spanish. It seemed to be infused with some kind of energy that didn't strike me as being genuine. It was certainly not what I hoped. But the congregation was enthralled and enthused with the exclamations of the young pastor. Suddenly, a loud and eurhythmic music swept the room, and some of the assembly began to throw themselves onto the ground, shaking and convulsing intensely. The scene seemed anachronistic, completely out of context, and hazardous, at least to me.

It was too much for me. I left in complete shock, with serious concerns about what else I hadn't seen as of yet in terms of religious practices. I didn't go out again until after Easter.

My next inquiry round took me to a number of churches across a wide range of denominations and idiosyncratic practices. Perhaps it was bias, skepticism, lack of faith, or spiritual intuition. I knew what I was looking for and couldn't find it. I visited congregations with worship practices that, to me, seemed bizarre. Others, from my perspective, appeared lost through years of mutations and confusion regarding their doctrinal compass.

One Sunday morning I found myself driving to south Los Angeles to meet a coworker. We had conversed somewhat about my religious inclinations and my unsuccessful search for a church to call my own. She insisted that I had to listen to her pastor. She claimed he was a renowned author and speaker. He even had his own TV program.

It didn't impress me, but it rather intrigued me. She seemed like a sober person, not given to the water cooler gossip or the abundant office soap operas. She was diligent, organized, and cordial—but at a distance. She was efficient in her work, but for the most part, she always appeared to be not very interested in it.

Finding the location of the church wasn't difficult. Finding a parking space was almost impossible. It wasn't a church. It was a covered baseball field with chairs all the way into home base. The place was imposing and noisy—almost chaotic. The dome was filled to capacity, and almost five thousand people sat elbow-to-elbow looking down intently for the pastor to appear. It was a rather claustrophobic experience, but I promised to endure to the end.

The pastor made his grand entrance accompanied by a recitation of his titles and academic acumen and a brass orchestra in the background. I couldn't help but smile quietly. A beam of light followed him until he had climbed a small platform with an acrylic podium. It looked like an announcement at the Oscars.

The sermon was a litany of scripture reading, comedic remarks, and verbal agreement and reaffirmation from the public. Laughter was the order of the day. The subject of the sermon was lost in the humor, at least for me. The pastor was charismatic, witty, sociable, and articulate. But I felt nothing. For me, I felt no connection with God.

Months went by. I longed to feel the warmth, safety, and renewal I had felt years before when I lay broken and alone on the jungle floor. I tried, almost without hope, to find His church—but it eluded me.

Years later, the hand of God led me to the dry and hot lands of the desert southwest. I thought my years in the military had prepared me for the rigor of desert weather, but I hadn't really experienced heat until I reached the desert in Southern California. I thought that kind of punishment was reserved for those who did evil and was to be dispensed to the wicked after death. *Well, I guess some of us will be punished in this life and the next*, I thought wryly.

Three months straight of over 110 degree weather has to be considered cruel and unusual punishment under the Constitution. Such is the norm in the Imperial Valley, but most people are quite content to live in that region. In fact, given the opportunity, they escape to other places but then gratefully return to visit and to resettle. I thought I was receiving a measurement of affliction for something I had surely done, and that God was holding me accountable. I went looking for job opportunities with the possibility of career advancement, but I was ignorant of the brutal environment. In time, I found much more. For three long years I complained to everyone about how hot it was—mostly to the wrong people, since they were used to the merciless weather. I did everything I could to avoid the heat and made my life quite difficult in the process.

In the spring of 1998, Grandma laid down to sleep one evening and God took her in the quiet of night. My brother described the occurrence, but he was more bewildered than grieved. She had cooked for him and some of his college friends that night. They had gathered to study for a test scheduled for the following day. Grandma said she was tired, which wasn't uncommon for someone a century old. My brother got up the next morning at around 5:30 AM to get ready for school. He reached the kitchen and it was still dark. He called her name, and she didn't respond. It was the first time in more than twenty years—since his birth—that she'd failed to get up by 4 AM. He knew right then that Grandma had died. His call came to me a few hours later, early in the morning.

I sat in my living room for almost two hours and tried to define how I was feeling. I had difficulty describing my current emotional state. More than anything, I wanted to be sad. I should have been despondent, but I couldn't find that emotion. My mind was flooded with memories—a lifetime of happy memories that spanned most of my existence. In fact, my earliest moment of awareness was waking up underneath the mosquito net on my bed, staring into my grandmother's soft blue eyes.

I wanted to cry, grieve, and long for her, but I couldn't. She was there, whole and clear in my mind—every word she said, everything she did, thousands of interactions and stories. They were all in the repository of my recollection, waiting to be shared and to become part of somebody else's memory one day.

I sat until midday, and then it became clear to me. She'd done her duty. She lived her life to the fullest, with peace of mind, clean hands, and a heart that had turned to God many years before her death.

"I'll meet God one day and cry at His feet. I'll tell Him that if I didn't know more about how to worship Him, then it was the fault of men, for they had lied and perverted His ways so that no one knew how to find Him anymore," she said. "Jesus died for all, even for me. If what I did wasn't enough, please, God, send me back that I may try to live better, but don't send me in darkness. Send me with a clear mind and the help of those who can hear Your voice," she concluded.

She didn't want to suffer in old age of illness and disease. She prayed that when her time came, God would take her in the garden, walking down the hillside, or in her sleep. I thought God had honored her request. As she slept, her spirit departed without sound or pain into the fold of God.

"Now you can rest in peace, Abuela," I uttered quietly as I arose from my prayer that morning.

For weeks, my mind dwelled on her. I laughed quietly while remembering her quick tongue and her almost innocent sense of humor. I could still feel warm when I thought about her familiar, weathered ebony face and striking soft blue eyes scrutinizing every corner of my mind, encouraging me to think beyond the obvious, beyond the mundane. Rather than sadness, I rejoiced in her memory and the life that we shared. I gave thanks to God Almighty for allowing me to be born of her seed in the land of our forefathers. I was never able to speak with her after I left for the States. But her words resounded clear in my mind, as if she had spoken them minutes ago.

Now and again my brother had relayed a brief message from Grandma. It was not much, but she was satisfied. "I taught your brother all that he needs to know to stay on the right hand of God," she would tell my younger brother when he'd inquire if she wanted to say something to me on his letters. "Just tell him to watch out for the shadows." That was always the message. "God does not dwell in obscure places, nor does He work by a sleight of hand," she would remind me. Stay in the clear always in all you do.

That was her voice, and I could still hear it.

THE LAMB OF GOD VIDEO

Ben Kingsley is one of my favorite actors. He is a small man, fragile almost, but has a powerful, convincing voice and a range of expression any actor would envy. His rendition of Moses was spectacular. I managed to purchase all the movies in the biblical series. They could have been filmed in my backyard.

I had found employment as a project manager for a large outsourcing and re-engineering consulting firm. The work entailed process redesign and improvement, as well as the relocation of the manufacturing operation across into Mexico. During my hour-long, hypnotic commute along a lonely stretch of the California desert landscape, I often meditated. I found little reason to stay in the area, and somehow I'd managed to do well. I had work that I enjoyed, friendly neighbors, quiet communities, and no traffic. Except for the inhumane heat, it was an ideal place to raise a family. I tried to explore my psyche and the deepest recesses of my mind about what kept me there, given the fact that I had other choices, many others. In the eight years since I had come from Cuba, I had managed to finish a graduate degree and was making my way through another advanced degree in business. By then I had a very marketable background.

Perhaps love kept me there. I had found that even in the most unusual places, there is indeed beauty and love. So it was in my case, for I found it in the desert. In 1995, I married and started a family. The comforts of family life kept my restless nature at bay.

During that particular drive to Mexico, my thoughts were interrupted by the flashing lights of a patrol car ahead on the road. The traffic, whatever little there was on that early morning, slowed to a crawl. As I drove slowly over the shoulder, I could see the wreckage of the vehicle, the blood spilled bright over the asphalt. I also saw a number of blankets covering bodies and parts of them scattered across the meridian of the roadway. I shivered with disgust, yet I was surprised.

Had it been so long since I'd seen a lifeless body? Yes, an eon ago. It seemed like another life, another me—bold, careless, unconcerned, and detached.

I wondered if the man who lay there was somebody's father, husband, son, or brother. Did he fall asleep with the burning sun on his face while driving? Was he on his way to work or home? Was his family still waiting for him, or did they know? A thousand questions assaulted my mind in those few seconds.

How do I protect myself from that? I realized that I hadn't depended on God, at least lately, as much as in years past. It felt safe everywhere, and my well-being didn't depend, at first glance, on a weapon or the sharpness of my senses. I had a well-planned and executed life, and God seldom seemed to intervene. Or did He? That could have been me there, broken and strewn all over the road. It could be me tomorrow, one week, or one month from now. Could God spare me again? Could He still hear me?

I was still lost in my thoughts when I arrived at my office. The accident scene had hit a strong note within me, well above my usual layer of rationalization and my self-aggrandized image. It brought back the reality of mortality, the fragility of my existence, and the need to seek protection. I closed the office door and prayed, a long and fearful prayer. I felt better, comforted, reassured, and rested. The weight of the anxiety lifted and hope was restored. My thoughts kept lingering on what I'd seen earlier. It wasn't a very productive day.

The accident scene flashed into my mind frequently for months. As spring approached, the urge to connect with God returned more intensely. I purchased a number of books dealing with religion and history and found myself spending time researching on the Internet and in the local library. God was occupying a significant amount of my time and attention. On a quiet Saturday afternoon, a TV commercial ran minutes before one of my favorite programs. It showed short scenes from the birth, teachings, and crucifixion of Jesus Christ. It was simple yet powerful. The reenactments were realistic and sincere. I ran to the counter to write down the number. I called and a friendly voice said the video would be delivered in one to two weeks. It was free, which made it a very desirable acquisition. A week later, a couple of young men dressed in white shirts and ties, and dripping sweat head to toe, rang my doorbell.

"Hello, sir, we're missionaries from The Church of Jesus Christ . . . blah, blah, blah," one of them said, trying not to faint.

They came with the almost melted video in hand and a smile out of context, given that they were riding bicycles. I was sure they were two minutes away from certain death due to heat exposure. My mind filled with conflicting emotions. I felt pity mixed with suspicion, since peddling in a 120 degree weather seemed more an act of lunacy than devotion.

Almost immediately, a distant memory of the boys wearing white shirts and ties, strolling downhill in the guerrilla-infested Guatemalan Highlands, flashed into my mind. A version of what I saw through the scope of my rifle then was standing right at my doorstep. So, the nutty nature of the missionaries was endemic. They must have some thrill issues, I thought.

I invited them in, and after they had gulped down several glasses of water, we spoke somewhat about my motivations for requesting the video and my expectations about it. I shared a little of my past experience seeking a church and my prior desire to feel closer to God. I was pressed for time, needing to prepare myself for an afternoon engagement. I pointed to the time and offered my excuses for not being able to converse with them longer.

They thanked me for my time and delivered the video and a book. Those items claimed to be about Jesus Christ and prophets who spoke about Him. We exchanged pleasant good-byes at the door, and I carried the book and the video into my room. I dressed and left for work. I anticipated watching the film later that night. But for one reason or another, I wasn't able to view the film until the weekend. I glanced at it several times. Now that it rested there on my kitchen counter, I felt better, reassured.

I sat on the floor close to the TV. The evening had been spent on trivial things. The wall-mounted clock silently marked that it was past 10 PM. It was only then that I found time to see this movie. I sat quietly, the unintelligible voices in Hebrew rumbling in my ears but the clarity of the images filling my heart. There, for the first time, I saw how it could have been when Christ was accused, tried, and executed on that fateful Passover weekend.

It all seemed so real, so plausible. There was no advocate, no defense, but in total submission to the Father of the Heaven, the Savior surrendered His life. The film was moving, thought-provoking. The brutality of the punishment, seldom imagined by anyone, was hinted although not depicted. The beauty of the Resurrection and the miracle of the tomb were there.

It was a short film, but its impact went well beyond the few minutes it lasted. I went out to the backyard and sat well into the morning. I pondered many things and wondered about what Grandma would have said if she had a chance to see this video. It was impressive. That Sunday after breakfast, I picked up the blue book the missionaries had left.

"The Book of Mormon," I read more or less aloud, as I sat in my home office.

I had never heard of the book, although Mormons were well-known American nomads of sorts of the mid-nineteenth century. As far as I knew, they were a sect of early religious zealots, also known for polygamy and isolation. That was, in a nutshell, my recollection from my American history class a few years earlier.

The title page was intriguing, but I withheld judgment. I skipped the testimony of all the witnesses and plunged into the book. I was a social scientist. I'd read hundreds of books and essays. I'd trained myself to assess the merits of the information presented to me rather than formulate an opinion based on hearsay or preconceived notions. Facts often stand for themselves and are able to sustain scrutiny without fear. I let the pages of the book speak to me.

Time flew. When I lifted my eyes from the book, the sun had dipped behind the mountains in the west, and twilight shadows played over the horizon. I took a deep breath. The book read like a well-woven story. It was plain, coherent, and fluid. Beyond a few early-century mannerisms, it was much easier to follow than the Bible. And the story—the story was like nothing I'd ever read before.

I ate little, my mind now connecting the characters and the plot of the book like a tapestry. The voice of the dying father, Lehi, to his sons resounded in my head with a very familiar echo:

> And men are instructed sufficiently that they know good from evil. And the law is given unto men. And by the law no flesh is justified; or, by the law men are cut off. Yea, by the temporal law they were cut off; and also, by the spiritual law they perish from that which is good, and become miserable forever. (2 Nephi 2:5)

The doctrine was sound, the flow impeccable, and the voice of the speaker real, human, pregnant with pain and sorrow like a father before a wayward son. I could hear Grandma pounding on the dining table, expounding in her own words about certain facts that were clear to her.

"There's no fence, son. You either listen to God or to the devil. You either live your life according to God's mandate, or, as some fools seem to believe, are free to break your neck. And break it you will. For to move away from God is to jump into the devil's playground," she said.

The words of this Book of Mormon drew from the depths of my memory well. It brought back hundreds of hours of conversations I'd had with Grandma when I read these words:

> Wherefore, men are free according to the flesh; and all things are given them which are expedient unto man. And they are free to choose liberty and eternal life, through the great Mediator of all men, or to choose captivity and death, according to the captivity and power of the devil; for he seeketh that all men might be miserable like unto himself. (2 Nephi 2:27)

I returned to the small room I called my office and flipped through the pages of the Book of Mormon, taking a few notes as I went along until I read something that literally took my breath away. There, almost at the bottom of the page, I found a very familiar name:

> And now, behold, I would speak unto you concerning things which are, and which are to come; wherefore, I will read you the words of Isaiah. And they are the words which my brother has desired that I should speak unto you. And I speak unto you for your sakes, that ye may learn and glorify the name of your God. (2 Nephi 6:4)

"Isaiah!" I exclaimed, jumping to my feet.

I flipped to the next page, and the next. I rested the book on the table next to me.

Who were these people? Why did they hold onto the words of a prophet lost to them hundreds of years before, and across the ocean, in a land they left behind? Why Isaiah?

A thousand questions came to my mind in a torrent, filling it with excitement. I scribbled frantically on a blank piece of paper, fearful that I might forget a question.

I kept reading. Different prophets spoke, and then simple folks, record custodians, wicked people who wrote scripture (that had to be a first), and then Mormon. Suddenly more lights turned on. The sequence became clearer; the chronology found synchronicity and the timeline in my head made more sense.

I kept reading until the lines of the text blurred again and again. My eyes were exhausted, but my brain spun furiously.

"This book and what it contains is mind-bending!" I exclaimed out loud in the quiet of the night. "How come I've never heard about it?" I murmured. It seemed almost a statistical improbability but there it was.

I nervously paced inside my small office, the verses flashing before my mind's eye, the voice of my grandmother stretching my thinking regarding "these things of God," as she called them.

I sat on the floor, leaning against the wall, pondering the things that I'd read, what they meant to me, and the symmetry with things I'd heard and learned from Grandma. Once more, here it was in pristine form, preserved for today, said by the mouth of the prophets fifteen hundred years before, and still as relevant today as the day it was uttered.

"Son, all we have, all we see, the very air we breathe was made by God. And it has been given to us by His merciful hand to have and to care for. All He asks is that we keep His commandments," she said. "Is it that hard to be kind, to be helpful, to share with and uphold those less fortunate? Whatever we have is His and not ours! We have no right to hoard it," she stated with steadfastness.

Throughout her life, Grandma employed hundreds of people in small business ventures of all kinds. From salting fish, to grinding peanuts and coffee, to making chocolate. It was all the same. Her concern was always the fact that the work helped provide for another family, not just ours. She never said no. Hundreds of times I saw her offer food to complete strangers, talk for hours to the brokenhearted, comfort those who had no hope, and smile on the face of adversity. As I read the words of King Benjamin to his people, I heard the voice of my grandmother echoing these teachings. I fell asleep on the floor, my mind occupied and restless. Morning surprised me. I'd had an unusual dream, but I couldn't remember it. It was chaotic and confusing and I awoke, my pulse racing.

I read of bands of robbers. I read of groups of men, thieves who murdered and plundered the land. They assembled themselves like wolves that prey on the weak and the defenseless, the simple and meek. They watched and lay in wait in the darkness of the holes of the rocks, in caves, and in the wilderness. They laid siege, killed, and destroyed again and again until the inhabitants of those townships had no choice but to abandon their lands and flee for refuge to other larger cities.

I saw how they then imposed by force their own government to exploit, to murder, and to intimidate all who opposed them. And thus, the rule of the weapon was imposed on entire peoples to rob them of their freedom and peace. That which the Book of Mormon recounts as it happened among their people I'd witnessed with my own eyes. That was the untold story of civil war, the senseless conflict that has prompted brother against brother, and the children of one mother to kill someone else's children for decades in Central America. And so it is to this day.

FOR GREAT ARE THE WORDS OF ISAIAH

As I read, I marveled at how much of the history of these people hadn't changed. Rather, it seemed like the children had failed to learn the lessons of their fathers. The land, by far, was marred by conflict and bloodshed. Instability, unrest, and lawlessness seemed the rule rather than the exception.

I read the book with the anticipation of a thriller. The climax, of course, was the great destruction and calamity right at the time of the crucifixion as it is told in 3 Nephi. Again, memory and experience found great resonance with the text. In years of roaming the jungle, I'd seen countless pre-Columbian ruins—truly impressive relics. Today, massive constructions remain buried under the tropical forest, hundreds of cities, of which just but a minute fraction has been excavated.

I've seen cities high in the mountains, some now submerged under water, some carved on the hillsides of the Andes, some deep in the Amazon, and some on the edge of the desert at the foothills of the Andean backbone. They're all silent witnesses to the great civilizations that once inhabited the continent. By the time of the discovery of the continent by the Europeans, these civilizations had all but disappeared. The conquistadors found squatters in those lands—groups that either through war or historical possession had come to occupy these majestic cities. It was obvious that the advanced knowledge and skills of their ancestors had since disappeared.

At the apex of the cataclysmic events, Christ appeared as prophesied. An impressive host of miracles, just like in the lands of the Bible, were displayed. He also talked simply about profound truths, issued commandments, and taught principles that didn't appear in the Bible as I knew it.

And then, without announcement or prelude, He rehearsed the words of the prophet Isaiah. He, the Christ, the Son of God, spoke to this people whom He called a remnant of the house of Israel, and said that through the Gentiles the gospel would be revealed.

I kept reading eagerly, now with the stir of echoes of my grandmother's voice of as she read Isaiah:

"I know, son, it doesn't make much sense to us. But the day will come when all these things we read from the mouth of this prophet will make perfect sense. God knows the beginning and the end—we're left to wonder what it may all mean. Since I have no prophet to explain to me these things, I pray that God Himself will give a little of His light so that I may understand. But, my son, mark my words—this prophet is talking to us today. We're the Gentiles, and God has not forgotten us. One day we'll be counted together with the people of Israel," she explained, her eyes burning with fire and anticipation.

I remember her frustrated travel plans to Israel and her disappointment when no temple was built there. I remember the sadness in her voice while recounting how she'd waited five decades for a sign from God that the gathering of the Gentiles had begun.

"It is written, and as it is written it will come to pass, son. God must rebuild His temple and invite all people from all nations. It's right here in the scriptures. And the temple will be a house of worship for all people who love the Lord and want to obey His commandments. Because there can't be true worship and communion with God without a place, a sacred place on the earth to gather and make offerings unto Him," she stated with conviction.

I read the familiar words of Isaiah, this time in the voice of Jesus Christ. What transpired constitutes, to this day, the most profound and significant spiritual experience of my life. As I read the words Jesus uttered a millennia ago to the people of the Book of Mormon, His admonition and commandment shook every fiber of my being.

> And now, behold, I say unto you, that ye ought to search these things. Yea, a commandment I give unto you that ye search these things diligently; for great are the words of Isaiah.
>
> For surely he spake as touching all things concerning my people which are of the house of Israel; therefore it must needs be that he must

speak also to the Gentiles.

And all things that he spake have been and shall be, even according to the words which he spake.

Therefore give heed to my words; write the things which I have told you; and according to the time and the will of the Father they shall go forth unto the Gentiles. (3 Nephi 23:1–4)

As my eyes crawled over the words of the passage, I felt myself begin to cry while the hair on the back of my neck and on my arms curled. A wave of emotion swept over my entire body, leaving me exhausted and trembling. I wept.

The sound of those few sentences reverberated inside my head and I heard the same message, just different voices. In an instant, years of teaching, conversation, and nurturing had come full circle. In the blink of an eye, thousands of miles away, and almost ten years later, the words of my grandmother had come to pass. Once more and according to His wisdom, He had placed before me the truth that she had sought all her life and the light she had promised I'd find one day.

"Son, go, and may you always be worthy of the protection of my God. I hope, son, that you never forget how merciful He has been with you. How patient and benevolent He has been with you. I've prayed for you since you were little that He may send you wherever it may be that the truth dwells. My child, we've lived in a dark country for many generations, and our fathers have lost the way of the true worship of God. And their fathers before then, so that we're blind and lost. But in my faith I've prayed always to my God. I've looked after Him and pleaded with Him for you. And I know, son, that He hears me and He has given me knowledge of the thing that must be. And this is why I know that there must be a church on the earth where the voice of God is heard. I know that there are men on the earth that converse with God and He hears them like you can hear me today.

"I know that just as He has heard my cry in the middle of the night and made my life easier, He will hear yours if you pray to Him with all your heart's intent. Go now, my son, without fear or concern, for He knows your heart. If you're willing, He will guide you to the dwelling place of His truth.

"As for me, I know that He will have mercy on me. I've tried to cleave to His every word according to the little knowledge I have. I sought after His Spirit and I've taught you all I know that you may not be deceived by these wolves in sheep's clothing. Son, there's no truth in this land, but surely God has not stopped being God. There's truth and I know, as certainly as the day's light, that you'll find it. And when you do, my son, it will fill your heart without measure. And you'll come to know that all the things I've taught you are true, that God has opened my eyes because of my faith in Him, and it will be the same for you.

"God brought our ancestors across the ocean five hundred years ago, but we're not lost to Him. He knows exactly where we are, and He has a plan for every one of us. His secrets, the hidden things of God, His miracles, and His power are reserved for those who have faith like mountains, those who aspire to have clean hearts and clean minds, those who are humble and thoughtful of the many things God does for them every single day, and for those who follow after everything that comes out of His mouth in the scriptures. My son, aspire to be one of them, and the shadow of His protection will be your defense. Always strive to do His will, to subordinate your will to His and you'll see. You will, my son, in a heartbeat, have a more perfect understanding of the things of God than I ever could. For you'll find those who know the truth, and I know that they are out there, for my God has given me peace of heart when I prayed about your future. Go now, my son, and know that He is always with you and you'll find Him."

I sobbed, curled up on the floor, my back to the wall in my room, simply overwhelmed by the intensity of the experience. I thought about the events of the last few days leading to it. I thought about the many years of reading and searching. It seemed like the walls of a dam had broken and a flood had rushed in, inundating every corner of the land inside of me.

The notion of a prophet in this era was simply a concept I'd never fully considered. It dawned on me that day that if the message was true, and I had absolute certainty that it was, then the messenger, Joseph Smith, was indeed a true envoy from God. The implications were many. Grandma was right: there were men on the earth who conversed with God, men to whom God unveiled His mysteries for the good of His children.

I went into the kitchen with the book in my hand. I opened a gallon of milk and drank most of it while my mind was still reeling. I continued to read for a few more hours until my body could no longer stay awake. I didn't eat, I didn't work, I didn't do much of anything until I closed the back cover of the book. I placed it on my dining table, my hands shaking.

Who do I call? Who do I tell that the words of my grandmother had come to pass? I wondered, my heart racing with excitement. I searched in my mind in vain since at the time I knew no one with as much religious curiosity as I had. I sat nervously staring through the dusty glass window of the patio door.

"I found it. After all this time, I've found it," I murmured quietly.

The next few weeks were just sheer anticipation. The elders of The Church of Jesus Christ of Latter-day Saints would starve to death if they were salesmen. They left no card, no number, no address, nothing but the book. I called the 800 number on the card that came with the video, but all they wanted to know is if I wanted more videos.

"No, I just want to get in touch with the elders," I said, trying my very best to camouflage my incipient frustration.

A sweet lady replied, "Oh my, I just don't know what to do but—this is the distribution center and—can I have your number?"

No luck. For the next three weeks I drove just about everywhere with my neck clear out the window looking for the elders. I'd seen them a thousand times around town before. You'd be hard pressed to find "normal" young people with white shirts and ties in the middle of the desert under one-hundred-degree weather. The elders seemed to be everywhere, except, of course, when I needed them.

I went over the book every day and made notes of passages in about every chapter of the book on a dozen handwritten pages. I had questions, tons of them. There were things in this Book of Mormon that were simply unbelievable according to the things I'd heard before.

Alma talks about the priesthood, how it is God's, and He points to who will be ordained from before the foundations of the world. You can't get it in the mail, nor in a seminary; you can't barter for it, nor do your robes make you a priest, like Grandma used to say. "It has to be in your blood or God must point His finger at you in public and call you a priest," she said. On the same subject, only he who is therefore selected by God can baptize. It's something administered by those who God Himself has given permission and power to do it. And then those baptized are written in the book of remembrance and become partakers of the fruit of life. That was profound, for I'd never been baptized. I wondered how much I should know in order to be baptized, or if just faith was sufficient.

I read the testimony of the witnesses, of those who knew the prophet Joseph Smith and who saw the gold plates. My mind burned with the idea of being able to see those plates. They were something sacred kept by God, hidden away from the world for a thousand years to be brought up in His own due time for a new revelation and a new era.

I drove rather haphazardly for weeks, stepping on my car brakes almost on reflex every time I saw a person wearing a white shirt and a tie. I couldn't do anything but bide my time until a fateful Saturday evening some three weeks later when the white-shirted, tie-clad individuals returned to my door.

"We're the missionaries of The—" the flustered young man started to say.

"Sit down, elders. I've been waiting for you for weeks now," I said, pointing to the living room sofa. "Some water?" I asked, walking toward the kitchen.

"Yes, thank you," they replied politely.

I returned with two glasses of water in hand, which I offered them. I observed them while they drank. They were young, much younger than I realized initially. Much too young to bear this responsibility of sharing such a solemn message with the world. I couldn't wait. The next few minutes were a mixture of truly intent questioning and a venting session of pent up frustration.

"Elders, what are you doing exactly? I mean, I know it sounds like a rhetorical question, but truly what is it that you do?" I asked, my eyes fixed on the one that seemed a bit more outgoing.

"Well, we teach people about Jesus Christ and our Heavenly Father. We explain to people that God has a plan for all and, that through the scriptures we can come to know His will for our lives," he answered.

The answer was good and somewhat logical. But my mind burned with the things that I'd learned from the book that went well beyond the simple and straightforward response I received from them.

"Elder, you're quite young and perhaps unable to gauge the impact of what you carry in your backpack," I said, pointing to their small packs on the floor. "Young men, how come there isn't a copy of this book under every streetlight in this country? God opened His mouth again, and from the edge of the universe His voice is heard once more, and I didn't know about it? Whatever you're doing, you've got to try harder! I've looked for this for almost ten years in this country. My grandmother searched for it her whole life, clear across the turn of the century, and died without finding it. Young men, do you know how many people are looking for the truth? Imagine it. Right here on this continent a prophet invoked the name of God and God answered him. Shouldn't everyone know about it?"

They listened intently, looked at each other, confusion clearly painted on their young faces. They looked for words for a few seconds.

"So—do you believe the book?" the more outgoing one said, cautiously.

"Of course I believe! Haven't you heard?" I shot back impatiently. "Elder, for twenty years I've heard the voice of my grandmother read the words of Isaiah. I heard her say that God would bless the Gentiles again and gather them with the people of Israel. And here it is again, in the voice of Jesus Christ Himself."

The missionary's face flushed as he fought hard to hold back his tears. His junior companion seemed to have swallowed a golf ball and started to breathe heavily. The silence was loaded with uncertainty and at the same time anticipation.

"Elder, I'm sorry. That didn't come out right," I said, softening my tone. I can only imagine the intensity on my face. "It was a harsh thing to say. What I meant was that this is, without a doubt, the most important Christian text ever since the Bible was printed." I tried to measure my words better this time. "I'm truly amazed that in spite of all my studying and exposure to academic learning, I've never heard about the Book of Mormon. It's almost inconceivable," I argued.

"Yeah, it happens—sometimes," he said softly, his eyes nailed to the floor.

We sat silently, not wanting to spoil the moment, unsure of what to say next or if something should be said. I looked at them now in more detail. They were really young indeed—perhaps not even twenty years old. Their shoes were dusty and they looked tired after a long day of penitence under the scorching sun of the desert. But their eyes sparkled with joy. The young men waited for me to say more.

"My name is Elder Cook and this is Elder Bentley. We're really happy to be here today," he said, nodding.

Elder Cook seemed not older but more seasoned, more certain and sure of himself. He shuffled with his backpack on the floor for a few seconds and then pulled out his scripture set. After he found the chapter he wanted, he looked at me without hesitation.

"We as missionaries often ask the investigators to read certain parts of the Book of Mormon so that we can begin a discussion. How far did you get in your reading?" he asked, staring at me inquisitively.

"I'm done, Elder. I finished the book a few days ago. I've gone over several parts a number of times, actually."

"Whoa! That's awesome . . . that's just great!" he said quite enthusiastically, the younger companion nodding in agreement.

They seemed energized now. The furniture seemed too small to contain their enthusiasm. They shifted and changed position several times before they decided how to proceed. They nodded continually. Their breathing was deep and rhythmic. They were brimming with exhilaration.

I gathered my notes. We spent several hours going over parts of the Book of Mormon and discussing some of my questions and observations. The exchange was warm, full of genuine affection, even love. I felt kindness in the voices and eyes of those young men, an embrace like I'd never seen before in the world. True, they didn't know as much as I thought they should, they didn't understand nearly as much as I assumed they would. Their statements had, however, the gentle conviction of one who truly had faith and knew without doubting

"Brother Leal, I know that the prophet Joseph Smith was a prophet of God, that he was chosen to restore the gospel in the latter days to His children, and that this church is headed by a prophet today through the power of the priesthood. Joseph did see the Savior and Heavenly Father. The keys of the priesthood were restored to him and remain on the earth today," he declared.

There was no hesitation in his voice. Although I was sure he'd articulated similar words before, it sounded driven by truth. There was no veil of pretense or rehearsal. The testimony of the young brethren resounds in my ear to this day.

They returned every day for the next two weeks to teach my family. They laid before my eyes the plan of salvation, the restoration of the gospel, and the keys of the priesthood. As the teaching progressed, our friendship did also. I realized how strongly they cared for me and my family, how deeply their spiritual roots went, and their desire for my progression. On Saturday night, they returned. I'd been reviewing some passages in the New Testament that related to the apostles attending the temple after the crucifixion. It was certainly contradictory, I reasoned. They were holding onto a Jewish tradition that no longer held spiritual value—or did it?

In my view, Christianity was no longer an extension of the Jewish religion of their fathers. As Christ hung on the cross, the veil of the temple ripped in half, exposing the most sacred relic of the Jewish religion—the Ark of the Covenant. This act in itself signified in my mind that the covenant was now shared with all, including those not of the house of Israel by birth or adoption. Mercy and forgiveness, and adherence to the law of God were now based on faith rather than blood.

On the other hand, Grandma's belief in the temple as an absolute necessity for the true worship of God was also quite logical. It was evident since Isaiah speaks about the Gentiles in the temple at length and in detail. It was one of those conundrums I loved. Grandma believed that only God could answer such things. Or, after much prayer, God could in many instances provide some insight while reading the scriptures.

I'd developed a great affinity and friendship with those young elders. They were truly my brethren. I'd come to realize that God had raised and preserved these young men in a safe place for a great purpose. They had grown unspotted from the sin and corruptive influences of the world. They were born in the fold of good, God-loving families. They had found me. Of all the people of the world and places where they could have been, they found their way to my door. Those thoughts often brought tears to my eyes.

The weather had changed. A slightly cooler breeze blew from the mountains in the west down onto the desert floor. It made for beautiful pink sunsets and a welcomed relief from the long, scalding summer. The elders came after dinner, fresh, happy, and eager to teach. After the usual greeting, they sat and gathered their scriptures.

"Elder, what about the temple?" I asked while scrolling my fingers over my notes.

"Yes, the temple," he said. "What about it?" he asked a bit puzzled. He didn't expect my question.

"Well, do you have a temple?" I asked point blank.

"Yes, we do. There's actually one in San Diego that's just absolutely beautiful!" he exclaimed.

He must have seen my consternation, for he launched into a more detailed explanation.

"I'm sure you have driven by it many times. It's right off the freeway going north toward Los Angeles," he tried to explain.

"Oh, yeah. I've seen it. I thought that was the famed Crystal Cathedral that they speak of on TV," I said, trying to withhold a chuckle.

"Nope," he said. "That's our temple—one of them, anyhow."

"There are more? What about Israel? Is there one there too?" I asked.

"Not yet. Our Jewish brothers and sisters haven't accepted Jesus as the Messiah. In time, perhaps," he offered.

"So, who's the temple for then?" I shot quickly. This was a hot button for me. Isaiah said that the Gentile—

"All the worthy members of the Church can go to the temple," he said, smiling. "I can tell you want to know more." His smile was wide and satisfying now.

I, on the other hand, fought back my tears. We talked about the history of the temple, the prophets, vicarious work, the spirit world, the priesthood, and the plainness of the scriptures.

Time went and the night advanced, so I finally let them go. They claimed to be under the threat of being chastised by the zone leader and the mission president for being out after hours.

I hadn't had a night like that in a very long time. Most of my burning questions were gone. My brain still spun furiously, and my excitement edged on intoxication once more. There was no simple explanation for what had transpired in the last few days. Out of nowhere, on impulse I had called for a video and my life had been taken down an unrecognizable but strangely familiar path.

In just a few days or a few hours, really, I'd found answers to lifelong riddles and subjects. After years of late night conversations, supposition, and hope, truth was staring me in the face. But how?

I wondered about this obscure religion. I knew no Mormons, and whatever American history had to say about them was neither enlightened nor polite. However, these young, unassuming, dedicated kids trod the streets of the desert community where providence (most likely God, Grandma would have said) had led me to settle.

"The Latter-day Saints," I repeated softly. It had a nice ring to it. It sounded gentle yet powerful, peaceful but imposing. I opened the Book of Mormon where I'd placed a post-it note and read:

> And it came to pass that he said unto them: Behold, here are the waters of Mormon (for thus were they called) and now, as ye are desirous to come into the fold of God, and to be called his people, and are willing to bear one another's burdens, that they may be light;
> Yea, and are willing to mourn with those that mourn; yea, and comfort those that stand in need of comfort, and to stand as witnesses

of God at all times and in all things, and in all places that ye may be in, even until death, that ye may be redeemed of God, and be numbered with those of the first resurrection, that ye may have eternal life—

Now I say unto you, if this be the desire of your hearts, what have you against being baptized in the name of the Lord, as a witness before him that ye have entered into a covenant with him, that ye will serve him and keep his commandments, that he may pour out his Spirit more abundantly upon you?

And now when the people had heard these words, they clapped their hands for joy, and exclaimed: This is the desire of our hearts.

And now it came to pass that Alma took Helam, he being one of the first, and went and stood forth in the water, and cried, saying: O Lord, pour out thy Spirit upon thy servant, that he may do this work with holiness of heart. (Mosiah 18:8–12)

As I felt the stir in my chest and my eyes began to burn, I wondered about the strange transformation that was taking place in me. I could feel my heart softening; I could feel the years of endless wandering and searching taking on meaning. After all, I had been searching and hungering for the truth, and every minute I spent on that search had brought me closer to this day.

That night I went into my room and prayed. It was a long and difficult prayer, for I'd neglected to pray for quite some time. I'd thought that since, indeed, God knew all my needs, no extensive pleading was necessary. Usually it went something like this: "Dear God, You know all my problems and troubles. You know my heart and how I want to be closer to You. You also know what I need. So please take care of it and help me." The end.

I had no disrespect in mind. I'd rationalized some time before that perhaps God had grown tired of the inaccuracies and practices that currently passed for religion. A simple fact—I'd thought that perhaps in this land of abundance we didn't need God as much. That was certainly my perception at the time. No one I knew spoke of God, at least not in any true sense that implied connection with or devotion to Him. For most, God was something, somewhere, somehow linked to humanity but absent and removed from everyday life. Grandma taught me otherwise, but somehow I'd forgotten.

But that night I needed to cleanse my heart and offer to God all my sorrow, all the pain from years past that hadn't gone away. I needed to rid myself of the grief, the nightmares, the faces that came night after night in a disquieting parade of sorts. I needed to place my past at God's feet. I couldn't carry it any longer. That night I felt the warmth and comfort I had experienced years before after being shot by the sniper, when my life drained away and my thoughts turned to God. I felt the gentleness of His Spirit embracing me in the dark.

I'd lived, more or less, a meaningless life. There was nothing significant, truly worthwhile, or honorable that I'd done. Kindness and gentleness weren't attributes I cared to cultivate. On the contrary, I wasn't a humble man. I'd lived a life designed to provide for me and consume based on what I thought I deserved. I'd taken credit for my accomplishments and often forgot or disregarded the true power behind my doings.

God had preserved me in the most perilous of circumstances. He had allowed for peace to come into my heart in moments of heart-wrenching despair. He had allowed rest for my troubled mind when the noise and the trembling of war deafened my ears and robbed me of solace. I know that He gave me clarity and sharpened my senses, He preserved me from the ingenuity and the weapons of the enemy. He spared me countless times when death cast its shadow over me.

My life has always been a witness to His mercy and compassion for me, for I knew I was nothing without Him, deserving even less, and He shielded me. Again and again my body recovered from the wounds of battle, and I knew it was He who healed me when others said I was beyond repair. He showed me that He heard my prayers and mended my torn flesh when others, if they were in my shoes, would have hoped for a quick death. He is the maker and the healer and in Him, according to His will, even the dead aren't dead forever.

He cleansed the blood off my hands and erased my offense. He forgave my alliance to strangers and forged hope in my heart in the midst of dreariness. I know that I owe my life to the unseen faith among shadows. I walk on the earth today and can see with eyes that pierce the veil of unbelief and ignorance that surrounded my forefathers. I heard His voice once and never forgot the sound.

I remained on my knees that night until I felt that all my torment was gone, until I could look skyward without fear. That night I was also convinced that I'd finally come face-to-face with the truth and the long-awaited word of God.

THE BRETHREN WHOM I LOVE

Night after night, the Elders returned. The following Sunday I attended church for the first time. The building was clean and simple, but inviting. There was no clutter, no excess, and light permeated every corner of the corridor filled with smiling faces. There were many different faces, and that appealed to me.

The missionaries met me eagerly and introduced me to my neighbor. Antonio was a neat, thin, friendly man I'd seen tinkering in his yard across from my house. His hair was prematurely gray, but his enthusiasm was contagious and youthful.

He was familiar to the other church members. Born across the border in Mexico, he ran his printing and copier business on both sides. After the protocol introductions, I took my seat among the gathering. No doubt the congregation took notice of my presence. I was an unfamiliar and quite peculiar face; however, I felt safe and welcomed. Language, words, history, and friendship overcame apprehension and apparent differences.

I made many new friends in a very short time. I saw men, young and old, strong and weak, offer prayers to God without inhibition or fanfare. I saw men singing hymns of praise to God with devotion, and crying tears of happiness and gratitude for the blood of Jesus Christ on the cross and His Atonement in the dark and lonely garden of Gethsemane. What I saw and felt in that church building sealed my testimony of the truthfulness of the message contained in the Book of Mormon.

A few days later, I was baptized by my friend and neighbor Antonio. He embraced me after lifting me up from the water, and I couldn't help but feel that I'd found my home. I'd been lost, cut off, and disconnected from God for most of my adult life. For once, I was certain I was in the right place.

And then I read the scriptures, sometimes day and night. I immersed myself in the doctrine with a hunger that has not left me since. I often thought of Grandma in the spirit world and her almost prophetic words about the knowledge and understanding that would be available to me in the future.

The brethren visited often, sometimes with their families, sometimes alone. They cared and loved me like I didn't know men could love each other. They strengthened me and guided me; they counseled and taught me with gentleness, hope, and faith burning in their eyes.

Bishop Zimmerman's soft but reassuring voice offered me a wealth of knowledge, insight, and inspiration that I'll treasure forever. I learned of patience, understanding, unselfishness, and dedication to the work of the Lord. Even in the face of adverse circumstances, he never uttered an unkind word or sighed in frustration, and his faith never wavered.

I found the older brothers that I didn't have. I found younger, gentler, kinder, more humble brothers I didn't know I'd longed for. I spent years enjoying the true fellowship of the Saints and the spirit of brotherhood in that obscure and apparently insignificant corner of the world where the Lord brought me into His fold.

I learned about their trials and their struggles, of their faith and frustration in the face of adversity. I also became acquainted with their quest to do better, to be better, and to rely on God for strength and power to overcome.

Although clearly a new member of the Church, my zeal and enthusiasm for the gospel and newly found truth all but consumed me. I sought after every opportunity to accompany the missionaries. My testimony of the gospel, of the Restoration, and the work grew with every passing day.

In what seemed to me an unprecedented occurrence, I was called to be the ward mission leader not too long after my baptism. That day I cried, a bit in fear, a bit in confusion. It appeared to me that God was laying upon me a task that was impossible for me to carry out. I accepted the calling, not because I thought I could do it but because I didn't know I could refuse. After I pulled myself together, I remembered the words of my grandma: "God will never set you out to fail, son."

I gathered my strength and realized that I was going to embark on an errand on behalf of the Lord and not something of my own design. I felt comforted and reassured. In time, the Lord showed me how seemingly impossible things come to fruition in His hands.

I labored with faith and renewed strength in what remains, to this day, my true passion in life: missionary work. I found redemption and forgiveness in the work of the Lord. With faith and dedication through the years, many have listened and believed the testimony I have shared. I've found great happiness in being able to bring but a few to the knowledge of God and of the Savior into the fold of the Saints.

Receiving the keys of the priesthood was, once more, the realization of almost prophetic promises made by my grandmother. To hold and to exercise the power of God unto the building of Zion, in defense of the weak, for the healing of the sick and infirm, to comfort and to build the congregation of the Saints has been without a doubt a life-changing experience.

Time pressed on with haste, and soon I was afforded the privilege of entering the House of the Lord. Attending the beautiful San Diego California Temple was an event that transformed my mind. As I crossed the veil into the celestial room, I felt as if the floor faded and the walls receded. I stood speechless in that breathtaking room surrounded by dozens of friends who had come to embrace me. I remembered then the words of the prophet Isaiah:

> Even unto them will I give in mine house and within my walls a place and a name better than of sons and of daughters: I will give them an everlasting name, that shall not be cut off. (Isaiah 56:5)

The meaning and the implications, as Grandma described it, became clear. I quietly praised our Savior for the gift that only God can give. For I'd received, as foretold by the prophet, a hand and a name that will endure in eternity according to my faith. And then I saw. My eyes were opened, I understood, and from that point on, the Spirit has whispered countless tokens of knowledge as they relate to the covenant.

Not too long after that, I embarked on the long drive from Southern California to the Salt Lake Valley to attend general conference. I figured that even if I only went once in my lifetime, I should go and see where the hand of the Lord had led the pioneers to settle and build the first stakes of Zion in the West.

Of course, I had other motives as well. Although modern means of communication allow for the General Authorities of the Church to speak to millions, I couldn't pass up the opportunity to see the prophet of God in the flesh. He was, at least as far as I was concerned, one like unto Moses calling the people to repentance and to labor in faith. I felt the compelling need to endure the day-long road trip to climb to the Mountain of the Lord.

There was one small issue. I required tickets in order to attend at the Conference Center. Since I'd already made up my mind for quite some time that I was going to Salt Lake, I refused to be discouraged by that minor fact. I packed my bags and headed north on Friday morning the week of the conference.

I drove through beautiful country. I listened to the same two CDs of the Tabernacle Choir for fourteen hours, since in my haste I'd neglected to bring any others. Between Las Vegas and Provo, there were no radio stations that could stay tuned long enough to enjoy, yet it was a trip made short by the anticipation.

On Saturday morning, I walked slowly up the hill from my hotel to the magnificent Conference Center near Temple Square. As soon as I cleared the slope, I choked when I saw the multitude. I'd gone to a rock concert years before in LA, but I don't think there were as many people there as outside that conference building. For the first time since I left my driveway a day earlier, I thought about how I didn't have tickets to the conference sessions.

I stood in the corner almost one full block away from the conference center, the crisp October air sweeping the leaves across the esplanade and my face. It was a beautiful sight to behold. Thousands of well-dressed, smiling families, friends, brothers, and sisters walked briskly to the lines forming in every direction from the building entrances. It was truly amazing. And they all had tickets.

I took a deep breath and started walking toward the small square by the main entrance. As I got closer, a thought entered my mind. I needed the Lord's intervention today to get a ticket, as bad as I'd needed Him for many other less critical things in the last few months. This was, after all, an act of lunacy or mountain-moving faith. I'd driven almost a thousand miles and was now faced with the uncertainty of whether I could actually get to the conference. I hoped the Lord wouldn't have me go to Salt Lake just for sightseeing—not that week. I did the only thing I could do given the circumstances. I prayed.

There I was, standing right below the beautiful waterfalls that decorate the magnificent building. Surrounded by thousands of my fellow Saints in the cradle of the restored Church, I felt happy, safe, and excited.

There I stood, in my dark blue suit and tie, my scriptures in hand, one more priesthood holder among thousands there that day. I smiled in satisfaction, and hundreds of faces smiled back at me genuinely. Where else in the world would that happen?

A gentle hand touched my left arm, calling my attention.

"Good morning," the tall, muscular man said. If one could get past the man's rather imposing physique, the soft hazel eyes behind his square face put you at ease. A young boy leaned on his leg as the man spoke with me.

I smiled back. "Good morning," I replied.

"Do you need tickets?" he asked. The man was a mind reader, or, indeed, Heavenly Father had heard my prayer.

"Yes! How did you know?" I exclaimed, almost jumping out of my skin with excitement.

"No worries. I'm Brother Spencer, and this is my son, Matt. Where do you come from?" he asked.

"From Southern California, close to the Mexican border," I answered, trying to offer some geographical references.

"Great," he said, smiling, while handing me two colorful tickets. "Glad you could make it and welcome to Salt Lake. We hope you enjoy the conference."

"Thank you very, very much," I said. He smiled and waved at me. He returned to the line where his wife and daughter waited. They all waved. I was simply overwhelmed.

After standing in a long line and being ushered through hallways with glass-like floors that were cleaner than I ever thought possible, I was shown the way to my assigned seat high in the mezzanine. The huge balcony protruded from the wall behind and tilted downward, suspended in the air. I breathed, deeply exhilarated. The view of the organ, the podium, and the choir was just awe-inspiring.

I was able to attend all the sessions of conference that fateful weekend. A kind elder, assigned to manage traffic in and out of the underground parking lot of the Conference Center, provided me with tickets to the Priesthood session. I sat six rows from the podium. I was able to sit, literally, face-to-face with the prophet of the Lord, Gordon B. Hinckley. That was, without a doubt, an experience for the family history book.

It was with great honor and humility that I later served in the bishopric of my ward. I had the opportunity to labor quietly with spiritual giants. These men truly consecrated all that the Lord placed into their hands for the building of His kingdom on the earth. They held back nothing, nor did they rest if the work of the Lord still had to be done. Until I met them, dedication, devotion, and commitment were mere adjectives. I found a home and place among them. I found inspiration, encouragement, and the true fellowship that most seek and few find in a lifetime of wandering in the world.

Although life, work, and the hand of the Lord have led us in divers directions, I carry with me memories unmatched. I found, in an obscure corner of the world in Southern California, all that I sought and needed to find the way of the true God.

EPILOGUE

It has taken me many years to find the courage to share glimpses of my grandmother's life story and an account of my search for truth, spiritual nourishment, and ultimately God. My life, both here and in my native land, has been fraught with struggles, disappointments, and bittersweet experiences. I've embraced this country as my own since in the land of my ancestors I have nothing but memories. Therefore, with immense gratitude I call this land my country.

As a keen and honest observer of the world around me, I can thus attest that our country has problems, some real, some imagined. I've traveled beyond these borders and into other lands. Thus I believe I speak with some authority on the issue. I can sincerely attest to the uniqueness and special character of this land. Failure to recognize how exceptional this country is, in my sometimes not-so-humble opinion, conveys an affront to God. This country, as some contend, may not be the best country in the world. But for those who will read these lines, and as one who gives witness to this truth, I can sincerely declare that there is not a better one.

The founding and development of this nation wasn't an act of fortuity. It wasn't luck or chance. The existence and emergence of this land was the result of careful planning and care on the side of the Lord. The coming forth of the Book of Mormon and the restoration of the gospel and all the miracles that accompanied those events had been foretold for millennia.

It's my testimony that the earth and all that is in it is the Lord's. We're

His offspring and thus equipped to attain, in time, a level of light, knowledge, and intelligence that will surpass in magnitude our current state. All knowledge belongs to Him and nothing is lost to Him. Although He had scattered the nations to and fro across the face of the earth and the oceans, He knows precisely where He has driven them.

I'm convinced that He pours a measure of His spirit of revelation to all those who seek Him with real intent and a pure heart. And it's that revelation that constitutes the seed of His word and the desire to come to know Him, the Eternal Father. There are men and women all over the earth in distant lands and on the isles of the sea who cry His name and He hears them. Therefore, it's our responsibility to seize the wind of faith and go on His errand to every corner of the world where His children call on His name for mercy and salvation. Such responsibility can't be abdicated, and in virtue of the abundant blessings that have been poured upon us in this land, we must obey.

I'm indeed grateful beyond measure that the Lord has led my steps to this land—that I've found the peace, truth, and knowledge that my grandmother desired for me. I'm grateful that the mercies of the Lord extend to those who have crossed the veil without the opportunity to receive the ordinances of salvation. The Lord has inspired His prophets to build many temples in high places where we may worship and perform under His watchful eye inside His holy mountain.

It's my witness that as before, the God of the universe has answered the prayer of the simple, the humble but faithful, and has spoken by the mouth of his prophets. I also testify that Joseph Smith was the one chosen to open the doors of the kingdom of heaven and allow the light and truth lost to memory to return. I have an unbending testimony of the restoration of the priesthood of God to the earth, and that such will be the foundation of His kingdom until Christ declares that the work is done. I express infinite gratitude to my Heavenly Father for allowing me to bear the priesthood in order to perform the ordinances of salvation here on the earth. I'm grateful for this endowment that allows me, for the first time in more than two thousand years, to restore to my ancestral line that which had been lost to my kindred dead.

I'm thus willing to declare with humility but with full intent that I've placed my eternal salvation and that of my family on the fact that The Church of Jesus Christ of Latter-day Saints is indeed the Church of the Savior. I've received, in faith and on account of my own life being in mortal danger, a personal testimony that Jesus is the Christ, the Son of the Eternal Father, and that He lives. It is He of whom we testify. It is He of whom we speak and say, "Master, Savior, and Redeemer." I declare that Jesus Christ is the instrument of salvation for the dying world, and I've pledged to dedicate my life to the work of spreading His gospel. He is the same that was crucified for the sins of mankind—past, present, and future—and none will be saved except he confess faith and believe in Him. We worship Him because He lives and guides the affairs of the kingdom through His prophets, seers, and revelators, Gordon B. Hinckley being the keeper of the keys of the priesthood and of the gathering in this day (2007).

I know that through Jesus Christ we're partakers of the covenant of the patriarchs, that in one measure or other, the blood of Israel runs through our veins and the blessings promised to them is also our promise. Thus we must remain faithful to the covenants, old and new, in order to receive the everlasting blessings of the gathering of Zion.

I've prayed that we may have the faith and strength to endure the trials that will surely come. I've prayed that we may not fear or heed the rumors of war and the power of tyrants and those that oppress. I've prayed that we may be sharp tools in the hands of the Lord to carve His word in the hearts of those who are looking for His truth. There are millions of men and women pleading in the dark for the light of the gospel, and to them we must give our account for our lack of diligence at the last day.

It is my testimony that if we are faithful and true to the stewardship that we've been given, we'll be counted among those present under the bright morning light when the trump will sound from the edge of the universe announcing the coming of the Lord Almighty and the resurrection of those who crossed the veil professing faith in Christ.

ABOUT THE AUTHOR

Malcolm Leal lives with his family in the foothills of the San Jacinto Mountains in Southern California. He is the principal and CEO of a Next Generation Network company that provides communications networks services and infrastructure to small and midsize domestic and international businesses.

He has served in The Church of Jesus Christ of Latter-day Saints in various callings since his conversion in 1998. This is his first and only work of nonfiction.

0 26575 52262 4